# Private Lord Crawford's
# Great War Diaries

# Private Lord Crawford's Great War Diaries

*From Medical Orderly to Cabinet Minister*

*Edited by*

Christopher Arnander

Pen & Sword
**MILITARY**

Published in Great Britain in 2013 by
Pen & Sword Military
an imprint of
Pen & Sword Books Ltd
47 Church Street
Barnsley
South Yorkshire
S70 2AS

Lord Crawford's War Diary Copyright © Lord Balniel, 2013
Commentary and Notes Copyright © Christopher Arnander, 2013

ISBN 978-1-78159-367-7

A CIP catalogue record for this book is
available from the British Library.

Typeset in Palatino and Baskerville
by Concept, Huddersfield.

Printed and bound in England by
CPI Group (UK) Ltd, Croydon, CRO 4YY.

Pen & Sword Books Ltd incorporates the imprints of Pen & Sword
Archaeology, Atlas, Aviation, Battleground, Discovery, Family History,
History, Maritime, Military, Naval, Politics, Railways, Select, Social History,
Transport, True Crime, Claymore Press, Frontline Books, Leo Cooper,
Praetorian P⌐                                              ⌐ and Wharncliffe.

For                                                         se contact

47 Chu                                                     2AS, England
                                                            k

# Contents

Acknowledgements . . . . . . . . . . . . . . . . . . . . . . . . . . . . . . . . . . .   vii

Abbreviations . . . . . . . . . . . . . . . . . . . . . . . . . . . . . . . . . . . . . . . .   ix

Timeline . . . . . . . . . . . . . . . . . . . . . . . . . . . . . . . . . . . . . . . . . . . . .   xi

List of illustrations . . . . . . . . . . . . . . . . . . . . . . . . . . . . . . . . . . .   xiii

Map: Prelude to the Great War . . . . . . . . . . . . . . . . . . . . . . . . .   xiv

Introduction . . . . . . . . . . . . . . . . . . . . . . . . . . . . . . . . . . . . . . . . .   xvi
Business as usual – Crawford enlists as a private in the RAMC –
the Lindsays – commitment to public service – The Royal Army
Medical Corps – one officer worth twenty men – vermilion
parasols – Crawford as a war diarist – back to politics – looking
back on the war experience.

Map: The Northern section of the Western Front 1915–16 . . . . . .   xxxii

I   2 May to 16 July 1915 . . . . . . . . . . . . . . . . . . . . . . . . . . . . . . . .   1
Departure from Aldershot – delays at Le Havre – alcoholic
temptations – prisoners – letters and parcels – political interlude –
venereal disease – journey to Hazebrouck – creating two operating
theatres – *Taubes* bomb Hazebrouck – promotion to Lance Corporal
– nurses – refugees – spasmodic fighting – many casualties –
Crawford's first louse.

II   18 July to 22 September 1915 . . . . . . . . . . . . . . . . . . . . . . . . .   25
From lace factory to seminary – fatigue and garden work –
Germanic names – court martial – thirty-one officers and nurses
lord it over twelve NCOs and men – Colonel's stretcher design –
trench fever and neurasthenia – *au revoir* to the horses –
looting and souvenirs – sailors revered – unofficial music –
French and British boots – the men's intuition about their officers –
loafing at GHQ – French railway guards – great troop movements –
Mother McCarthy rattles the nurses.

**III  25 September 1915 to 2 January 1916** . . . . . . . . . . . . . . . . .  63
*Der Leichenfeld von Loos* – morale of wounded men – Hazebrouck
groans under British occupation – dental red tape – visit of an
august personage – hospital crisis – lice, flees and scabies –
Churchill's speech horrifies – inspection trip with General
Porter – boot problem and foot problem – French cartoons and
posters – French replaced by Haig – Crawford granted leave.

**IV  2 to 12 January 1916** . . . . . . . . . . . . . . . . . . . . . . . . . . . .  103
A week's leave in Scotland.

**V  12 January to 23 March 1916** . . . . . . . . . . . . . . . . . . . . . . .  114
Officious military police – clothing reform – NCOs and men will
win the war, not officers – follies of GHQ – gathering troops –
Crawford proposed as RAMC quartermaster ... and Viceroy of
India – contradictory routine orders – attack on Ravenna's cathedral
and other atrocities – carnage at Verdun – dentistry the pariah of
medical services – French press attitudes – British government
confusion over conscription – French courage and endurance.

**VI  24 March to 6 June 1916** . . . . . . . . . . . . . . . . . . . . . . . . .  146
The Anzacs and Canadians come to town – twelve months in the
ranks – Australian indiscipline – second trip with General Porter –
Zeppelin over Edinburgh – local currencies – Anzac lung troubles –
German brutalities anger America – Dublin shame – Crawford's
family want him home – complex accoutrement – preparing for
Somme – promotion to corporal – Jutland's stupefying losses.

**VII  7 June to 9 July 1916** . . . . . . . . . . . . . . . . . . . . . . . . . . .  178
Lord Kitchener's death and assessment – his succession – colonel's
stretcher plagiarized – colonel's well earned promotion – French
press urging British action – Russia's success at Czernovitz peters
out – allies bogged down in Salonica – Crawford offered
commission in Intelligence Corps – Battle of Somme – Crawford
accepts cabinet post, encouraged by his senior officers.

**Postscript** . . . . . . . . . . . . . . . . . . . . . . . . . . . . . . . . . . . . .  196

**Map: Aftermath of the Great War** . . . . . . . . . . . . . . . . . . . . . .  198

**Illustration Credits and Source Notes** . . . . . . . . . . . . . . . . . .  200

**Index** . . . . . . . . . . . . . . . . . . . . . . . . . . . . . . . . . . . . . . . . .  201

# Acknowledgements

My principal debt is to my first cousin, Robin, the current Earl of Crawford & Balcarres, eldest grandson of the 27th Earl, or Bal, as he was generally known to friends and family. He showed me our grandfather Bal's diary of his service as a medical orderly in the British Army between April 1915 and July 1916. Not only did Robin and his son, Anthony, authorize its publication, but he carefully read several drafts and suggested a mass of improvements. He also gave me access to Bal's unpublished personal letters to his wife Connie and provided some of the illustrations. His support has been unfailing, detailed, creative and enthusiastic.

Three other grandchildren of Bal – Francesca, Eliza and Hugh – read the drafts and provided many excellent suggestions, for which I am immensely grateful. Hugh's father, Bal's second son, James Lindsay, wrote a fine history of the Lindsays, *A Family Story*, which was most helpful, as was Nicolas Barker's *Bibliotheca Lindesiana*, the story of the Lindsays as book lovers and collectors over four centuries.

The original manuscript, in very small handwriting and full of abbreviations, was deciphered and typed in the early 1990s by the distinguished judge, Sir David Edward, and his wife. Without the benefit of this huge and selfless task, I could not have contemplated editing the book. I am most grateful to the National Library of Scotland for providing me with an indispensable copy of Sir David's work, for use of images from their collection of official First World War photographs, and the maps of Europe on pages xiv and 198. The map of the Western Front on page xxxii was adapted by my wife Primrose from an original map of the United States Military Academy, Department of History, West Point.

I owe a lot to Professor John Vincent, who edited the 27th Earl's diaries from 1892 to 1940, under the title *The Crawford Papers*. They have become essential reading for those interested in the political, artistic and social scene of his era. They have given give great pleasure to Bal's descendants and the wider Lindsay clan.

Bal spent most of his military service in France, at Hazebrouck, about fifteen miles behind the main section of the British line, running south from Ypres. Marc Enjalbert showed me the town most hospitably and led me to its archives. Georges Degroote and Jean-Michel Saus provided several illustrations, mainly from www.hazebrouck-autrefois.com, a website with a superb collection of historic postcards of Hazebrouck. I was fortunate to join a tour of the Flanders battlefields, with lectures by Nigel Jones www.historictrips.com; he also provided valuable advice and gave or lent me much interesting material about the Great War. The web site www.scarletfinders.co.uk is an invaluable resource for students of nursing in the Great War, including the diary of Dame Maud McCarthy chief matron on the Western Front. Anne Powell, author of *Women in the War Zone*, provided me with helpful comments and essential corrections.

David Beech of the British Library briefed me on the Crawford stamp collections and philatelic books. Karen Moran of the Library of the Royal Observatory Edinburgh provided images of the 26th Earl, its greatest benefactor. The Royal Borough of Kensington's library has been invaluable for its collection of political biographies and memoirs as have the libraries of the Army Medical Services Museum, the National Army Museum and IWM, London. The Wigan Leisure & Culture Trust gave access to their archives and contemporary local newspapers.

I was greatly assisted by Roni Wilkinson who guided me through the Taylor Collection at Barnsley, helping me select images and using his magic to improve the quality of photographs nearly a century old. I am very grateful to the editorial team who have helped me so much at Pen & Sword Books. Henry Wilson, Matt Jones, Irene Moore and Jon Wilkinson; they have been most tolerant of my chopping and changing.

It is rare for professional historians to make overt acknowledgement of Jimmy Wales, Sergei Brin and Larry Page, but amateur historians, such as myself, are most grateful for the extraordinary easing of their work afforded by the founders of Wikipedia and Google.

Nowadays it is a fashion to apologize for the sins of our forefathers. Ministers feel that they must apologize for acts of slavery, colonialism or slaughter committed centuries ago. In this spirit, I take this chance to apologize for my grandfather's slur on my wife Primrose's grandfather. Soon after joining Asquith's coalition government in July 1916 as Minister of Agriculture, Bal, a firm Conservative, called on the Chancellor of the Exchequer, Reginald McKenna, a Liberal. Britain's food situation was desperate and Bal sought guaranteed agricultural wages and prices to encourage home production. Of this meeting he notes in his diary 'I am bound to say that these radical wretches improve on acquaintance', though he could not secure the necessary guarantees.

Apologies, then, to Primrose and unbounded thanks for her tolerance and for her shrewd and practical advice throughout what has been a lengthy and solitary project.

*Christopher Arnander*
*London, July 2013*

# Abbreviations

| | |
|---|---|
| ADC | Aide-de-camp; assistant to a general or other very senior officer |
| ADMS | Assistant Director Medical Services |
| A and D book | Admission and Discharge book, recording those entering and leaving a CCS |
| AJB | Arthur J. Balfour, former Conservative Prime Minister, ally and patron of Crawford |
| ANZAC | Australian and New Zealand Army Corps |
| AOC | Army Ordnance Corps |
| AS | Average Soldier, or Tommy; this refers to the privates and junior NCOs |
| ASC | Army Service Corps |
| AT | Ambulance Train |
| Batman | Officer's servant |
| BEF | British Expeditionary Force |
| Blighty | Slang for Britain, from Indian *bilati* much used in the British Raj to denote home |
| CB | Confined to barracks |
| CCS | Casualty Clearing Station |
| C-in-C | Commander in Chief |
| CO | Commanding Officer |
| Cpl | Corporal |
| DADRT | Deputy Assistant Director Railway Traffic |
| DMS | Director Medical Services |
| DSO | Distinguished Service Order – for distinguished service during active operations |
| Estaminet | Bar or café or bistro, of modest standard |
| FA | Field Ambulance – a mobile hospital rather than any form of vehicle |
| FO | Foreign Office |
| FP | Field Punishment – for soldiers convicted at a court martial (various forms) |
| GDO | Group Duty Officer |
| GH | General Hospital |

| | |
|---|---|
| GHQ | General Headquarters, from where the war is conducted; for BEF, in 1915–6, it was at St Omer, then Montreuil |
| GVC | *Garde des Voies De Communication*, which guarded the French railway system |
| HLI | Highland Light Infantry |
| KCB | Knight Commander of the Bath |
| KOYLI | King's Own Yorkshire Light Infantry |
| L/C & L/Cpl | Lance Corporal |
| Lt | Lieutenant |
| MO | Medical Officer |
| MP | Military Police or Member of Parliament, according to context |
| No. 1 | Shorthand for No. 12 CCS's main unit in Séminaire St François, Hazebrouck |
| No. 2 (or 'officers') | Shorthand for No. 12 CCS's officers' unit in Maison Warein, Hazebrouck |
| NCO | Non-commissioned officer – all grades of corporal, sergeant and quartermaster |
| P of W | Prince of Wales |
| PPCLI | Princess Patricia's Canadian Light Infantry |
| Pte | Private |
| QM | Quartermaster |
| RAMC | Royal Army Medical Corps, also shorthand for French military medical services |
| RE | Royal Engineers, regiment or individual member of it (also known as 'sappers') |
| RFA | Royal Field Artillery |
| RFC | Royal Flying Corps, predecessor of Royal Air Force |
| RGA | Royal Garrison Artillery |
| RTO | Rail Transportation Officer |
| S of S | Secretary of State |
| SM | Sergeant Major |
| Tommy | See AS |
| VC | Victoria Cross – awarded for extraordinary courage in battle |
| VD | Venereal Disease |
| WO | War Office |
| YMCA | Young Men's Christian Association |

# Timeline

## (period of Crawford's military service in italics)

1870    Franco-Prussian War, necessitating French reaction, sows the seeds for
        the First World War.

1871    October – Birth of David Alexander Edward Lindsay (hereafter 'C'), at
        Dunecht, near Aberdeen.

1892    On graduating from Magdalen College, Oxford, C does social work at
        Oxford House, Bethnal Green.

1895    June – C elected MP for Chorley in Lancashire – 'the youngest in years'

1896    C private secretary to Gerald Balfour, First Secretary for Ireland, brother
        of Arthur J. Balfour, later Prime Minister.

1897    In Parliament C presses reform on South Kensington Museum; leading to
        separation of art and science activities and to the creation of Victoria &
        Albert Museum in 1909.

1899    C appointed Trustee of National Portrait Gallery, his first appointment to
        a major art institution, to be followed by National Gallery, British
        Museum and several others throughout his life.

1900    C marries Constance Pelly. Introduces legislation for Monuments
        Protection Act.

1903    C's book on Donatello published. Co-founds National Art Collections
        Fund (now the Art Fund), which buys art for British museums.

1909    Victoria & Albert Museum opens, largely due to C's work in promoting
        reorganisation of South Kensington Museum. C's book 'The Evolution of
        Italian Sculpture' published.

1911    C becomes Chief Whip of Conservative Party; major issues – Ireland,
        Parliament Act, military budgets and replacement of Balfour as leader by
        Bonar Law.

1913    January – on death of his father, C becomes 27th Earl of Crawford &
        Balcarres and ceases to be MP.

1914    June – Assassination of Archduke Franz Ferdinand in Sarajevo
        precipitates World War One.
        August – Britain declares war on Germany on violation of Belgian
        neutrality.
        September – First Battle of the Marne checks German assault on France
        and both sides withdraw to trench line, which remains virtually
        unchanged for three years.

1915 *March – British attack on Neuve Chapelle results in 13,000 casualties with no ground gained; depressed and anxious to serve, C decides to enlist in RAMC in the ranks, aged 43.*
*April – C trains as RAMC private in Aldershot. Troops land at Gallipoli, Dardanelles campaign.*
*May – C assigned to No. 12 CCS and sails for France.*
*June – First Liberal/Conservative coalition formed, headed by Herbert Asquith; C declines offer of ministerial job.*
*June – After a month's delay at Le Havre, No. 12 CCS established in Hazebrouck; C in charge of two operating theatres and promoted to lance corporal.*
*September – Battles of Loos and Artois.*
*October – British forces land in Salonica to help Serbia; large resources tied up there.*
*November – Dardanelles campaign ends in failure; C's criticisms of Winston Churchill.*
*December – British-Indian force besieged in Kut for almost five months, ending in large losses.*

1916 *February – beginning of Battle of Verdun (ended November.)*
*April – C promoted to corporal, declines potential quartermaster promotion.*
*June – death of Lord Kitchener. C accepts commission in Intelligence Corps.*
*July – C witnesses beginning of Battle of the Somme (ended November).*
July – C joins first coalition, headed by Herbert Asquith, as Minister of Agriculture.

1916 November – Appointed Chairman of Royal Commission on Wheat Supplies, set up to secure UK's food supplies, retaining this position until 1925.
December – C joins second coalition, led by Lloyd George, as Lord Privy Seal and holds other ministerial positions until 1922.

1918 November – Armistice brings an end to the war.

1922 October – C retires from politics at the end of Lloyd George's last ministry.

1924 C refuses Stanley Baldwin's offer of ministerial job.

1925 C seen as 'Uncrowned King of British Art' and, over his remaining lifetime, is involved in many of the nation's art institutions. C chairs committee on British broadcasting.

1927 C's committee recommended formation of British Broadcasting Corporation (BBC); C declines its chairmanship.

1930 C's family business, Wigan Coal & Iron Company split and merged into Lancashire Steel Corporation and Wigan Coal Corporation, after three years of losses, at instigation of Bank of England.

1939 September – Start of Second World War.

1940 February – C, formerly critical of Churchill, recognises him as the nation's only possible leader.
March – C dies at Haigh Hall, Wigan.

# List of Illustrations

## Plate section between pages 94 and 95

1 Private Crawford, RAMC
2 Man about town
3 Whipping the Conservatives
4 Wigan Coal & Iron
5 Stretchers on & off the train
6 Makeshift operating theatre
7 'Red Beard', astronomer
8 The 26th Earl, 'Red Beard'
9 St Bartholomew & St Andrew
10 Neuve Chapelle
11 Fisher & Churchill
12 AJ Balfour
13 *The Imitation of Christ*
14 The diary manuscript
15 The V & A Museum
16 Grande Place, Hazebrouck
17 Officer chats up a nurse
18 A puzzling complaint
19 One of the army's three curses
20 The foot problem
21 Tommy tempted
22 Horse ambulance bogged down
23 Microcosm of a hospital
24 Dullish work for the crews
25 Treatment in the trenches
26 Under canvas
27 A seminary turned hospital
28 Lemire, hailed as King or Pope
29 Slouching Australians

30 Australians enter ruined Ypres
31 *Taube* over Hazebrouck
32 *Taube* downed
33 King of Montenegro with Haig
34 The Grand Duke too late
35 French crowd at the bank
36 *N'oublie pas de souscrire*
37 Verdun – *On les aura*
38 A venerable *poilu*
39 A mobile laboratory
40 The ownership of teeth is a luxury
41 Ideal for the horsey
42 Promoting French inoculation
43 Pathetic refugees
44 The execution of Edith Cavell
45 Sant'Apollinare Nuovo, Ravenna
46 The Boche's desire to smash
47 A near miss for Connie
48 Zeppelin at home
49 The *Sussex* somehow regained port
50 Uncle Sam extracts a tooth
51 The Bishop blesses an ambulance
52 Very hot in the X-Ray van
53 Reprographer protected
54 Connie's home hospital
55 Wounded Sikh
56 A cushy time for our soldiers
57 Kitchener sets out for Russia

## Illustrations in the text

| Page | |
|---|---|
| xxxiv | RAMC evacuation system |
| 13 | Cattle truck for 40 men or 8 horses |
| 26 | Plaque to commemorate RAMC occupation of seminary in Hazebrouck |
| 32 | Campaign to give fresh vegetables to the allied soldiers |
| 39 | King George V jettisons his German titles |
| 45 | Field Punishment |
| 85 | Staff officer, as seen by Bruce Bairnsfather |
| 94 | The Prime Minister's letter, promoting a new cartoon book by Raemaekers |
| 96 | Tracing lost family members |
| 105 | Warning against loose talk |
| 118 | Germany is beaten |
| 129 | The Pope's outrage |
| 134 | 'Wait and See'…'Too Late' – Asquith and Lloyd George |
| 148 | Cheeky chappie from Down Under |
| 151 | *Endure Fort* – The Lindsay family motto |
| 158 | Two franc note issued by the Chamber of Commerce, Marseilles |
| 171 | Germany tries to induce Holland to give up its neutrality |
| 179 | England staggered by Kitchener's drowning |

# Prelude to the Great War

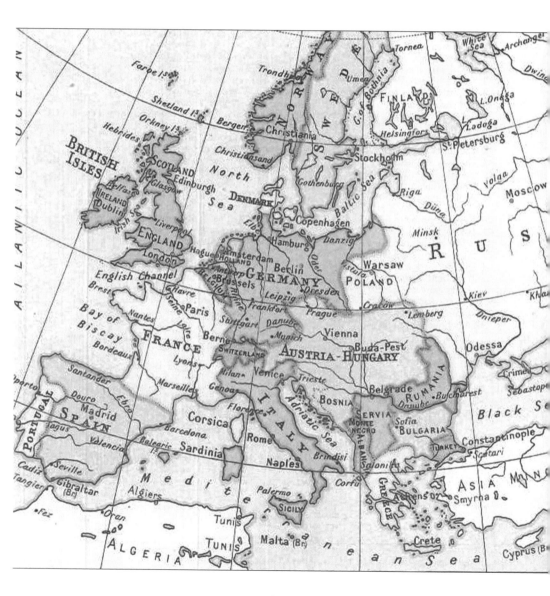

The 'big five' European powers, locked into alliances, were preparing for a general war that none of them wanted.

- The *Central Powers* were **Germany**, the new economic power house, which yearned for empire and feared being surrounded, and **Austria-Hungary** which was divided at the top and worried about minorities inside and abutting their kingdom
- The *Entente Powers* were **France**, which desired revenge after defeat in 1870 and the recovery of Alsace & Lorraine; **Russia**, which feared revolution and the risk that Constantinople (Istanbul) might fall into the wrong hands; and **Britain** which focused on empire and finance and wanted a balance of power in Europe, with no military involvement.

Secondary states jockeyed for position. **Italy**, wobbly in its loyalties, sought grandeur through seizing Libya in 1911 from the **Ottoman Empire** which, thus weakened, had its Balkan estate lacerated in 1912 by **Bulgaria**, **Greece** and **Serbia** which, in their turn, in 1913, fell out with each other over their Ottoman spoils. In the same year, **Romania** and **Montenegro** took advantage of the chaotic situation in the Balkans to add to their own territories.

Most European states contained three sources of power – military, parliamentary and monarchical – which pulled in different directions. Inconsistency of policies led to mistrust and misunderstanding between states, accentuated by religious and language differences. Nationalist ambitions and hatreds added to the mix.

In this unstable environment, what might have been a containable crisis – the assassination, on 28 June 1914, of the Archduke of Austria-Hungary – became the trigger of the Great War. The alliance system launched a process of mobilization which no mediation could stop; there was no arbiter, such as the United Nations, to hold the ring.

In the first days of August 1914, almost all thought that the war would be over in three months.

# Introduction

*Business as usual – Crawford enlists as a private in the RAMC – the Lindsays – commitment to public service – The Royal Army Medical Corps – one officer worth twenty men — vermilion parasols – Crawford as a war diarist – back to politics – looking back on the war experience.*

## Business as usual

It was all going to be over in a month or two.

The German Emperor, Kaiser Wilhelm II, told his soldiers as they set out for battle that 'you will be home before the leaves have fallen from the trees'. The *Liverpool Daily Post & Mercury* reported that a couple of maiden ladies from Birkenhead had resolved to remain in Switzerland 'until the end of the war', but anticipated being home by Christmas. As a 26-year-old lieutenant (later field marshal) Bernard Montgomery remarked 'at least the thing will be over in three weeks'. They had not allowed for the unstoppable mobilization unleashed by the main participants: Germany and Austria-Hungary, the Central Powers, France, Russia and Britain, the Allied Powers.

In August 1914, Germany and France had huge standing armies, while Britain's was in size less than a tenth of either and its priority was the defence of (or addition to) a global empire. Volunteers were needed. Hundreds of thousands of men came forward and dozens of new battalions were formed. For women, it was a unique chance to play a bigger role; there was no greater opportunity than in nursing for which, in London alone, more than 50,000 women volunteered. The recruits, male and female, were moved by a great wave of patriotism but many of them also hoped for a little adventure in a short war with no idea of the horrific reality to come.

In the previous decade the British fleet had been strengthened in response to Germany's growing navy, and the army had been totally reorganized, which made it possible to send out a British Expeditionary Force to assist France within a week of the start of the war. But Britain had no aspiration for a European war – the very idea was anathema to most people – and had not strained every muscle to prepare for it, as had Germany; thus, in the War

Office, there was little interest in war's new technologies. The services of a brilliant Dutch aircraft designer, Anthony Fokker, were declined by Britain, so he worked for Germany. Britain's top general, Sir William Nicholson, thought that military aviation was 'a useless and expensive fad'. Arthur Pollen's technique to enable naval ships to fire accurately while bobbing about on the waves was not properly exploited. The Army had scant use for the machine gun, which, in German hands, was to be an instrument of slaughter. Across the plan submitted by the tank's inventor, an official wrote 'this man is mad'.

A small but well-informed minority of realists took a sombre view of the future. Sir Edward Grey, the British Foreign Secretary, observed to a friend that 'the lamps are going out all over Europe; we shall not see them lit again in our lifetime'. Perhaps that was overstating it, but three of the top commanders did not doubt the seriousness of the war. Whatever they might say in public, France's Joffre privately feared a war of 'indefinite duration' and Germany's von Moltke 'a long wearisome struggle', while Lord Kitchener, on becoming Secretary of State for War, shocked the British government by stating that the war would last 'three years to begin with'.

Among the realists was David Alexander Edward Lindsay, 27th Earl of Crawford & Balcarres, the premier earl of Scotland and an experienced politician. A Lancashire MP for eighteen years, he had been Chief Whip of the Conservative party in the House of Commons, until his father's death in 1913 translated him to the House of Lords and forced him to give up his parliamentary seat of Chorley in Lancashire. He knew continental Europe well; only a month previously, he had had to dash back prematurely from a visit to Bayreuth, his journey complicated by the mighty German war machine as it mobilized. On the day that war was declared he was horrified by 'the insouciance and lack of foresight in the patriotic crowds'. He wrote to *The Times* criticizing the complacency of the 'business as usual' attitude and asserting that 'the bulk of the country does not realize the tremendous menace which confronts us'. He urged the government to tell the people what was at stake, singling out Lloyd George as the ideal person to take the message up and down Britain.

The realists were soon proved right. The Kaiser's supposedly foolproof Schlieffen Plan required the German forces to invade France through Belgium. Germany would take Paris in a few weeks before the Russians could mobilize their forces. But the Kaiser underestimated Belgian resistance, did not expect Britain (though bound by treaty to preserve Belgian neutrality) to declare war and faced unexpected resistance in the east from Russia. So France, with its British and other allies' help, was able to check the Germans at the first great Battle of the Marne in September 1914. Germany withdrew to a fortified trench line, comfortably within French territory. By the year's end, the forces on both sides had dug in for a long war of attrition on the Western

Front. Britain had lost the cream of its standing army and would now depend on territorials and unseasoned recruits. Meanwhile, the war spread from Europe into Africa, the Middle East, China and the vast expanses of the oceans. It was the first global war, with the antagonists too evenly matched for a quick end and too proud to accept any compromise or American offers of mediation.

### Crawford enlists as a private in the RAMC

Crawford longed to do something productive. He had no official position and was well outside the normal criteria for enlistment in the Army, being 43 years old and married with seven (soon to be eight) children. For months he agonized about where he could be useful. As head of a large family and chairman of a major company, it was difficult to get away, particularly as winding up his father's estate was complicated. He served as a special constable in London, spoke in the House of Lords and lobbied his political friends, among whom he opposed the idea that the Conservatives should form a coalition with the Liberal government of Herbert Asquith – as was to happen in May 1915. He participated in recruitment meetings, though his searing integrity might have put off some of the young men; at one meeting in Manchester he depicted 'not the glories of war, but its horrors', to the consternation of John Hodge, the Minister of Labour (as recounted in his memoirs), who was sharing the platform with him.

In March 1915, after a lull of several months, the British launched an attack on German positions at Neuve Chapelle, in support of a French campaign to the south in Champagne, with a view to recapturing the important town of Lille; instead, the British gained a few yards in return for 13,000 casualties, but were unable to consolidate their gains through lack of reserve troops and ammunition. The Neuve Chapelle disaster (painted as a victory by some governmental sources) depressed Crawford greatly and induced in him suicidal feelings. It was clear that his warnings were correct, that the nation was indeed facing a 'supreme crisis', as he had put it in his *Times* letter, and that the war would be a long and terrible one.

So, with the somewhat anxious support of his wife, Connie, he enlisted as a private in the Royal Army Medical Corps. He was the first peer to enlist as a private and the only cabinet minister (as he later became) to serve in the ranks in the First World War. He was following four of his gardeners who, a few months previously, had joined the RAMC, describing it then as 'a noble service where courage and charity are intertwined'; three of his brothers, Walter, Eddy and Lionel also enlisted as privates in infantry regiments though all were over age. As a natural member of the officer class, from a 'family of warriors' (as the *Wigan Observer* put it at the time), to enlist in the ranks must have seemed to his contemporaries an unorthodox move. But then Crawford was chief of the Lindsay clan and over the years the Lindsays were never afraid to take an unorthodox line.

## The Lindsays

The Lindsays were of Flemish origin; they came over from France with William the Conqueror and gradually expanded over much of central Scotland. The Crawford title, dating from 1180, is Scotland's premier earldom. In 1320 David Lindsay joined a handful of barons and freeholders in signing the Declaration of Arbroath – a plea to the Pope for Scottish independence, which included these words 'for, as long as but a hundred of us remain alive, never will we on any condition be brought under English rule'. The Lindsays had truly nailed their colours to the Scottish mast by participating in this bold assertion of Scottish independence. Lindsays have, over the centuries, been active in most walks of Scottish life but also in Britain as a whole. Clan Lindsay societies have been established in Scotland, Australia, USA and Canada to meet the aspiration of clan cohesiveness which prevails even amongst the remotest of cousins.

In the late eighteenth century, Alexander, the 23rd Earl, branched out in a new direction. After serving as a soldier in the American Revolutionary War, he married his first cousin, Elizabeth Dalrymple, heiress to the Haigh estate, near Wigan, Lancashire, rich in coal although its exploitation had fallen into decay. He restored the mines and built a foundry – tasks interrupted by spells as Governor of Jersey and of Jamaica. Most aristocrats of the day wanted to buy broad acres of land, but he preferred to buy small parcels which might have coal or might inhibit a potential rival's acquisition strategy. As an assembler of mining rights he was a true precursor of the Gulbenkians and Texas wildcatters of a later era.

He and his son, the 24th Earl, laid the foundations of the Wigan Coal & Iron Company, which grew to employ more than 10,000 people. The 25th Earl devoted much time to collecting books and pictures, in search of which he began travelling to continental Europe while still a schoolboy; he made the *Bibliotheca Lindesiana* one of the greatest private libraries ever assembled. He was also a scholar and wrote several books about history, family and religion. His son, Ludovic, the 26th Earl (still known by his descendants as 'Red Beard'), was an esoteric collector, who assembled a huge number of French Revolutionary and Napoleonic manuscripts, among other historical, religious and cultural documents. His unique collection of stamps made him the virtual inventor of modern philately, earning him the nickname *The Premier Earl of Philately*. His 4,500 philately books are now a prize possession of the British Library.

Ludovic was also an amateur scientist, becoming a Fellow of the Royal Society at the early age of 30. A keen astronomer, he took groups of scientists to the South Seas to view eclipses and gather specimens on his giant steam yacht *Valhalla*. Several species of birds were discovered and named after him such as *Dendroica vitellina crawfordi* . In London, he helped set up the Grosvenor Gallery, instal electric lights there and found the London Electricity Company (now part of EDF), which pioneered the distribution of electricity in London. Its first general manager was an Anglo-Italian inventor, Sebastian de Ferranti, who was later to create his own great electrical business. Ludovic's interest in spiritualism was distinctly unorthodox, causing Lord Derby to wonder if he was not of 'latent unsoundness'.

## Commitment to public service

Ludovic's son, the 27th Earl (known as 'Bal' to family and friends), inherited from his ancestors a commitment to public service, a great interest in the arts and sciences, an international outlook, combined with a strong feeling for his family, clan and business. Crawford was also a man who, though confident in his opinions and ready to express them – as Lloyd George put it in his memoirs 'with clarity and suavity' – was shy and loath to push himself forward. As Conservative Chief Whip he led 'a life of abnegation with no desire to get on' in politics. His desire to avoid the limelight and his high standards – 'I dislike leaving a job half finished' – led him to refuse ministerial office in 1915. When offered it again a year on, he at first thought it repelling, but was urged to take it because of his knowledge of the war in France which would be unmatched in government circles. He even hesitated before accepting promotion to lance corporal until sure that he could do the job. Yet such were his intellectual and diplomatic skills that he was regularly sought out for leading roles in British political life and cultural institutions such as the National Gallery, National Portrait Gallery, British Museum and more than twenty others, regional and national. He also chaired the committee on broadcasting that led to the creation of the BBC.

Perhaps, like his father, he might have been suspected by some of 'latent unsoundness' as the first peer to join up as a private instead of taking a commission or doing a grander job at home, but he found great satisfaction in his work and humble position. He wrote to his wife Connie about the ease of 'being on terms of equality with the big section of the world' and 'how natural one's conversation becomes by wearing the uniform of rank and file'. His adaptable personality enabled him to deal equally with casualties, colleagues, officers and politicians of every rank. As a French speaker, he established good relations with the local people whose lives were so disrupted not just by the German invasion, but also by the British Army's requisitioning of accommodation and supplies – not to mention occasional looting.

He was a deeply religious man, a Christian of a robust type, with a distaste for 'floppy, slushy churchmanship'. He was much influenced by Thomas à

Kempis's *The Imitation of Christ* (managing to read a few pages of it in Latin most days). He had a practical desire to 'improve the condition of those less happily placed' than himself – after university he spent nine months in social work at Oxford House, Bethnal Green. He devoted much effort to opening up museums so that the people could get 'their share of the beauties of art'. His abiding interest in other people is shown in his attitude to a young German prisoner, Leutnant Buchholz, whom the RAMC cook protested at having to feed, in his kindness to Private Chany, whom he arrested and who pressed a tip into his hands after his court martial, and in a chance meeting with an artillery man who was scratching his heels with such violence that 'I asked for a peep. It was our old friend scabies . . . I gave him the usual advice.'

## The Royal Army Medical Corps

For centuries doctors had been involved in tending wounded soldiers in Britain's wars, but it was not until 1898 that the Royal Army Medical Corps was formally established. Within a short time it had its first big test in the Boer War, but it was the First World War that brought an enormous growth in its size, importance, status and activities. Over the war its strength rose from less than 20,000 to 163,000. On the Western Front alone it handled 5.5 million casualties (including repeats) of which one third were directly due to battle injuries and two thirds to disease, illness and infection. The RAMC helped save millions of lives – and, in the spirit of the Hippocratic oath, not only British lives, as pointed out by one RAMC poet, John Finley:

> *I bear the stretcher and I bend*
> *O'er Fritz and Pierre and Jack to mend*
> *What shells have torn*

The RAMC had prepared itself to play a full and immediate role in the British Expeditionary Force. By the end of 1914, when the opposing sides had dug themselves into their trenches, the RAMC had devised an effective method for evacuating casualties from the front line. Stretcher bearers brought the wounded into a sequence of help points – the regimental aid post, the advanced dressing station, the main dressing station, the field ambulance (a mobile hospital, not a vehicle), each of them a little further back, but very close to the front line. If the soldier needed further treatment he was sent back to the nearest casualty clearing station (CCS), or he might be able to go straight back to duty.

The CCS has been described as the 'operating power house of the army medical service in the war'. It was usually located at least seven miles behind the front line, beyond the enemy's big guns, near a railway siding (but not so near as to constitute an obvious bombing target). Its function was to check the wounded, record their details, patch them up for return to the front or send them to a base hospital in France or, as most soldiers hoped, to England, known as 'Blighty'. In fact, because of the desirability of treating wounded men as soon as possible, CCSs themselves became virtual hospitals, under canvas or in huts or requisitioned buildings, with up to 1,000 beds. At the start of the war, a CCS's theoretical complement was eight officers and seventy-seven other ranks; in practice, the staff could be supplemented by surgeons, anaesthetists, dentists, nurses, extra stretcher bearers, drivers, an engineer and an interpreter. A CCS could consist of over 100 people, with often a horse and a servant for each officer, as well as grooms for the horses. Crawford was struck by the number of these 'non-effectives' in his CCS, accounting for at least twelve per cent of the unit.

It was into No. 12 CCS that Crawford was recruited as a private in April 1915, gaining promotion to lance corporal and then corporal over the next year. His prime responsibilities were to set up and maintain its two operating theatres. Throughout his service with the RAMC, after six weeks training at Aldershot and a long waiting period at Le Havre, he was at Hazebrouck, a town in French Flanders, about fifteen miles behind the trench line. Crawford undertook many a task such as stretcher bearing, preparing the wounded for surgery, assisting the surgeons, fetching, unpacking and mending equipment, managing drugs and instruments, portering, delivering laundry, making splints, x-raying, carpentry, painting, whitewashing and scrubbing. Once he had to hold the horse of an officer out shopping, earning a fifty centimes tip for his pains.

Under the pressure of events the RAMC resorted to a good deal of improvisation. Unqualified NCOs carried out operations; Crawford's sergeant major 'eradicated' Private Head's carbuncle with a pair of scissors. Strict recruitment criteria were waived. Dr Kelsey Fry was asked only one question at his interview: 'Do you ride?' He did not, but gave the brilliant answer that he hunted regularly with the Quorn and the Pytchley. Once accepted by the RAMC, he had to have some quick riding lessons, but horsemanship was irrelevant to his duties. His equestrian deficiencies were more than made up for by the skills that he developed as a surgeon of jaw injuries. Orderlies, such as Crawford, were often over age. The RAMC was one of the few regiments where the normal age limit (38) for recruitment into the army was overlooked.

'How many new complaints have sprung from this vile war!' exclaims Crawford – the new ailments were indeed a huge challenge for the RAMC. Trench foot, a most painful condition arising from permanently wet feet, unavoidable in the muddy trenches of Flanders, despite regular foot inspections and sock changes, rendered many soldiers immobile. It led to amputations of rotten toes and feet. Trench fever debilitated a man for at least a week; its symptoms were high fever, severe headache, pain in the eyes, legs, knees and back and it could take a month to recover. It took until the end of the war to learn that the louse was its cause. This knowledge might have saved a huge number of troops from trench fever.

One feature of bullet wounds was that they carried scraps of infected clothing and soil into a wound, which could cause gas gangrene or tetanus. Antibiotics were not yet available and blood transfusions in their infancy. Many deaths resulted from infection rather than wounds. Inoculation was a great success, despite 'the hostility of cranks and fanatics'.

One of the most puzzling of the new ailments was the overwhelming exhaustion caused by extended stays in the trenches which left a man incapable of doing anything. It was known as neurasthenia or shell shock or NYDN (Not Yet Diagnosed – Nervous) or, informally, as PWU (Permanent Wind Up) or GOK (God Only Knows). It could be hard to distinguish it from cowardice or malingering, while Crawford thought it was confused with nicotine poisoning. Some medical leaders were totally dismissive, such as Sir Andrew McPhail 'a manifestation of childishness and femininity', and Sir Arthur Sloggett who described sufferers as 'lunatics'. There was scant sympathy for the condition among the rank and file, or even among medical officers; one wretched man could only blurt out 'I've lost my hat, sir. My hat! I've lost it ...' to which the doctor roared 'And what do you take me for? A bloody milliner? Get out before I have you put on a charge'. Some sufferers were executed for supposed cowardice, but gradually, towards the end of the war, the condition came to be understood. Now it is known as post-traumatic stress disorder.

The RAMC presided over enormous advances in medical knowledge and skills. Its front line stretcher bearers were incredibly brave; King George V thought that they should be eligible for the Victoria Cross, but that would have resulted in thousands being awarded to stretcher bearers which would have changed the emphasis of the award. Many awards were made to RAMC officers and men for gallantry, including several VCs. The war inspired poets and poetasters throughout British regiments, including the RAMC. Their men's courage and devotion was extolled in the simple and moving poem by Corporal W.H. Atkins, whose second verse illustrates the role of the hospital orderly, such as Crawford, 'doing his bit'.

> Oh! it's weary work in the whitewashed ward,
> Or the blood-stained hospital base,
> To number the kit of the man who was hit
> And cover the pale, cold face
> Or hand out fags to the brave boy in rags,
> Who'll stick it and cheerfully grin,
> As the deftly used knife cheats grim death of a life
> While the grey of the dawn creeps in.

*To hold the hot hand of the man who talks wild*
*And blabs of his wife or his kids,*
*Who dreams he is back in the old home again,*
*Till the morphia bites, and he loses his pain*
*As sleep settles down on his lids.*
*The 'Hospital Orderly' doing his bit,*
*Of VCs not many they score,*
*Yet are earned every day in a quiet sort of way*
*By the Royal Army Medical Corps.*

## One officer worth twenty men

Crawford enlisted in the ranks as a Tommy or, as he describes himself and his colleagues, an 'average soldier' or AS. As a private, quite soon promoted to the rank of lance corporal, he inevitably developed a certain hostility towards officers. However, his hostility was not to his RAMC officers, mostly doctors, dentists and surgeons, whom he told his wife were a 'thoroughly good lot'; nor was it to experienced career officers, but to the spoilt young 'swankers' from combat regiments who came for treatment to his CCS. Crawford believed in the hierarchy of the army and the need to keep the respective roles of officers and men, but expected an officer to behave properly, which many of these young, virtually untrained, officers did not do, and to show proper respect for long-serving NCOs, privates and their own military servants (batmen).

By tradition, officers, who were mostly educated at public schools, were more valued than men, who were mostly working class; the British Army encapsulated the class system in its most perfect form. Crawford refers to 'the disparity between the treatment of officers and men based on the old theory that one officer is worth twenty men'. But by 1915 the regulars had been nearly wiped out in the battles of the previous year and most of the newly recruited officers were young and inexperienced. Some of them knew their limitations and deferred to the more experienced NCOs, but others threw their weight about and put much extra work on the RAMC men when they arrived wounded or ill at the CCS.

A constant irritant was the excess baggage that officers brought with them, well beyond the limit allowed by regulations. Long hours were spent by RAMC men unpacking their cases, many of them in a disgusting state; Crawford made a special point of disinfecting them, as he was a stickler for hygiene and wanted to maintain the standards of his 'clean little community'. One major, 'proprietor of the biggest kit we have ever handled', arrived with 'a little under a quarter of a ton – five great lumps of vanity', including his own primus stove to sterilize his food and drink in the trenches. One captain came with two horses and a groom; another brought two polo ponies in tandem with a dogcart, which struck him as unbelievable in wartime. Crawford was outraged by one patient, a general, who complained that 'our brand of champagne was not to his liking! What are we coming to?'

Crawford and his colleagues were constantly vexed by the standoffish demeanour of 'so many who never commanded more than a squad of clerks or accountants ... and whose heads are turned by the importance of their position as sub-lieutenants'. It did not help that many of the RAMC men were twice the age of most of the new officers. After six months Crawford had come across hundreds 'who are utterly incompetent to lead men, to inspire confidence or respect, to enforce discipline, to behave even as gentlemen.' He felt that the war would be won by the NCOs and men, not the officers, and 'commissions should only be given to those who have passed a certain period in the ranks' – rather an unorthodox view at the time.

Officers with leadership qualities were respected by the men, but there was resentment that officers could go off for short leaves to Paris, that their home leaves were more regular and that their correspondence was subject to a lesser degree of censorship than that of the rank and file. Crawford got into trouble early in his military career for signing a telegram to his wife 'Bal', his nickname. In *Corky's War*, Private Percy Cawkwell, a RAMC stretcher bearer from Hull, is quoted as ending a letter to his adored Tilly with the word *Vergissmeinnicht*, German for 'forget me not', and had it sent back by the censor with a black line through the offending word. Crawford and his fellows 'in the underworld' knew almost nothing about what was going on; he felt that the officers were much more likely than the men to be indiscreet and leak information of value to the enemy.

The staff officer was a particular *bête noir* for the rank and file; 'lions led by donkeys' was a description that Crawford might have appreciated. Inexplicable instructions were a constant cause for dissatisfaction. One day Crawford's CCS suddenly received an order from GHQ to inventory all officers' kits. This procedure would have been impracticable without a trebling of the staff in the pack store. 'Some smart young major on the General Staff must have done this ... without the smallest regard for the waste of time and energy', noted Crawford. A week later, the order was withdrawn; it transpired that it was supposed to refer only to deceased officers, but GHQ forgot to insert the word 'deceased'. Leadership, both military and political, was indecisive and incompetent; the pleasant faced British generals made a 'small impression' on the men compared with their opposite numbers – 'What we want are generals with the faces of tigers or vultures or alligators' like Germany's Hindenburg or Italy's Cadorna.

The British Tommy was no revolutionary, but the privileges of the officer class were noticed, if not resented. When Winston Churchill resigned from political office and secured command of a battalion, he asked his wife to send him a pair of trench wading boots coming right up to the thigh – a protection against trench foot that average soldiers could not readily obtain. However, the war was a great leveller and there was equality of sacrifice from all sides of the armed forces – indeed many of the spoilt young 'swankers' were particularly heroic in battle. Grumbling rather than mutiny was the average British soldier's reaction to any unfairness in the system; one safety valve was a fuller democracy at home, with the Liberal and Labour parties competing for the vote of the working man, and, in due course, woman.

## Vermilion parasols

A notable feature of Crawford's war diary is the antipathy that the men felt towards the nurses. He makes it perfectly clear that there is no hostility to nurses as such and that they perform a necessary function in the base hospitals, but they had no place in a CCS whose function the RAMC official history calls 'recording, treating and distributing casualties.' Often the casualties could be passed on within hours to their next destination, be it the front line or a base hospital; at the CCS itself the wounded did not need much nursing attention. *The Sketch* imagined a wounded man muttering to an orderly, as an angel of mercy was descending on him *'Lummy, 'er Ladyship again? Look 'ere, George! Be a sport. Go and tell 'er I'm too bloomin' ill to be nussed today.'* Many of the nurses were high born or educated women; in Crawford's unit one newly arrived nurse was 'very grand'. Some arrived with tennis racquets and vermilion parasols – 'What do they expect to find here?' he wonders. Working class wounded felt uncomfortable being nursed by them.

The complaints were about the nurses' bossiness, dirtiness, noise, wastefulness and evening parties with officers (leading to a scandal, darkly hinted at by Crawford, which involved a nurse having an officer in her 'bunk' till 3.30am). Nurses took iodine from the dispensary to stain chairs, bandages to polish furniture, ether to clean table cloths and used milk to clean the leaves of potted plants. Crawford was infuriated when they ate chocolates and left cherry stones in the operating theatre which it was his job to keep clean; he found it 'droll' that they told the orderlies not to put their hands on the banisters. Their officer status enabled them to order the men about, though their functions and powers were unclear. Few of the men would have had any previous experience of taking orders from a woman let alone one younger and less experienced than himself.

It was not just Crawford and his comrades who were upset by the inexperience and frivolity of some nurses. Grave doubts were expressed in *The British Journal of Nursing* about the wisdom of sending 'intensely ignorant' nurses out to the front line 'in the stern work of war, only those who are of use are acceptable, others are not only not wanted, but hinder and hamper the genuine worker'. The same journal has lively exchanges on the relationship between orderlies and nurses. At the time, there was widespread prejudice against women doing serious jobs. A War Office official rebuffed the offer of one qualified surgeon (and suffragette), Elsie Inglis, to set up all-women medical units on the Western Front with the words, 'My good lady, go home and sit still' – but the French and the Serbs welcomed her efforts.

However, there was a grave shortage of nurses and unqualified nurses were better than none; also there were strong political pressures to place nurses near the front. The RAMC addressed the organizational problems and, by the time of Crawford's departure from his CCS, improvement was already becoming apparent. The desirability for surgery at the first possible moment after many sorts of wound also enhanced the role of nurses in a CCS. A key figure in improving the nursing service in France was the chief matron of the British Expeditionary Force, Maud (later Dame Maud) McCarthy; she appears a few times, not altogether unaffectionately, as 'Mother McCarthy' in the diary. By March 1916 she felt that everything at No. 12 CCS was in 'excellent condition' – for which Crawford and his comrades could have taken much credit.

## Crawford as a war diarist

Crawford kept diaries for all his adult life from 1892 to 1940. They include interesting and acute observations on family and social life, politics, business, British cultural institutions, education, art and literature. They are considered by historians as important sources for the study of Britain's political and cultural history. They were edited by Professor John Vincent and published as *The Crawford Papers* by the University of Manchester Press in 1984 – Crawford had a special connection with that great northern city, having served for many years as Chancellor of Manchester University and as chairman of the nearby Wigan Coal & Iron Company.

Crawford's service in the RAMC was only partially covered in *The Crawford Papers*. During his time in France he wrote up his diaries as best he could with limited time, light and space at his disposal, often very tired and constantly interrupted by colleagues or air raids or the call of duty. Entries were written in small notebooks and in tiny handwriting. The deciphering and typing of these notebooks was carried out in 1990 by the distinguished judge, Sir David Edward, and his wife.

To help the general reader the many abbreviations and repetitions have been culled or massaged, while retaining stylistic authenticity. Yet the reality of his life was repetitive – the hard physical work ('hands like metal files'), the grinding monotony and frustrations of daily tasks, stretcher bearing, scrubbing the theatre floor, carrying and unpacking luggage and the unremitting pressure of casualties and patients. This daily physical repetition and the stagnation of a static posting must have been difficult for a middle aged man whose life had been spent in stimulating political, artistic and social circles. Fortunately he was fit and did not get ill, as did some of his RAMC colleagues. It helped that he was an abstemious eater and drinker, though enjoying his regular cigarettes (whose threat to health he notes, though not yet scientifically proven).

At the start of his career in the ranks, he was concerned that his status as a peer should not be discovered and he asked his wife Connie to address his mail so as to disguise it. Of course he knew that it would come out, but wanted to have a few weeks during which he could establish relations with the NCOs and the rest of the men on his own merits. This he did successfully and his colleagues treated him as their equal, as he did them. Once one of his comrades, Private Hyde, a schoolmaster in private life, was asked insistently by the new matron, MacCrae, to confirm that Corporal Crawford was in fact also Lord Crawford; Hyde loyally (and rather impolitely) gave her short shrift. Crawford's presence in the CCS soon became known in senior military circles; once, to his fury, he was paraded before General Plumer 'as though I were a prodigy or a freak', being one third nude as he was doing heavy work on a hot summer's day. He clearly came to be much valued for himself and soon received promotion. Later he was encouraged to become a quartermaster, but preferred 'the scientific work of the operating theatre' and felt that 'the post should go to old and experienced soldiers, upon whom it is the greatest compliment to confer commissioned rank'.

While most of the entries deal with daily activities, he also writes about external topics, for example, the 'aged, ragged and untidy' *poilus* who guard the French railways with 'the utmost vigilance and efficiency' or the differential propensity to suicide of officers and men or the awe felt by soldiers for sailors. He elaborates on the characteristics of the louse and the flea. There is the continuing saga of Colonel Grech's efforts to develop and patent a better stretcher which Crawford christened 'Gretcher'. There are conversations and observations about politics; the antipathy felt by him and his political colleagues towards Winston Churchill (then at his career's lowest ebb, as scapegoat for the Dardanelles disaster) is a recurring theme.

There are graphic vignettes – cheering recruits arrive at Hazebrouck station and their mood swiftly changes when they see the platform full of bandaged men from the front – a man loots a very large church bell, gets it back to England, but is forced to restore it. Music making boosted morale; the mouth organ of 'an incomparable Lancashire lad', Darkie, improved marching by fifty per cent. The group's restricted band (at one point twenty strong) of tooth combs, tin kettles and penny whistles, to which Crawford contributed a deep bass hum, greatly impressed French cottagers who came out in their scores to listen to *ces Anglais*.

His love of arts, literature and language shines through the diary. As a young man he called his horse Giotto after the Italian painter. There are passages about the reconstruction of the Cloth Hall at Ypres, the Austrian attack on the church of Sant'Apollinare Nuovo at Ravenna and the local architecture. He takes pleasure in the little garden behind his CCS; though a bit disappointed in the lack of horticulture, he understands that the priority lay in boosting agricultural output. He enjoys the cartoons in the French newspapers contributed to the war effort by Jean-Louis Forain, Abel Faivre and Louis Raemaekers. He admires the artistic skill in French war loan posters. Literary references and foreign words spring off the page, not to mention rare English words such as 'umbratilous', 'pleach' and 'chopin' which may cause some readers to resort to a dictionary.

## Back to politics

Family and friends often tried to get him back to Britain to take a more important job – even the King questioned his role in the RAMC ranks – but he was content to continue with the RAMC. Early in his RAMC service he expresses the hope that he would end the war as a sergeant, but later he became more susceptible to a change. However, as he mentions in his diary, it was not possible for a member of the rank and file, even if he wished to do so, to apply to serve elsewhere; Crawford was loath to break the chain of command by going over the heads of his superior NCOs and officers. Early in his service he was summoned back to London by A.J. Balfour, the former Conservative Prime Minister, who proposed that he should join Asquith's coalition government of May 1915, as Civil Lord to the Admiralty; his refusal of the job was seen by Balfour as 'not defensible on any ordinary rules of conduct', but he understood Crawford's personal reasons. He was also proposed as Viceroy of India by Lord Curzon and Austen Chamberlain (he is amused by 'a very piquant contrast – the squalor and discomforts of Hazebrouck followed by the spacious glories of the East').

In June 1916 he was called to be an officer in the Intelligence Corps and to foster relations with the French press. This was a job which would have suited his diplomatic skills and understanding of the French people and language. As he was about to take it up, he was invited back to London by the Conservative leader, Andrew Bonar Law, to become Minister of Agriculture in the Asquith coalition and a member of the Privy Council; he remained in politics until 1922 as a minister. He also served as Chairman of the Wheat Commission, a dominant factor in the global wheat trade during and after the war; he was responsible for promulgating the 'standard loaf' – bread was a subject that he deals with from the point of view of the average soldier while serving in the RAMC.

On his return to London, his political associates and personal friends all wanted to pick his brain about his life as an average soldier in France – 'for every fact of the actual situation out here they know, I know twenty'. There can be no doubt that, as the sole cabinet minister to have served in the ranks in France, Crawford would have brought to the table a unique understanding of the thoughts and feelings of the rank and file, 'the underworld', as he calls it, to which he belonged for fifteen months.

## Looking back on the war experience

The First World War was an appalling experience for its direct and indirect participants, be they combatants or civilians. It touched a larger number of people and places than any previous war. There were thirty-five million casualties of the war and at least fifty million died from the influenza that stalked the globe immediately after it, its spread hastened by the war.

Yet for many, despite its horrors, it was among the most rewarding experiences of their lifetimes. People felt that they were doing something really important and worthwhile in the 'war to end all wars', as they saw it. Mary Brandon, a wealthy American novelist who used her fortune to set up a French Army hospital, spoke of her real happiness in trying to save the lives of horribly wounded French soldiers; she repeated her noble service to the wounded in the Second World War. Harold Macmillan, the future British Prime Minister, loved the camaraderie of war service and the 'sense of teamship and the sense of triumph'. Private Cawkwell of the RAMC, thought his time as a First World War stretcher bearer in the front line 'the adventure of a lifetime and I am all the better for it'.

Crawford had similar emotions. He took great pride and satisfaction in what he felt that had done for his RAMC unit. Of one of his operating theatres, he wrote 'I love every corner of the little place – I have painted its windows, whitewashed its walls, scrubbed its floor scores of times, and, when not working, I have contemplated all its perfections and closed my eye upon every shortcoming.' He had an enormous respect for the etiquette and discipline of the Army; he was filled with admiration for the 'courage, character and good will of the average soldier'.

He greatly missed his family, friends and home, but established cordial relations with his RAMC superiors and colleagues. Most of them were from different backgrounds to his own, but united in the camaraderie and shared pains of war, such as being squeezed thirty-one to a cattle truck or bombed by German planes or worn down by constant exhaustion. One of his comrades, forty years on, by then a British Rail porter at Blisworth, recalled nostalgically carrying stretchers with him in France. Crawford enjoyed the limited available fun (he called it 'thin sport') behaving like a schoolboy at Corporal Lisgo's fortieth birthday party or delighting in his new uniform like a schoolgirl getting a gift of fashionable clothes or contributing his deep bass to his unit's choral activities – a striking contrast to Wagner's mighty music that he had enjoyed at Bayreuth a year earlier.

After he left the RAMC in France he referred to his time there as a 'grim experience upon which I look back with infinite tenderness'.

# The Northern section of the
# Western Front 1915–16

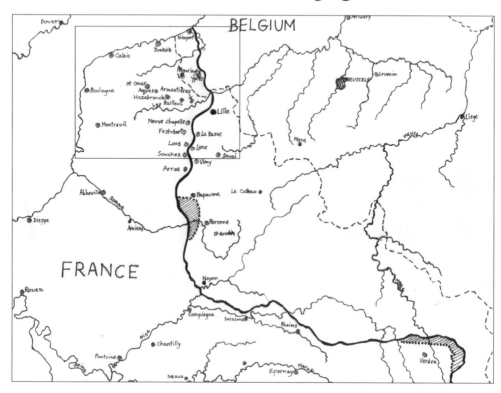

The trench line, which stretched over 400 miles from the English Channel to the Swiss border, was virtually unchanged during Crawford's time with the RAMC. Constant fighting resulted in huge casualties and little territorial gain on either side.

His base at Hazebrouck was very near to the main areas of British activity in 1915 comprising major battles at Neuve Chapelle, Ypres, Aubers, Festubert and Loos and several lesser ones..

In 1916 there were two gigantic campaigns: at Verdun and on the Somme. The smallness of the contended areas in these two campaigns (shaded opposite) is to be contrasted with the casualties – in each case about one million between both sides.

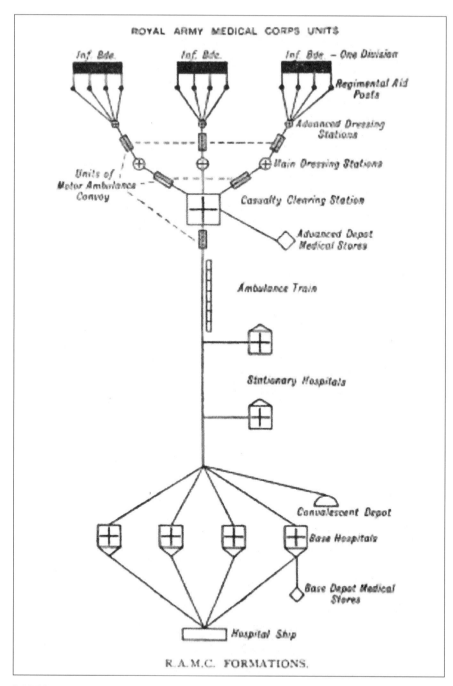

RAMC evacuation system

# I

# 12 May to 16 July 1915

*Departure from Aldershot – delays at Le Havre – alcohol and venereal disease – prisoners – letters and parcels – political interlude – boredom – nightmare journey to Hazebrouck – creating two operating theatres – bombing raids by* Taubes *– promotion to lance corporal – nurses – sad groups of refugees – spasmodic fighting – many casualties – Crawford's first louse.*

Crawford enlisted in the RAMC at the start of April 1915. On 12 May, after six weeks training at Aldershot, he set sail for France with his unit, casualty clearing station (CCS) number 12. He then resumed his life-long practice of keeping a diary which he had abandoned because of depression induced by the disastrous Battle of Neuve Chapelle in March.

At Le Havre the unit hung around for five weeks, increasingly frustrated at its inactivity and failure to move nearer the front line. Crawford was chosen to be in charge of the operating theatre. On 17 June his unit embarked on a thirty-six hour train journey to Hazebrouck, in the Flemish part of France; it was 'a night of nightmares' for Crawford and his colleagues, with thirty-one to a cattle truck, while the officers travelled in comfort, causing a 'great deal of unpleasantness'. It gave Crawford an early taste of the different treatment of officers and men.

Hazebrouck was to be Crawford's home for the next year. A meeting point of several railways, the town was about fifteen miles behind the front line. Thus it was a natural focal point for British troops and casualties, as well as German bombing and observation planes. In addition, it received many refugees (21,000 in the first year) mainly from Belgium and Lille. In 1918 the town was to be completely abandoned under a German onslaught and its 25,000 inhabitants themselves became refugees. The town and its British visitors were fortunate in that there was a highly respected mayor, Abbé Jules Lemire, also a member of parliament, who provided the practical and spiritual leadership needed in a period of great difficulty.

On reaching Hazebrouck, Crawford set about preparing the operating theatre, its equipment and supplies, in a requisitioned lace factory. On 23 June he was promoted to NCO status as a lance corporal. A few days later nurses started arriving; the resulting friction between them and the men permeates the diary. A separate, smaller, officers' hospital was also established in what had once been an orphanage, Maison Warein, named after a great benefactor of the town. It was where Crawford spent much of his time, though he was quite soon to have responsibilities across both hospitals, often referred to in the diary as No. 1 and No. 2 (or 'new station' or 'officers'), respectively.

In May, while still at Le Havre, Crawford was affected by a political crisis at home. The leadership of the Liberal Prime Minister, Herbert Asquith, lacked energy and coordinating ability; his reaction was too often 'wait and see'. There had been a failure to supply enough shells to the troops of which there were, in any event, too few and lacking experience. Confidence was rocked when Lord Fisher, First Sea Lord, resigned over the failing Dardanelles campaign, for which Churchill, First Lord of the Admiralty, was held responsible. Asquith was forced to admit several Conservatives (who had hitherto suspended party politics) into a coalition. Churchill was demoted to Chancellor of the Duchy of Lancaster and A.J. Balfour, a former Conservative Prime Minister, became First Lord in his place. He wanted to recruit Crawford into his department and Crawford was unexpectedly summoned to London to see him, but he refused the task. This uneasy Asquith coalition – which Crawford considered a blunder – was to be replaced eighteen months later by one led by Lloyd George.

The Dardanelles campaign was one of several diversionary strategies designed at the start of 1915 to weaken Germany's allies and divert her troops from the Western Front. Another such strategy was invasion of the Balkans, via Salonica, to build on Serbia's initial success against Austria-Hungary. Both had the aim of defeating Turkey, 'the sick man of Europe', helping Russia and securing Greece, Romania and Italy as allies, while neutralising any threat from Bulgaria. Both were to fail, at great cost, because rivalries and disagreements between the services, the politicians and the allied powers led to delay, compromise and uncoordination, without which either strategy might well have succeeded.

Notwithstanding these diversions, by far the biggest theatre of war was the Western Front, comprising a trench line stretching over 400 miles from the English Channel to the Swiss border. It incorporated a lot of French territory, including the important industrial city of Lille and most of France's coal and iron ore resources. The trenches were such that it would be very difficult for either side to make a breakthrough. The German trenches were stronger and on higher and drier ground – and ground of their choosing – than the British and French ones, with superior backup trenches; the Germans had made great efforts to hone their trench digging skills over the previous eight years. They had fewer men by a third, but better armaments than their opponents, notably the machine gun, whose devastating capabilities were not at first appreciated by the British leadership.

The British sector had witnessed a series of big battles in the three months before Crawford reached Hazebrouck – Neuve Chapelle, the second Ypres battle (where gas was first used), Aubers and Festubert – all of them with insignificant gains and large casualties. Thereafter, major battles were avoided in preparation for a big autumn offensive, but spasmodic hostilities took place. Much of the fiercest fighting took place in the region of the Ypres salient, which both sides wished to control, being the last piece of unoccupied Belgium and a gateway to the Channel ports. The town of Ypres was largely destroyed.

The French strategy was to drive the Germans from their homeland at all costs and in all haste (Georges Clemenceau, then a newspaper editor, blazoned across his front page regularly the headline *Les Allemands sont toujours à Noyon* a town 100km from Paris). The British strategy was to support the French, but delay the attacks until sufficient men and materiel were in place. The German strategy was not to lose a single inch of French territory held and, if lost, to recover it no matter what the cost. It was a recipe for continuing stalemate and huge casualties.

## Wednesday, 12 May 1915

Left Aldershot at 8am after two hours packing hospital stores. Noted as singular that our officers never visited or inspected us during this heavy work. Difficulty of combining military and medical duties exemplified in deplorable waste of men's time at Aldershot. After school of instruction is finished, men on draft attend incessant parades, at which they have stood at ease over two hours a day, for three days in succession – it should be practical continuation of stretcher drill and bandaging.

*Nona's Queen*, certified for about 500 passengers between Liverpool and Douglas. This time we took about 1,300 passengers – an old paddle tub built in 1885. No wireless as far as I could see – very few boats, some rafts and insufficient life belts. Two lower decks covered with men and equipment –

men sleeping over one another and crawling about like crabs on a fish-monger's counter. We were also allowed on the upper deck, but no smoking for certain reasons. The marvellous searchlight at Havre Point.

## Thursday, 13 May 1915

Journey in the open sea about six hours, but actually in transport for twelve hours. Crossing so good that there were no ruined tempers or kits. Wasted several hours unloading equipment, then marched through dull drizzling heat to the rest camp No. 2 at Sanvic, some four miles, mostly uphill – very tiring and our men in bad temper. The burden of route marching in formation of fours, while wet and heavily loaded, is not fully appreciated by the lightly clad and dry-shod officer at head of column. I wondered as we marched up if we are popular in France. Familiar we must be – the spectacle of British troops can no longer be a novelty; but I thought I detected signs of *ennui* and some malevolent glances.

## Friday, 14 May 1915

Amazed by the number of rats at the ASC's place. Slept in a very wet tent. Talked much while on duty with French territorial guarding the water tower. Later in day our colonel talked to me with great consideration.

## Saturday, 15 May 1915

Wired to CC&B and signed it Bal. Interview with censor (a major I think, deaf, choleric, inept). He censured me with great animation for having signed a telegram by a 'ridiculous nickname.' Two other officers there and a RE NCO who threw up his eyes to the ceiling when my scolding began. Evidently he was accustomed to these outbursts.

CC&B stood for Constance Crawford and Balcarres, née Pelly, also known as Connie, whom he married in 1900. Bal was his nickname by which he was widely known among family and friends. They had a very happy marriage for forty years and had eight children. One feature of the war was the huge number of gifts sent to soldiers at the front from Britain. Connie sent regular food hampers from Fortnum & Mason, which were shared by Crawford with his colleagues, as well as crockery, linen, bandages and a football. The ladies of Cheltenham College provided his unit's x-ray van and two Misses Heath of Southfields, a novel 'for the Tommy or Reggie who receives this book … such anonymous kindnesses touch the heart', observed Crawford, 25 May 1916.

4

## Monday, 17 May 1915

Heavy rain again last night and the camp like a marsh. How this adds to our discomfort and alike to our work – we have to sweep out our tent fifteen to twenty times a day. Our colonel addressed us on VD, liquor, enteric etc. Very strict injunctions to avoid dangerous things like shellfish and watercress. About VD he was admirable – I have never heard the case so well put – such an event is a breach of contract on our part towards our King and country. He is a strong personality and impressed us very much.

## Wednesday, 19 May 1915

We are here a week today, very irksome. The efforts of our men to learn French are most amusing. I have a class of four boys who live in my tent and what amuses one most is the extraordinary things they want to be able to say in French.

Tommies loved messing about with the French language. Marshal Franchet d'Esperey was nicknamed Desperate Frankie. The stenciled notice on their cattle trucks *40 hommes 8 chevaux* became 'it'll hold 40 Tommies or 8 she oxes'. Each verse of the popular song *Mademoiselle from Armentières* has a wonderfully pointless last line, for example:

> *You might forget the gas and the shell*
> *You'll never forget the Mademoiselle*
> *Hinky, Dinky, Parlay-Voo*

The camp at Sanvic with very strict boundary rules is without attraction. Watched French territorials and *poilus* marching. They trudge along with no effort to keep in step, '*Pousse-Cailloux*' [foot-sloggers] they are aptly nicknamed, but it is astonishing what distances they can cover in their aimless rambling style – up to twenty-five miles a day for a week in succession. Few if any of our troops could do this, certainly none formed of these elderly gentlemen over forty. French bayonet a terrific weapon.

## Thursday, 20 May 1915

Our camp has now got some money – yesterday was the pay day. Five francs apiece handed round. Result a certain ominous hilarity. Some of our men don't yet realise the tremendous danger of breaches of discipline. There are prisoners working in Le Havre dockyard who have been sentenced to fifteen years – among them an officer convicted of rape. If a prisoner tries

5

to escape he is shot. There have been two or three cases. Our men know this, but the temptation to imbibe is so strong that they are ready, largely from heedlessness, to run these tremendous risks. These last few weeks have much disposed me to support Lloyd George's stringent proposals.

Lloyd George, Chancellor of the Exchequer, thought that the effect of alcohol on industrial productivity was more damaging 'than all the German submarines put together'; he declared that 'we are fighting Germany, Austria and drink; the greatest of these deadly foes is drink'. His idea of nationalizing the trade was opposed by the brewers, while temperance supporters did not want the state to 'sully its soul' by getting into the drinks business. He proposed new taxes on drink, most of which were shot down. The abstemious Crawford often notes the bad influence of alcohol on the troops; as a young man, he had done social work in Bethnal Green and was shocked at the devastating effect of alcohol on the poor.

### Friday, 21 May 1915
We marched five or six miles this morning; it was the first parade, except for the roll call, in eight days. Such a pity that our life is so idle, we are getting soft, with too much meat and too little exercise (also no vegetables) – bread is very compact and tough, but good quality. A Cabinet crisis in England. Thank heavens that I am out of this political turmoil. A coalition government seems a fait accompli. Blunder – it will silence much criticism which is essential and cloaks the collapse of the government brought about by disloyalty and intrigue.

Crawford told his wife that he had, several months previously, helped 'nip in the bud' the proposal of a coalition – unsuccessfully, as it turned out.

### Saturday, 22 May 1915
The colonel paraded me and Gray. I am to be put in charge of the operating theatre. If I can stand the work, it will be a responsible post – better anyhow than the pack store to which I was previously allotted.

### Sunday, 23 May 1915
Prisoners. One lot of our own – a melancholy procession of men occupied in the menial services of the docks, clearing up the latrines and passing along with a moody hangdog air. The other set of prisoners was a company of

German soldiers who were being marched onto the quays to unload a cargo of cotton. Their sleekness and physical prosperity struck one immediately. Their moral abjection no less noticeable. I was standing with another RAMC man as they passed by. Suddenly they realised who we were – the French they treated with sullen apathy or disdain. Towards us their eyes glittered with insensate, almost demoniac, malice. I recalled another train of prisoners seen long ago in Siberia.

> He visited Siberia in 1899 as he anxiously waited to learn whether Connie would change her mind and agree to marry him, their engagement having been broken off.

## Monday, 24 May 1915

Letters and parcels from Connie and the children. She sounds well – well enough anyhow to remove anxiety from my mind. No transport had come in when we left this morning; one certainly should have reached the docks. I hope no mishap. Three days ago the submarines made sailings from Southampton impossible.

> The British government had made great efforts to build large battle-ships, in competition with Germany, before the war; there was to be only one big naval battle, at Jutland in 1916, whereas the threat from submarines, ultimately of far greater consequence, had been underestimated.

## Tuesday, 25 May 1915

Went on pass into Le Havre – sauntered about, had my hair cut, more than ever *en brosse*. Most of the men in No. 12 have had their heads shorn. It is ugly and, were one unexpectedly returned home, one would have a frigid reception – but the practice has its advantages. Le Havre is a fine town and the docks are magnificent. People well turned out. There is an air of capital importance and prestige in all these large provincial towns of France. I find our men compare Le Havre with their impressions of London or Edinburgh. They should compare Le Havre with Sunderland or Bristol – then what a contrast!

## Wednesday, 26 May 1915

Great perturbance as a censor's stamp has gone astray – the rubber stamp which franks letters, evidently a dangerous implement to fall into hostile or unscrupulous hands – but rather amusing for those who groan under the censor's vagaries. Over eighty-one in the shade – bathing parade, superb sea view from magnificent cliffs.

## Thursday, 27 May 1915

Our letters are failing to reach home. Wrote to Connie asking her to make enquiries in London, as the delay does not lie with our censors here and correspondence doesn't go through French hands at all. Our uniforms begin to get shabby. How can they be replaced? Our boots begin to wear. Our tempers remain calm and equable. We are prepared to face our trials of immobility with patience and long suffering. Reading Thomas à Kempis on these virtues, but how different is the English translation from the sonorous Latin, how washy and thin.

## Friday, 28 May 1915

Bitterly cold night, slept in my overcoat. Two hours on committee settling details of our athletic sports. These began in the afternoon – to be finished tomorrow. The Northumberland CCS left this morning; we gave them some good cheers. Their destination quite unknown to us. They must have been kicking their heels here for six weeks or more. Who knows – perhaps our fate will be even more tedious than theirs. But we gradually accustom ourselves to life in a rest camp. But why should those who have done no work be in a rest camp, while there are units at the port who have laboured incessantly and without twenty-four hours' change, for six and even eight months? This lack of repose is killing our men of sheer fatigue, and in the RAMC (for the moment at least) reserves and substitutes are ample. We base our hopes of migration on an acknowledged fact which may appeal to the common sense of our masters.

## Saturday, 29 May 1915

I unexpectedly find myself in London. Last night, I got an order to proceed forthwith to London to report at WO. Started at once for Le Havre, drew my warrant at headquarters in the town, and boarded the *Hantonia*. We were chased or rather observed by a submarine ten or fifteen miles out.

To WO at 11am. I was passed from man to man, all quite ignorant of causes – till luckily I stumbled upon George Arthur who told me AJB wants me to become Civil Lord of the Admiralty. A nice sort of proposition to consider at an hour's notice. Went to see Ned Talbot and, while there, was summoned to see AJB at the Admiralty, where I found him surrounded by maps and Admiralty chess boards. He was very kind – appreciated my difficulty of consenting to discharge from the army, still more my apprehension that my heart is no longer in parliament – which makes me feel I should do the work under reluctant protest. Indeed this was my first and now is still my abiding sentiment. He refused to accept a yes or a no at such short notice. I am to see him tomorrow. Lunched with Ned Talbot who pressed me very strongly to consent. On argument his plea is strong; on psychology mine seems to myself irresistible. One thing he said quite reminded me of old House of Commons days. Macnamara, it appears, is to stay at the Admiralty. Ned is most anxious to have an experienced hand to watch AJB lest he fall a victim to M's guile. After a most distasteful morning went to Hillbrook, where I found Connie and the children in good health and spirits.

> Sir George Arthur was Lord Kitchener's biographer. Arthur Balfour (commonly known as AJB), the new First Lord of the Admiralty, wanted Crawford as his Civil Lord of the Admiralty. Thomas Macnamara, a Liberal MP and Parliamentary and Financial Secretary to the Admiralty since 1908, was vastly more versed in its activities than AJB. Lord Edmund ('Ned') Talbot succeeded Crawford in 1913 as Conservative Chief Whip in the House of Commons; later, as Lord Fitzalan of Derwent, he became the last Lord Lieutenant of Ireland, before the position was abolished in 1922.

## Sunday, 30 May 1915

Connie would like me to stay in England and a life of ease and security would indeed be agreeable, but I should hate it and work without zeal or enthusiasm. I do not want to think of my own wishes, but I feel sure that after a fortnight in England, I should feel as suicidal as after Neuve Chapelle. She agrees, so I refuse. Came to London at 4pm, wrote to AJB and talked to Ned Talbot on the telephone who is really sorry I don't see my way to joining the government.

> Balfour was surprised at Crawford's apparently irrational decision – ministerial job offers are rarely refused – and described it in rather laboured terms as 'not defensible on any of the ordinary rules of conduct, but I recognise that there are inward intuitions and impulses which cannot be argued out on paper, but which, nevertheless, carry with them an authority which cannot be, and ought not to be, ignored'.

## Tuesday, 1 June 1915

On the boat back to France, a long talk with some newly enlisted REs, all colliers from Tamworth and district. They are skilled in use of rescue apparatus and their special job will be to reopen tunnels destroyed by the Huns.

Reported to No. 9 GH, which is surrounded by barbed wire and guarded by armed sentries. There are at this moment some 1,200 VD cases. They include sixty officers, one a lieutenant colonel. What an odious and detestable place. There have been as many as 2,000 cases at a time. I had occasion to pass through the officers' lines. What can they think of themselves! I took my mental revenge by refusing to salute.

I brought back a football from London which had a tremendous ovation. Paraded before the colonel to report on return for duty – very sympathetic. I quite realise the adverse comment I shall encounter from those who cannot understand.

In the stratified class structure of the time there might be criticism of Scotland's premier earl enlisting as a private. He was the first peer to enlist as a private; it was a thoroughly unorthodox step for a senior aristocrat and politician to take. He also feared that his CCS might be dispersed and he would have to make new relationships.

## Sunday, 6 June 1915

Service at 7am. 8.30am to docks for twenty-four hours guard. Saw No. 23 general hospital packed into train for Etaples – twenty-nine to the truck.

## Tuesday, 8 June 1915

Colonel Grech took Gray and me to see the hospital over the Gare Maritime d'Escale. We were shown all the sterilising plant, operating theatres etc. But when are we going to use our knowledge? The frogs begin to croak. The young bull frog has almost the note of a bullfinch. The araucaria at Les Roncherolles, just outside our camp, shows its fruit pods already.

## Wednesday, 9 June 1915

Route march through the fascinating Forêt de Montgeon. Just as we were getting out after spending three to four hours in losing our way in the labyrinth, rain came down in torrents and Lieutenant Beale took us for shelter in to a delightful shady estaminet where we entertained ourselves with temperance drinks and our hosts with soldiers' choruses. All our march was to the strains of a mouth organ played by an incomparable Lancashire lad called

Heaton officially, but known as Darkie. It is unbelievable what a difference is made by such a slight and restricted type of band. One's marching on a tiring route is improved fifty per cent.

Our system of medical treatment is vague and un-business-like. Instead of the sick man being placed in charge of one particular surgeon, he is examined everyday by the officer in waiting. As this officer is changed every twenty-four hours, one may guarantee that diagnosis and treatment constantly vary. This is a pity and in some cases may well be a danger.

## Friday, 11 June 1915

It is a month since we landed. Movement to have a photo taken of our unit – a good idea for never after leaving Le Havre shall we have an opportunity of a joint portrait. What will happen to many of us? There is good evidence that every unit of the RAMC has its time fully occupied at the front indeed there is ample scope for reinforcements during these times of heavy casualties.

> The second Battle of Ypres, which ended in April, was followed by the Battles of Aubers and Festubert – all with heavy casualties and negligible ground gained.

## Sunday, 13 June 1915

Early celebration and church parade at 10.45am. Another idle day. We are too otiose, but the circumstances of our sojourn here – not knowing if we may not be called away at a few hours' notice – make it impossible to follow out any definite scheme of drill or lectures. If the WO could tell a unit on arrival that a month perhaps would elapse before moving, our officers would arrange a regular scheme of work which greatly increases our efficiency – what prevents anything of the kind is our uncertainty. Now after several weeks a feeling of lassitude is being followed by unrest. One hears complaints (for the first time).

A young man of the YMCA sold me a pair of candles. One was partly consumed. I protested. Apology followed by conversation ensued and he ended by snap-shooting me with a Kodak – a most irregular proceeding as our camp commandant is all against these small amusements and amenities. He has gone so far as to forbid us to kick our football about before 4pm.

## Tuesday, 15 June 1915

My friend Jock, a NCO in the YMCA, tells me of a sweep-up of men employed on quasi-civilian work. He was wounded and for many weeks past has been serving soldiers behind the counters. Wherever one goes one sees men to whom strength and vigour have returned, but who have dropped out of sight and are performing very insufficient functions. The Army Pay Corps, the ASC, the AOC each has many men, especially NCOs, who seem quite unoccupied and whose services would be much more profitable at the front. Surely women and elderly retired soldiers could do much of the work being done by these able bodied men. I am greatly struck by the number of non-effectives. In our own small unit, the officers' servants and grooms amount to twelve or fourteen per cent of our strength!

## Wednesday, 16 June 1915
On camp guard all day long. Very dull and tiresome work. My neighbour in No. 9 tent caught a louse on his neck. I tickle all over with apprehension.

## Thursday, 17 June 1915
In the evening we got orders to be ready to move. Great satisfaction in camp for our life has been burdensome and our inactivity excessive. I notice that the excitement stimulates the use of bad language. The paucity of the soldier's vocabulary drives him to use swear words whenever his emotions are too strong for his powers of speech. Hence ugly, stupid and obscene language – limited to a very few foul phrases repeatedly employed. The ordinary adjectives and adverbs don't exist to a particular type of soldier – they are replaced by 'bloody' instead of the words 'very', 'quite', 'rather', 'somewhat' and others which provide all the gradations of light and shade. The man thus impoverishes his own powers, makes himself impotent to give a consistent and living account of any normal incident. Our unit does not seriously err in this matter – indeed our language is on the whole decent and measured – moreover there is quite a strong feeling against bad language.

## Friday, 18 June 1915
Early to the docks in full kit, all our spare clothes wrapped into our coats which made us ache all over. Loaded our heavy equipment into three or four railway wagons – a very heavy job which took us five hours or more – by 4pm we got to our siding to entrain. Thirty-one in a cattle truck (covered). Tomorrow perhaps I will jot down my recollections of what is likely to be a night of nightmares. Our feet are in a continual wrangle. There is the card playing section, the eating section, the sleeping section and the quarrelsome gang. Vermin also seems probable. The day has been cool and the night will be frigid.

At embarkation, No. 12 CCS comprised seventy-six NCOs and men, eight officers, one warrant officer, one interpreter and nine horses – eight nurses would join them shortly in France. The WO diary records that on the crowded train, as they left Le Havre, there was 'a great deal of unpleasantness' because a lieutenant of the ASC insisted on his batman having a private compartment to himself, while thirty-one of the men were packed in a cattle truck. The truck was almost certainly one of the standard French wagons which held eight horses or forty men. Crawford and his comrades were lucky to be only thirty-one. An American soldier, Charles Hoyt, described conditions there graphically – 'Men were stacked in and piled up in a manner that would have brought protests from a self-respecting sheep on the way to market'. The same wagons were used for deporting Jews in the Second World War.

### Saturday, 19 June 1915

What a night! The disposition of our nether limbs occupied us from 9.30pm or so until midnight. The shindy, swearing, singing, shuffling of feet, losses and recovery of temper all at once and all continuously – they leave me with an indelible recollection of complete chaos. Our sergeant is dull and lacks initiative. Nothing would have been more easy than to distribute us in a symmetrical way – it would have given rest to many. Daylight at 3am. A few troop trains, an ambulance train and some hundred German prisoners. The weather gets hot. We reached Abbeville by midday – a huge long train with a locomotive of very moderate power. It is now 4.30 in the afternoon and we are awaiting for departure. Our destination is said to be Hazebrouck – a pleasant little town, but I doubt if we shall stay there long. It seems rather off our line. A little knot of gamblers, all very youthful, cause a good deal of resentment among their contemporaries. I notice that the winnings generally fall to the same man. Gambling is illegal – we have been warned against it, the punishment is severe.

## Sunday, 20 June 1915

We reached Hazebrouck about four this morning having passed slowly up the line, branching off at Boulogne or just south of it. I went into the decorous little town and had coffee. Much Flemish spoken – in fact the place is Flemish in all essentials. Back to our railway siding where we stood about till midday when we began to unload our railway wagons. Put the goods (30 tons) on to the ground and in the afternoon we began to reload them into motor wagons – this went on till 6pm when we walked to our hospital – a distance of a quarter of a mile or so. It is a lace factory – a large top lighted building like an ordinary weaving shed – say 250 by 80ft. There are three little office rooms attached and deplorable sanitary arrangements. There is a well in the middle of the floor from which strong odours arise.

Heavy gun firing audible all evening. We are all very tired not having had our boots off for sixty-five hours. Slept wonderfully – never did a feather bed feel so soft as the uncommonly hard floor.

## Monday, 21 June 1915

Spent practically the whole morning scrubbing walls, windows and floor of the apartment which is to be called the operating theatre. It is a makeshift place, but I am in charge thereof and must do my utmost to produce a clean and sanitary room. The light is bad – drainage very insufficient. Every pailful of water has to be mopped up from the floor – fresh water, however, is laid on but it is undrinkable and requires boiling.

## Tuesday, 22 June 1915

Awakened at 3am by the great German gun which spent most of the morning bombarding Cassel and Dunkirk. Some time ago this German monster was put out of action by our aviators. She is now repaired or replaced and is again erupting. Busy all day in the operating theatre, very tired at night.

## Wednesday, 23 June 1915

There was a terrific bombardment in the Arras region between 1am and 2am this morning. Much the heaviest firing I have yet heard. Yesterday a *Taube* dropped two bombs at our victualing store on the railway. They fell just on either side of a train standing in a siding.

> *Taube* was a German aircraft, which was excellent at mounting observations from a great height and difficult to spot because of its translucent wings; they subjected Hazebrouck to many bombing raids. 'Taube' is the German word for dove, which it resembled at a distance. It was soon replaced by more powerful aircraft and became a training plane for German pilots.

Four hours in the morning getting out stores and instruments for the theatre. The colonel wishes me to become a lance corporal. I don't like the idea. I am in charge of the operating theatre and as such should be an NCO, which gives sufficient rank to confer the power of giving orders. The operating theatre staff is too small to make any promotion necessary; however, I shall have to give way though I begged him to wait for a week until he can judge whether I am capable of the work. Some men's stomachs make such a task impossible. I must have spent twelve hours in the operating theatre today. Cannot get into the town. Badly want a bath. Our latrines odious. This afternoon some devious sewers, running haphazardly beneath the floor of our great ward, were opened and somewhat purged. The place still stinks notwithstanding much Cresol. It is rumoured that we are to send a detachment to Bailleul and also that we are to man an infection hospital in Hazebrouck. This would denude us so much as to make an end of our CCS. How much I should regret the severance of many ties which have grown up in these six weeks abroad; to be placed in another unit, where I know I have no friends and indeed might meet ill-wishers, would be distressing.

## Friday, 25 June 1915

Ten hours in theatre setting out instruments and sterilizing. Called away during each of my three meals to talk to Lieutenant Dawson – rather hard! Got permission to go into the town. Wonderful hot bath after seven days' dirt. A little rain, enough to make our camp into a quagmire. General Traherne here yesterday expressed astonishment at the transformation we have effected in four days. He saw the filthy unpromising place the day before our arrival.

## Saturday, 26 June 1915

Finishing touches to the theatre. I anticipate some friction between the surgeons – all wish to operate and Dawson, it would appear, expects to do it all. Another source of trouble may arise from the nursing sisters, six of them, now on their way. They bully the orderlies and complain to the officers about trivialities which cause them offence. So far as soldiers are concerned there is not the smallest doubt that they would prefer to be nursed by the RAMC orderlies – but the British public imposes these nurses on our units. They cause difficulties in commissariat, lodging, sanitation and everything else.

## Sunday, 27 June 1915

The colonel has been looking for a new scene of operations, our factory being cramped, water-, light- and drain-less, with a miserable access – altogether the most unsuitable place. We should do much better to have our own encampment in some field outside the town. It was suggested to him that we should become the depot for cases of ordinary sickness. He on the other hand is anxious to do some surgical work for which our unit is qualified and for which our entire equipment has been prepared. Accordingly he proposes to the authorities that we should establish an officers' hospital.

## Tuesday, 29 June 1915

At the new place I have to take charge of the theatre. It is disheartening after a week's incessant work in the main theatre to begin afresh in a vilely dirty hole. The light however is good and perhaps we may do good work. Our fatigue party of twelve began to clean out the garrets which have not been touched for twenty years. The first floor is filthy, the ground floor wants a thorough cleansing.

This evening a couple of hundred refugees trailed into the town – a sad shocking spectacle – old shattered men, young mutilated children, women dragging their wearied children along, the children carrying bundles as big as themselves – a cruel sight, especially the young people dazed with fear and fatigue. Some village near Béthune has been bombarded and these poor souls have lost their all. If only some of our slackers could realise the atrocities of war surely they would abandon their apathy.

Our food arrangements have been changed to our advantage. We live very well. I like Hazebrouck better every time I walk in the streets. Had a good omelette. Heard a political sermon in the great church, but the man's French was very bad and I could make little of it, as my place was too far back. Besides, he spoke with a strong Flemish accent.

## Wednesday, 30 June 1915
At No. 2 hospital most of the day. The colonel, a man of energy and decision, means to make the officers' section a marked success. Let us hope he may – there is some scepticism as to whether our personnel will be adequate.

Two nurses arrived to the horror of the unit which intensely dislikes the nurses at this stage of the firing line. Further back and when the wounded men are convalescent and anxious to gossip, the help of nurses is invaluable – but at the earliest stage after being wounded, the patient doesn't want to have to be on good behaviour. Orderlies and men alike dislike nurses and from all accounts with good cause.

> The feeling may have been mutual – Nurse Jentie Paterson of No. 5 CCS commented in a letter home that 'orderlies to my mind are all very well but they can never take the place of women nurses ... they lack education, perception and conscience ... being of a different social status to us, his ideas of cleanliness differ and he never, not even the best, grasps 'surgical cleanliness' – in fact, Crawford constantly stresses the need for cleanliness in a surgical environment.

Do I detect certain nonchalance in the frequenters of the cafés and market square? We are near the line, widows who walk in the streets are innumerable, shops and factories are shut – yet with all this evidence of war and with incessant gunfire dinning round us, there is a happy go lucky bored feeling among the *indigène*. He is accustomed to war and no longer thinks much about it, externally at any rate. There is no rush or anxiety to read the telegrams. A man buys a newspaper, folds it up puts it in a pocket and walks away without ever glancing at a headline. One can understand it. The French are confident. *Joffre les tient!* And here in Hazebrouck they are making lots of money – but let one of the new German shells shriek into the town and we shall see much more human weakness.

## Thursday, 1 July 1915
Spent some time in the new hospital which is being cleaned from garret to cellar by a squad of twelve men, aided by three painters from the town. It is astonishing how our fellows are dispelling the squalor. Also to be dispelled or else expelled are three professors who occupy three precious rooms on the

first floor. They are really elementary school teachers but, as their establishment is an endowed orphanage managed by the municipality, their title and style are grandiloquent. Steps are being taken to get rid of them. They are making a desperate fight but the help of the mayor has been invoked, l'Abbé Lemire, a man of some position in France, and we hope to acquire this Naboth's Vineyard without undue scandal. Without these rooms our work will be cramped – with them the place will just be a physical success. Water and drainage remain the chief problems. Hazebrouck hasn't got a plumber left and our men will have to rearrange the gas, water and drainage system. I doubt not they will do it quite as well as the natives.

> Abbé Jules Lemire was a teacher of philosophy and rhetoric. He was mayor of Hazebrouck and, for thirty-five years, a French member of parliament. He promoted laws, among many others, to help children, to restrict obscene publications, control working hours and protect small investors against risky South American bonds. He was a pioneer, internationally and in France, of the allotment movement (*jardins ouvriers*); he wanted all the French to be able to own a plot of land and grow their own food.

Nursing sisters keep arriving – there are now seven of them. We groan at the prospects before us, for the orderly is looked upon as a scullery maid and treated far worse, for he can't turn up his nose and give warning. Why is it that so bitter a prejudice exists against them? I don't fancy it is jealousy for there is no conflict or competition as our duties scarcely overlap – neither is there this kind of hostility on the hospital ships or ambulances or base hospitals. In all these the nurses show their authority much more than their status justifies, but they are not looked upon as unwelcome or harsh agents. It is in the CCS at or close to the line that the patients themselves are so unsympathetic to the nurses and the nurses retaliate on the orderlies. Among their luggage were vermilion parasols and tennis racquets. What do they expect to find here?

### Friday, 2 July 1915

To St Omer with the colonel and our interpreter, Vicomte Braga De Souza, to buy a hot water geyser for the new hospital. We were two hours or more over the job, but finally brought one away. The problem of fitting it up will not be simple.

It pleased me, St Omer. We had five minutes in a cathedral which is full of most interesting things. The Jesuit church is magnificent – a marvellous glow from its red brickwork in the evening sky. Curiously Roman in architecture. Now secularised – used as a garage alas. Domestic architecture decorous and often dated. Streets irregular but determined in line. Solidity in the town hall, placidity in citizens, cupidity in shop keepers. Dear little Hazebrouck is outshone, but still holds my affections.

## Sunday, 4 July 1915

Stifling oppressive weather. Making aluminium splints all morning. All afternoon wounded men kept pouring in – but the bulk appear convalescent or strong enough to be passed on to a base hospital. Many medical cases which only require trifling attention. The problem is whether the station should temporarily treat itself as a hospital and give such cases a good treatment or pass them back forthwith. In point of fact the latter is correct. We are not a hospital and are not equipped as such. The CCS is merely a milestone in the baseward career of an injured man, and the quicker we evacuate these men the better for us and for them also. The Northumberland CCS have received and evacuated as many as 1,000 cases in twenty-four hours.

> There was a continuing debate as to whether it was better to operate on a wound at the earliest possible moment at the CCS or to send the patient back to a base hospital, where there would be better facilities for surgery.

## Monday, 5 July 1915

Our men rather tired by the strains of yesterday – to receive a man every third minute for five or six hours, to register, wash, re-clothe, feed, diagnose and put to bed such a number means hard work; it was especially hard as our organisation is still defective and whereas some men were overwhelmed with work, others were almost idle.

## Tuesday, 6 July 1915

Lieutenant Dawson told me that the sisters are at liberty to use the theatres as a sitting and serving room. It is therefore quite natural that they should look upon my colleague Gray and myself as interlopers. But we have had our revenge; Gray made a wonderful mattress for the operating table, a paragon in mattresses – thin yet feeling thick, hard yet feeling soft, narrow but conveying the impression of breadth, and into the bargain, light clean and graceful. These good ladies set out to make a duplicate and produced a heavy hillocky macadamised switchback. They realised their discomfiture and appealed to us for help. We put their tumuli under the field fracture box – the closest substitute for a traction engine, and this morning the mountain ranges had vanished only to reappear when they tried to squeeze the thing into an ill-designed pillow case. Assisted at the operation on a RFA man, for removal of two cists below right eyebrow, very bad case. Thirty-five minutes, no ophthalmic instruments available; those which should have come had been omitted by oversight at home.

### Wednesday, 7 July 1915

I see controversy in the London press about waste of food in the army. Though the scandal is considerably reduced, the waste continues on a serious scale; both at Aldershot and in France, I am puzzled to find a solution for a serious state of affairs. I confess that I see no simple solution. In England, especially in provincial camps, the destruction of good food has been tremendous and the odd thing is that synchronous with waste there has been constant hunger. What is destroyed at dinner is badly wanted at tea. There has been plenty of food for supper but it got messed up at breakfast and by midday was in the incinerator.

Here at Hazebrouck we eat together. We cut off the bread from loaves on the table. At Aldershot a whole loaf was given me every day – much was wasted. Here I cut off the three or four slices I require and cause no loss. We also distribute our surplus among the refugees in the town. This is much appreciated. At home no army food may be given away for fear that government property may be converted into cash. That is the terror of the War Office, and the sergeant cook and quartermasters are the object of suspicion lest victuals be converted into cash, and these precautions and restrictions hamper all effort to economise where there is now waste. Moreover, the indefeasible right of the British soldier to his pound of bread and his morsel of pepper is too sacred to be lightly impaired – Parliament might ask questions – colonels might get into trouble, all sorts of terrors might ensue, and meanwhile the waste continues.

### Friday, 9 July 1915

Another tiresome and rather vexatious day. Nurses rather overpowering – they ate chocolate all over the operating table and dropped cherry stones on the floor. I always thought it an unpardonable offence to bring food into a theatre. The place is a club room, a cloak room, a serving room and now an estaminet!

## Saturday, 10 July 1915

A German aeroplane dropped three bombs at the railway station close by us. One fell in a garden and did no damage. The second broke through a roof but failed to explode. The last blew a hole in the road, smashed a hundred panes of glass; two small children were injured slightly, but were able to eat their dinners with gusto.

## Sunday, 11 July 1915

Two hundred cases arrived today. I was in the theatre all day – five cases under anaesthetics, two of amputation of fingers, two on one man, three from another – also a terrific bullet wound entering the back of the thigh and issuing above the knee after travelling round thigh bone. This operation was conducted with promptitude and skill by Dawson, but it is still likely that the man will lose his leg.

What sights, what horrors, what a continuous nightmare these convoys of wounded men pouring in, batches of fifteen, twenty and thirty – weary fellows stumbling down our entrance passage on the verge of collapse then shown to a stretcher where they subside in complete coma. Their clothes are taken off and washed, often destroyed in the incinerator. They are given hot beef tea, and, as far as circumstances permit, the orderlies wash them where they lie.

Then there is the stretcher case – the man who can't walk and has to be carried from the car to the stretcher allotted to him in our ward, one doesn't see the tragedy so markedly in these cases – something like a corpse passes – it is anonymous and too passive to make an impact on the imagination. Those, on the other hand who can walk, have the wan haggard features of paralysis – a curious stiffness of countenance as though the mobile features of the face, particularly the mouth, had been frozen, eyes likewise are glazed.

## Monday, 12 July 1915

There were two operations today – one of gangrene, the actual operation being amputation of two toes, and drainage of the leg below the knee with thirteen incisions. This seemed well performed. The man was still lying un-conscious on the table when the order came to evacuate him to the base hospital by train. I was rather shocked – but the decision was right. The man could safely travel for three or four hours. If, as is possible, his leg has to be amputated below the knee clearly the man should be in a hospital where he can receive attention and special nursing quite impossible at a clearing station.

One hundred and fifty men left today for base hospitals and only a few came in, but I was hard worked all day – yesterday was a tremendous effort for us all and I am afraid there are signs of excessive hilarity which mark our reaction from stress. Tonight my opposite number, who has been doing the work of ten men, has imbibed too freely – some of the NCOs are too often the worse for liquor. I confess I laughed like a fool when a merry man from the next tent tied Pte B. . . . . . by his braces to the tent.

## Tuesday, 13 July 1915

Two dental cases this morning, lasting two hours! The anaesthetic apparatus broke down badly and we had to send a patient away without having concluded. I was rather disgusted, but the man (who had come to his senses twice during the operation) behaved splendidly.

Tired this afternoon, for these days have been strenuous – not merely the unfamiliarity with operations but standing for hours in a room loaded with chloroform, and with our steam sterilizers hard at work all the time. There are the peculiar and often overpowering vapours which rise from a gaseous wound, not to mention what comes from pails full of blood. Thank God I have not failed in my duty. I have throughout been able to do my work – I don't say efficiently, but with interest and zeal.

Two processions tonight in the streets. One is evidently a group of aged pensioners – evacuating a Belgian village close to Bailleul – forty or fifty old men and women, all looking seventy years of age, some of them one might say centenarians. Some walked along with the confident stride of honest and healthy maturity, others broken down in health and morale. Here and there the pathetic figure of some poor old dame being wheeled along in a decrepit bath chair – all this grim tragedy of fright was escorted by a dozen nuns, old as their flock. Where will they go, where will they find their resting place? The second one is not a procession exactly, but a series of groups of men all moving to the town hall – these are young Belgians who are foregathering from all parts of northern France and are about to undergo their first military training. I talked to some of them, very merry and rather excited young fellows – all eager for the fray with that enthusiasm for fighting which is seldom found among those who know what it really involves. After inscription at the town hall, they were to go by train to some place in the south of France but could not tell me the name of the place or how long they would stay there. They passed along, a succession of brave fellows of whom again the future is uncertain and must be precarious. Let us hope they may avenge the cruel fate of their aged compatriots whom they passed in the streets as they marched so confidently towards their destiny.

## Wednesday, 14 July 1915

This I must record as an inevitable landmark in my military history. For the first time I am lousy and very damnably itching. Many of my friends laughed, others shuddered, but to us all the day of trial must come. How long it will be protracted is the most urgent problem. Spent all afternoon arranging the theatre at No. 2. The floor is irregular, the place faces south, the light is divided and the room is a passage, no water is laid on which adds to one's work. I shall be sorry to leave our tiresome and inconvenient kitchen at No. 1, which we have laboriously converted into my *beau idéal* of a theatre. In spite of all its impossibilities I love every corner of the little place – I have painted its windows, whitewashed its walls, scrubbed its floor scores of times, and when not working I have contemplated all its perfections and closed my eye upon every shortcoming.

I look forward to my migration to the Maison Warein with some apprehension. It will be a genteel place with many nurses and few orderlies. The patients will be officers with whom I cannot speak on terms of equality – such is the etiquette of the army of which I cordially approve. On the other hand there will be officers who will try to pick up an acquaintance for one motive or another. Of this I staunchly disapprove. Then again I shall be largely cut off from all the good fellows with whom I have lived so happily in France for the last two months; but I must try to keep in touch with them. The places are only half a mile apart and I ought to manage to see something of them several days a week. It is a pity that our unit is to be further broken up. Already we have nearly forgotten the existence of sixteen of our colleagues who are running the observation camp at Bailleul, and, now that our third establishment is to be started, our unity must be irretrievably lost – until indeed the time comes for us to move forward. But under these circumstances, shall we move forward? It is simple to replace a centralised and single CCS by a fresh unit – but to call on a fresh CCS to take over three establishments, two of them very highly specialised, is to expect too much; in fact the more efficient our work, the more immobile we become. I don't want to sit in Hazebrouck till the end of the war.

Tonight the colonel suggested that I should give him my letters for technical censorship. He would frank them without perusing them on receiving my general assurance such as the officers give that no improper news of a military character is included. The thought is kind, but embarrassing. I never write indiscretions (military), and I have long since overcome any reluctance at the idea of my correspondence with Connie being scrutinised. At first I disliked it intensely but the censors, after a week or two of amusement, come to read our letters with an automatic nonchalance – gathering the general sense of the missive and only really reading the letter when something special attracts their attention. They say that unless something specially funny occurs they can't remember a syllable after putting the paper down.

## Thursday, 15 July 1915

Spent much of the morning clearing the operating table for the new theatre and all the afternoon scrubbing its black marble floor – picturesque but unsuitable, since the floor is much worn and will collect pools of blood.

At midnight last night awakened by the rain coming through the tent. I found it had poured a wine glassful into my boot, a liqueur glassful into my haversack and a teaspoonful into my cap – last night's rain fills our reservoir, immensely relieving our labours. For some days past every bucketful has had to be brought from the neighbouring gendarmerie, a walk of 340yds. Late last night a new nurse arrived. A corporal and six men were ordered out to meet her, carry luggage and escort her to her billet. While on their way to the station they met the lady, being accompanied by two officers and the sergeant major. Our officers are unwise in their zealous attentions to these nurses.

General Porter came over the wards yesterday and visited the theatre. I believe he expressed pleasure. This afternoon I saw the Black Watch march in. They looked superb; seldom have I seen so powerful a body of men. I think they were the 9th Battalion and got to France a week ago.

> Robert Porter, like so many RAMC officers, was Irish. He had already served more than 30 years as an army surgeon when he was appointed Surgeon General of the Second Army in 1915. The Black Watch was destined to suffer great losses in the forthcoming Battle of Loos.

## Friday, 16 July 1915

Five dental operations under anaesthetics. In many ways they are most trying – there is a personal violence directed against the patient which somehow doesn't seem necessary in the average anatomical case. One of the most pathetic sights I ever saw – 200 patients struggling to rise from their stretchers on Sunday night when, at the conclusion of divine service, the national anthem was played. Persistent rumours of an impending effort along the front, and great confidence among those who tell us about our prospects.

# II

# 18 July to 22 September 1915

*From lace factory to seminary – fatigue and garden work – Germanic names – court martial – thirty-one officers and nurses lord it over twelve NCOs and men – colonel's stretcher design – trench fever and neurasthenia – au revoir to the horses – looting and souvenirs – sailors revered – unofficial music – French and British boots – the men's intuition about their officers – loafing at GHQ – French railway guards – great troop movements – Mother McCarthy rattles the nurses.*

In late June the French and British high commands had agreed to launch a major joint offensive. The French wished to do it almost immediately whereas the British wished to wait until the following spring, when far more troops and weapons would have become available. Eventually, September was chosen for what, to the British, was known as the Battle of Loos. In order to be better prepared for the big volume of casualties expected, No. 1 theatre of No. 12 CCS moved from its small lace factory to a capacious seminary in the middle of town. The officers' station, at Maison Warein, was also completed.

Hazebrouck was 'bristling with troops' during the late summer of 1915. The town was regularly visited by German planes which dropped bombs and observed the military preparations under way. Spasmodic fighting continued a few miles away. The German bombing was not yet very effective and the big guns too far off to harm Hazebrouck. The town maintained a certain normalcy and the locals were making a lot of money out of the British presence – 'how they rob us', complains Crawford, since the barber charged the British troops one franc for a haircut, while the locals, even the local millionaire Vanook, paid only 50 centimes. The flow of refugees, the grief of the bereaved, the worries of split families and the floods of casualties, however, were daily reminders of the horrors of war.

Crawford's frustration at the absence of movement on the front, and consequent static life, was relieved by a visit to St Omer with the station's washing (the prices were evidently too high in Hazebrouck). St Omer was the location of the GHQ and he was astonished at the number of staff officers loafing around and the hundreds of cars, which were never being used, but subject to endless cleaning by their drivers. The wastefulness of the army's activities, much of it perpetrated by staff officers, constantly irritated him.

The medical content of his work turned out to be at least as large as the surgical; many of the soldiers, because of the conditions in the trenches, were very vulnerable to diseases. Several diseases were unfamiliar, such as trench fever, a sort of very bad flu which could put a man out of action for a month; it affected a quarter of all British troops. He makes his first acquaintance with shell shock, triggered as much by the horrors of life in the trenches as active fighting, which was at first often mistakenly diagnosed as malingering or cowardice.

## Sunday, 18 July 1915

We vacated our lace factory after 9am and our men proceeded to the Petit Séminaire in the Rue St Omer which is being vacated by the South Midland CCS. This is an important change for us as our capabilities for work will be much enhanced – we shall be able to do credit to ourselves. Our little station is taken over by No. 17 CCS beside whom we camped for several weeks at Le Havre. They were delighted with the place, little realising the strenuous ten days we spent in making it habitable – I spent most of the day there and

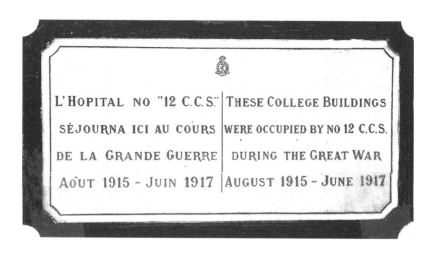

L'HOPITAL NO "12 C.C.S." SÉJOURNA ICI AU COURS DE LA GRANDE GUERRE AOÛT 1915 - JUIN 1917

THESE COLLEGE BUILDINGS WERE OCCUPIED BY NO 12 C.C.S. DURING THE GREAT WAR AUGUST 1915 - JUNE 1917

we left the theatre intact for No. 17 to use while getting out their kit. There were three operations. In one case a man had forty shrapnel wounds – the whole of his right side and back – both legs. It was a serious affair but well handled by the surgeon and with good treatment this man will he walking about in three weeks. A new nurse has arrived – very grand.

The Petit Séminaire St François accommodated not only No. 12 CCS, but also a French medical station and continued to provide education for young priests some of whom had to lodge in local cinemas.

## Monday, 19 July 1915

Spent much of the morning helping No. 17 in our theatre. Working also in our own new officers' theatre. An ingratitude. We left our theatre dispensary intact in order that No. 17 might make a good start. I stayed there twelve hours, Gray was there twenty-four, Sergeant Tidy kept the dispensary going twenty-four hours and slept in it. In fact we gave No. 17 as good a start as any CCS has ever had in France. We had to remove our instruments and I went down at three this afternoon to evacuate them. There were six or eight heavy panniers. I asked the sergeant major if he would let me have the help of a man to put them into my van – no he said – he hadn't got a man to spare. I began to do it myself. Half a dozen men, ashamed of their SM's churlishness, hurried forward and my car was loaded with expedition. Tonight a nasty operation in our new quarters – bullet into thigh, bruising femur, and lost in back of leg. Dawson could not locate it – a dangerous case. We got our theatre ready in two hours – good.

## Tuesday, 20 July 1915

Spent most of the day at No. 2, painted many windows and did much fatigue work. Saw many visiting officers. It will become a resort of officers who will give us a lot of trouble when they visit their friends. Many Australians in town – talked with five or six of them at a tea shop late this evening. Nice quiet and sober fellows, very different from those Martha described as seeing at Cairo.

Australian and New Zealand troops, most of them drunk, had rioted in the red light district of Cairo recently. Martha was the wife of Sir Ronald Lindsay, one of Crawford's brothers, who was then serving as Under-Secretary for Finance in Egypt; later, he became British Ambassador to Turkey and Germany, head of the Foreign Office and, from 1929 to 1939, Ambassador to the USA.

27

## Wednesday, 21 July 1915

Endless morning collecting stores for the officers' place. Our theatre still badly equipped, though at a pinch we could perform an operation. Convoys came in with a few German prisoners. A Gordon came across a slightly wounded German, who promptly and in excellent English implored the Highlander to spare his life. 'What did you say', I asked him. And I smiled at the answer to the Boche. 'Yes, I will spare your life if you will give me all your bloody buttons.' Whereupon he cut off everything in the nature of a souvenir the German possessed and marched him back to the guard.

Slept at officers' last night, Maison Warein, for the first time. Our funny bedroom is really a garret without a proper ceiling, which Sergeant Nunn and I occupy to keep watch over our stores and the kits of wounded officers (none of whom have as yet arrived). We are opposite the great parish church of St Eloi, patron saint of blacksmiths. We are dominated by its tall pierced steeple and haunted by its clock with the eccentric bells which strike at impossible hours. Old Warein, who made the wondrous wine cellar here, and who left his great fortune to found an orphanage, inserted a paragraph in his will forbidding church bells at his funeral as he had suffered so acutely from them all his natural life. We sympathise with him – but the dreamy old town of Hazebrouck doesn't seem to mind midnight being tolled at two o'clock in the morning.

## Thursday, 22 July 1915

There is always a morbid curiosity about operating rooms – ours has no locks and it is moreover used as a passageway between the main building and the dining room. People going to and fro are apt to be mischievous, and need one add, import dirt on their boots. Then again it is essential that the broken nerved patient should be prevented from messing about in rooms where there are instruments or poisons. There have been many suicides among officers – few among the rank and file. It is not that the officers are more neurotic than their men – but the fundamental difference is that the rank and file on entering hospital find themselves on improved rations. The comfort of the stomach revives, cheers, consoles and encourages him – even those suffering from terrific wounds rejoice in their victuals if it be only beef tea. The officer does not enjoy this inducement to struggle for life. So his depression is more acute and sad cases are relatively far more frequent. The man we operated on for the bullet wound in the thigh died early this morning – such a nice, young fellow and with a beautiful face. I should like to write to his mother. I wonder if he has one. He died of a secondary haemorrhage. Put on my new uniform tonight – my old one is rapidly becoming a disgrace. But working as a porter, painter, artisan and scullery maid does take the shine out of one's clothes.

### Friday, 23 July 1915

Worked hard all day but at non-essentials; still preparing No. 2 for patients who never come. I painted, whitewashed, unpacked stores, carried furniture, and, as regards the theatre, did nothing but go over instruments and sterilise. Spent some time at No. 1. I am afraid that there is some friction there. Conditions have been against us. Our predecessors (the South Midland CCS) are still on the premises awaiting orders to move up the line. Their kit lies all over the place; they sprawl and sleep all over their kit, while ours is scarcely unpacked and our men tumble all over the packing cases. Meanwhile, men come in at the rate of several hundred a day and corresponding evacuations take place. Our sergeant major quarrels with the quartermaster, our sergeant cook bickers with both. There is some jealousy between various officers and everybody is overwrought. In a week's time, when the invaluable Corporal Newby has reformed the sanitary system, and when a better method of receiving and despatching patients has been devised, there will be a marked improvement in our morale.

### Saturday, 24 July 1915

Same day as yesterday – painted, washed, sterilised, received and prepared some terrific instruments which Major Turner has had sent from home – but alas, Turner is leaving us; he is to command a field ambulance. Last night he celebrated his promotion and came home *en belle humeur*, tumbled into an empty packing case we had left at the front door, apologised to the orderly, climbed our rickety staircase in the dark, and slept the sleep of the very just. I am sorry he is going for I like his cold grey eye, his clear cut features, and they say he is an admirable surgeon.

Our personnel at No. 2 as follows:

Sergeant Nunn

Corporal Lisgo – dispenser

Lance Corporal Evans – clerk, Lance Corporal Crawford – theatre.

Privates Baxter, Farley, Hill, Moorby, Markin, Mordle, Webster, Lockyer (cook), GDO and nursing orderlies.

This morning Sir Anthony Bowlby came to inspect the hospital – a dry man – I doubt if he is a great one. He ranks as colonel and travels from station to station, operating where necessary and generally acting as expert consultant. Dawson complained today that he asked his advice about a poor fellow who was shot through the neck and paralysed downwards – an operation was clearly impossible but perhaps some alleviation might be devised. All Bowlby would vouchsafe was 'well he won't last very long', and nor he will. He will probably die of pneumonia tonight – aided let us hope by a merciful injection of morphia.

> Sir Anthony Bowlby was consultant surgeon to the British forces in France, author of many works about surgery and, from 1920 to 1923, President of the Royal College of Surgeons.

The nursing staff dined in the station tonight. This caused much work and more dissatisfaction. Alas how I groan under the domination of my own, very own old woman – Alexander by name. She hails I fancy from Scotland, just over the border. She is full of virtues and on the whole knows her work pretty well. She worries the surgeon and bullies the orderly, all with a smiling countenance. She is rather deaf. Covetousness is her failing – or perhaps an inordinate acquisitiveness. Nothing in the ward is safe from her clutches. She pinches all she can see – for the benefit of the theatre, and now Dawson pinches from us for the benefit of No. 1. The pincher pinched. At times, I permit myself a dim smile.

> Sister Alexander was known informally as Bully Beef.

### Sunday, 25 July 1915
Another long day of hard work honestly performed. Went to service in the town hall this evening. Our padre preached. I dropped off into a sweet slumber and was only just rescued in time by L/C Evans, as I was dropping off my chair.

### Monday, 26 July 1915
This morning, our big howitzers passed to the south followed by twenty-five French siege guns, all with nicknames, Chantecler, Berthe, Alouette and so on, and sure enough a few hours later a *Taube* came sailing over the town to make certain which road the artillery had taken. There was a tremendous fusillade, but the German airmen sailed serenely round and round while our shells burst innocuously – generally behind him, and always a hundred yards short.

## Tuesday, 27 July 1915

Lieutenant Dawson after all is to take charge of No. 2. That was the original plan, but it was abandoned when we took over the big responsibility of the South Midland station. Then Major Turner was appointed and forsook us – now Dawson is back again. The situation is piquant for as soon as he found he would not be here he began to pinch choice instruments and equipment from our theatre. Now he finds it necessary to restore them, and I hope that there is an occasional prick of conscience. He has not behaved handsomely by us. Last night our harem had a hair washing parade in the officers' bathroom and this morning I found a sink full of advertisements of cosmetics, *postiches*, pin curls and other whatnots of coiffure.

## Thursday, 29 July 1915

It is said that Lord Kitchener and Sir John French have been in the town today. I did not see them – perhaps it was imagination. Spent some hours removing furniture from the apartment of three professors – their rooms were essential to the proper organisation of No. 2 and there has been a good deal of difficulty in getting them to evacuate. At last we have succeeded – we had to load up three motor lorries full of their trash, and heavy stuff too. They tipped me five francs to be divided by the four of us who carted their stuff away for them.

> Lord Kitchener of Khartoum was appointed Secretary of State for War on its outbreak. He made an immediate impact through his recruiting methods and his forecast (unique among ministers) of a long war. He had a huge reputation from his service in imperial outposts, India, Egypt, Sudan and South Africa, but lacked political skills and was reluctant to take on new ideas. Sir John French was C-in-C of the British Expeditionary Force in France. He had had a distinguished military career. He served as a cavalry officer in the Boer War and was Chief of the Imperial General Staff before the war. He was blamed for military failures in France and replaced by Sir Douglas Haig in December 1915.

## Friday, 30 July 1915

Fearfully tiring day. I should like to do a little pruning and arrangement in our garden. We have some nice trees – walnut, cut leaved walnut, an American buckeye, *euonymus europaeus*, purple beech, purple hazel, a gawky Wellingtonia, magnolias and several ordinary trees. Next door to us is a well-kept place which we envy from our upper windows. There are few flowers and trees in Hazebrouck, nor even window boxes; there is utilitarianism, stern and uncompromising, in the use of the land to which the very old and the very young have devoted most loving care during the absence of able bodied soldiers.

> The lack of flowers was doubtless due to Abbé Lemire's *jardins ouvriers scheme* which encouraged people to grow fruit and vegetables; he supported a scheme, sponsored by the French President, to improve vegetable supplies for allied troops.

# Œuvre des Légumes frais
## aux Soldats alliés

A big service in St Eloi tonight, I imagine for those in mourning. The town is crowded with old men and older women. There is a pathetic little scene on the market place every week, what one might call the widow's market. At the southeast corner, the kerb is occupied by a long row of egg sellers. The women stand on the edge of the pavement, their baskets on the ground just below them. They are crowded into a short length – there may be forty or fifty of these women – out of the fifty at least three quarters must be widows – it is a forlorn spectacle, and how often do these poor souls fail to sell more than a fraction of their slender stock. No casualty lists are published here but the ill news, though less effectively organised than ours, finds its way quickly to the friends and parents of those who are killed in action. The French soldiers write constantly, generally postcards, and often enough the first indication that a son or husband has been killed is the cessation of letters. Veuve d'Assonville was telling me this morning that her third son hasn't written for ten days and she has almost given up hope! Poor woman, and there is a town full of the same sad cases.

### Saturday, 31 July 1915
Add to my list of trees elm and weeping elm, acacia, sycamore, hawthorns and laburnum, *ailanthus, celtis occidentalis*, and an outer fringe of poplars – no bad collection!

Exceptionally tiring day. Some of us are pronouncing ourselves as 'fed up'. Our place is controlled by the women and they have never allow a man to finish the job – and each woman seems authorised to give as many orders as she pleases to any man she selects, with the result that the wrong men are told off to duties to which they should not be allotted. They forget or abrogate their own orders and every now and then try to be sarcastic at our expense. They get no reply to their sallies. We are much too frightened of being accused of disrespect or bad language. There have been many cases where a wretched man has been traduced and then reduced that every sneer has to be borne in silence.

And the officers? We have no protector or advocate. Dawson doesn't give us a thought – even now we only have one leaky bucket to wash in, and that at the courtyard tap *coram populo*! He takes no interest in us. He is about the only man I have ever met whom I have never heard to say 'thank you'. It is a pity. Much good honest work has been lavished on the place – we have created a model clearing station which excites the warm and sincere admiration of every visitor. Yet our efficiency is impaired and the future harmony of the place grievously threatened because no thought is given to the comfort or decencies of the staff – this morning for instance we only had one and a half loaves of bread for nineteen men. That is inefficiency and clumsy organisation, but what adds bitterness is the insufferable domination of ill-tempered women. If only Captain Cole or Lieutenant Beale were here our troubles would be removed for they both realise how much more depends upon the men than on the nurses in an advanced surgical base. Officers – we have only had a few through our hands and they make a bad impression on me. I am watching the animal which has very peculiar characteristics.

## Sunday, 1 August 1915

Stifling day. Not well. Corporal Lisgo administered calomel which shook me. I hope with good results. Miss McCarthy came – the matron in chief. At church in town hall, Evans had to wake me up once or twice during the sermon. One part I heard was a panegyric of Esau.

> Maud (later Dame Maud) McCarthy, an Australian, was chief matron of the British Expeditionary Force in France.

## Wednesday, 4 August 1915

Who should walk into our courtyard but Arthur Lee *déguisé en Général*! I didn't recognise him, but he greeted me with enthusiasm. We walked together on the road towards Paris. What is Paris saying? They watch our labour troubles with amazement. They do not lay the blame at the feet of our artisan population, but rather direct their criticism, discreet and veiled in the press, open and unconcealed in conversation, against the country which, despite parliamentary government and democracy over so many generations, has failed to produce the great leader of men. 'What surprises me about this war', said Asquith the other night when visiting headquarters here, 'is that this war should have failed to produce a great soldier.' 'Yes', said Henry Wilson. 'And it has equally failed to produce a statesman.' Cabinet cohesion and collective responsibility are breeding this fatal compromise and there still lurks the demon which makes men's minds hinge on the future. What will be the fate of parties, Conservative, Liberal, Labour, Nationalist? How many still harbour this obsession, whereas it matters not a jot who runs our domestic affairs for five years after the war? The nation should concentrate on defeating Germany. Months ago, in August or September, I wrote a letter to *The Times*, protesting against the 'business as usual' catchword. How right I was!

Arthur Lee, a Conservative MP, had been sent out by Lord Kitchener to report on the medical services in the field. He was a trustee of the Wallace Collection and the National Gallery; he helped set up the Courtauld Institute. He left his home, Chequers, and its contents, to the nation as the British Prime Minister's official residence. Henry Wilson, of Irish origin, served forty years in the British Army, becoming Chief of the Imperial General Staff, a member of the War Cabinet and Field Marshal. As Director of Military Operations from 1910, he planned the deployment of a British Expeditionary Force in the event of a European War. Such was his dedication that he would spend holidays cycling around northern France and Belgium to improve his understanding of likely battle terrains. In 1922, soon after being elected MP for North Down in Northern Ireland, he was assassinated by the IRA.

## Thursday 5 August 1915

Hazebrouck bristling with troops – a new division has just marched in and the square looks for all the world like the crossroads at Aldershot. Quantities of Lancashire men. They passed our place singing – occasionally shouting out that cry which still survives in England 'are we downhearted?' followed by a loud 'no' in unison. We are not downhearted, at least I hope not – but the exclamation makes me sick at heart, likewise singing in the ranks. There is no song among those who have spent a few months here except when we come together some evening and fall unconsciously to singing hymns. At our old station, we used to do this, and from its open position, we were within range of forty or fifty houses – their inhabitants used to pour out to listen; touching and indeed skilful it was.

Three explosion cases came in this evening, a major and two lieutenants, Lorett and Chapin. Lorett whom I had to wash and put to bed had the most lithe figure I ever saw – poor fellow, but he will recover. Chapin, elderly and corpulent, must have had his skin punctured in 200 places, 200 wounds, all from earth and gravel which a faulty petard threw up in our own lines at grenade practice. He will lose an eye I fear. Such courage and fortitude; it did me good to staunch his wounds.

How the evenings are drawing in, how early the sunset, how mature the grapes and pears begin to look. Technically, I fancy we are in autumn – the spring campaign collapsed, the summer campaign misfired, the autumn is upon us and we are moving inexperienced and unseasoned troops into the line within a few days of their arrival and all the time, with half her army smashing the Russians, Germany holds us securely and indeed constantly attacks. That is the feature of French and British reports. German attacks and counter attacks repelled. How is this damnable war to end? Is it merely to be attrition along the existing line? The east apart, German losses greatly exceed ours. Because they have the men, their haste is greater than our own and they dare any and everything – but the prospect is lamentable.

### Friday, 6 August 1915
Drawing stores at No. 1, Franck, our QM, threw up his hands in horror at the scale and variety of our requisitions. Our CCS is becoming a base hospital or a convalescent home. The old sergeant major spirit and the economical mind of the WO employee surge within his breast when he thinks of our outlays. Moreover, he seems the only person in the unit who remembers the poor taxpayer and who dreams of his groaning two or three years hence. He says there will be a scandal – a port wine and *pâté de foie gras* scandal – we must moderate our demands, lead a simpler life and evacuate our patients more quickly.

### Saturday, 7 August 1915
We are making use of the officers' servants who accompany their bosses from the front. By a polite fiction we propose to retain the services of some of these men after their masters have been evacuated to the base. At No. 1 there are no less than twenty-five convalescent orderlies who do much fatigue work, and indeed without whose assistance the machine would break down. In this

35

case they are generally lightly wounded patients, who, though fit for light duty here, are all the better for being out of the firing line for an extra week or two. They secure this rest in return for their work and thoroughly appreciate the change. If they grow idle they are immediately sent to re-join their units and willing substitutes can always be found. The assistance of these men is invaluable, and, without them, it would be impossible to deal with 1,000 to 1,500 cases a week.

Here at No. 2 our problem is the same, but we are in a difficulty for when an officer goes to a base hospital, his servant returns to his headquarters. He is not ill, and he has not reached us as an invalid – our control of his movements is therefore small. We use the men for the two, three or four days of their officer's sojourn. As soon as the batman has learned the lie of the land, the geography of house wards, drains and water, he has to go and we wearily begin the education of his successor. Nothing could be less satisfactory, both from his point of view and ours – for he never knows quite what he has to do, nor we what he is actually doing. Amidst other multifarious duties I have to keep an eye upon this changing and evanescent squad.

He is an odd creature the officer's servant, or 'batman', as he is familiarly known in the army. I always imagined he was a smart soldier, a valet by training and a hero by instinct. Not a bit of it. He is a thoroughly normal type of the British soldier. In nine cases out of ten they seem to be chosen by chance and have no more idea of being a soldier servant than the man in the moon. Many don't know how to handle a tea cup without chipping it or to perform the usual avocations of domestic work – cleaning clothes, waiting at table and so forth. They are just plain honest soldier boys, differing in no whit or capacity from any of the thousand others with whom we rub shoulders.

I noticed during the last ten days how very grey my hair is becoming. It is a bit *coupé en brosse*, very short indeed, and as such not causing much growth and vitality. I grow white. It is not anxiety and mental distress since I joined the army, for my mind has been at rest – perhaps I am now beginning to show the external signs of decay the seeds of which were laid in the autumn. I am well. My appetite is under restraint, I sleep on a wooden floor and feel it as soft, softer indeed than a feather bed at home. I work hard – manual labour for my theatre work for the time being is at its minimum.

## Sunday, 8 August 1915

Out at 7.45am to have coffee, took a private of the Worcesters with me, such a good fellow. He comes from Evesham so I turned him on to asparagus and plum trees, the only topic on which he can wax eloquent. Intelligent talk with the colonel this morning, who says that, during the early stages of the war many of our men behaved very badly, looting and destroying during the retreat, and giving themselves and us a most evil reputation. It was partly excitement and nervousness, partly too that among the younger officers were men quite ignorant of our military traditions, and who forgot into the bargain that they were moving through an allied country. At one moment the advent of *les Anglais* was feared almost as much as an irruption of Germans.

Some officers were actually cashiered for looting the houses in which they were billeted. In one case pictures were cut out of their frames. I am surprised. The French acknowledge the magnificent contribution of the BEF to the saving of Paris and now they say that the soldier here in Hazebrouck is of a much better quality than before. We have no inducements to rob our local neighbours and I am bound to say that the demeanour of our men is beyond all praise. And judging by our reception from the inhabitants, they have forgiven, if they have not forgotten, the sins of our predecessors.

The British helped the French thwart the German Army at the Battle of the Marne the previous September, thus saving France from defeat.

### Monday, 9 August 1915
Tired again. Regamey said to me today, 'Why, you are getting quite white: is it old age or whitewash?'

### Wednesday, 11 August 1915
Bands playing in the town square of Hazebrouck, giving an atmosphere of gaiety. There was some competition I imagine and when I was there the East Lancs were playing. There is a case at No. 1 of a man suffering slightly from shell concussion – but the fumes were so much impregnated with valerian that it has been almost impossible to keep the poor fellow in the ward, so unbearable was the stench.

### Thursday, 12 August 1915
General Plumer came to inspect No. 2 accompanied by an imposing staff. I had never seen him before but I remember his saying some very kind things about Robin soon after his death, for which I felt grateful then and now.

I got caught by him – captured between the kitchen and pantry just as I was warning the boys to be prepared – but he got inside quicker than I expected and I was paraded as I was – wearing my vest as I was fatigue working. Afterwards the colonel apologised for this pursuit, it appears that our RAMC brass had told Plumer I was here. Plumer, who had never heard of me, thought that he had a hint to call me up. We exchanged two or three colourless remarks. The colonel much affronted at our surgeon general for this persecution. Why should I be paraded one third nude as though I were a prodigy or freak? What is the name of this tiresome general? I have seen him here once or twice. I thought him civil and soldierly and did not detect the weak strain he betrayed this morning.

Plumer commands the Second Army. I suppose he replaces poor Smith-Dorrien. He looks a good steady sober soldier, I dare say suitable for siege warfare, but too slow in gesture and mind to be a great or inspiring leader. What a pity we can't use the ingenuity and resource of Baden-Powell, who would be invaluable in trench warfare, but I suppose it was impossible to give a command to so relentless a chatterbox.

Herbert Plumer's kindness about Crawford's brother Robin, who died in 1911, suggests why he was so popular with the troops who referred to him affectionately as 'Plum'. In 1917 Lloyd George wanted him as Chief of the Imperial General Staff but he declined. His ruddy appearance led people to think that he was the prototype of Low's cartoon character, Colonel Blimp, but appearances were deceptive; he was an effective and admired general. Robert Baden-Powell, on retirement from the British Army in 1910, devoted himself to building up the Boy Scouts Movement which spread all over the world. Sir Horace Smith-Dorrien was held responsible for failures on the Western Front and abruptly was relieved of his command. The real reason might have been that he held up the German progress at Le Cateau the previous year, contrary to Sir John French's specific orders, and thereby saved the day.

Gleichen came to see a patient. He is now a brigadier general – but what a misfortune to hold a German name and German rank too – I heard men in his division speak of him with great disrespect. The lull in casualties continues – our patients are chiefly medical and a very dull lot of cases from the scientific point of view.

People with German names encountered hostility and violence during the war. Count Albert Gleichen, son of Prince Victor of Hohenloe-Langenberg and a British mother, had been a regular soldier in the British Army since the age of eighteen. As a kinsman of King George V he had to anglicize his title to Lord Edward Gleichen. The royal family changed its name from Saxe-Coburg-Gotha to Windsor and jettisoned their German titles. Many others with German names made similar changes. The *Financial Times* referred to the 'growing agitation for purging the City once and for all of men of alien enemy birth'. The paranoia extended even to food – Apfelstrudel gave way to Apple Charlotte (people perhaps did not know that this pudding was named after a German lady, Charlotte, Princess of Wales). Even pets were at risk – the novelist Graham Greene reported on a dachshund being stoned in Berkhamsted High Street.

## Sunday, 15 August 1915

Much of yesterday evening and all this morning messing about with a man under arrest, a London Cockney, a four good conduct stripe man, an old soldier and a cynic, Chany by name. He stayed out the other night – was put under open arrest, and then broke bounds again. I arrested him and marched him to the police station, and then a voluble Belgian refugee came to charge him with robbing her of 100 francs. This morning I took the fellow his breakfast. He passed the night in the French clink at the town hall – plenty of straw, doubtless much vermin and no light.

Then to No. 1 under police escort – the accusing woman picked him out instantly from a file of twenty men. This civilian charge supersedes the military offence and we shall not have to deal with the man if as seems probable the charge of larceny is substantiated. The whole thing is a wretched business – it is painful to run in a man with whom one has associated. He was our cook and had only been with us a week yet he belongs to our unit although not RAMC.

The strain continues unabated. Today there are twenty-five officers at No. 2, five nurses, one resident medical officer – thirty-one people in all who are entitled to give orders to twelve NCOs and men! Surely such a condition of things can have seldom existed before – one does not get a moment's peace, and when one man has given one an order a nurse promptly countermands it, and in doing so fires off two or three extra commands. I watch these women with amazement. They spy upon the staff, they give the patients no repose. They pinch our rations as though they were accumulating a privy hoard for themselves. They are tireless in issuing instructions but themselves do little beyond entertaining the inmates. They fatigue the gramophone as much as they tire us. They scold us like children and expect us to do the work of giants. Were we absent, the hospital would collapse in an hour. Were they promoted elsewhere, hardship and friction would disappear in five minutes and the patients would sing a *Te Deum*, for they often enough have reason to complain of these pushful busybodies. At No. 1 the sisters are a small force, confine themselves to their proper duties and fulfil a useful function.

Rather a curious procession this afternoon. Starting from the great church just opposite us, proceeding round the town square where a service was held, and returning to the church square to disband. There were things that pleased me in this modest affair, notably the group of orphans, and bringing up the rear a big congregation of men and women all dressed in deep mourning. I suppose this is some church festival; is it St Joan of Arc? There was an element of intercession, a note also of confidence in the little drummer boys, dressed up as Zouaves, who rolled their drums with vigour and assurance. I was in the parish church the other night for an intercession service and noted how for a certain period the congregation stood with outstretched arms. Rather a *beau geste*.

One other melancholy point. Abbé Lemire, the Hazebrouck deputy, labours under partial excommunication by the retrograde and bigoted bishop of Lille. As the procession started he passed along beneath the trees towards the square, returning with them, and standing ten minutes by us at our front door as the conclave returned to the church square. People saluted him as though he were a king or pope – there he stood watching it all with a wistful gaze and, as the end of the procession drew near, he passed forward as though unwilling to see the dean who displaced him. He has a fine face, Lemire, priest, deputy and mayor.

As a 'Christian Socialist', Lemire was reviled by some traditionalists; in the local newspaper *Le Patriote de Flandres* he was bitterly criticized for his *'lamentable rôle'* in moving girls from the Warein orphanage into lay schools when Crawford's unit took occupation of it.

### Monday, 16 August 1915

Spent most of the morning at No. 1 concerned with the charges of breaking barracks and larceny brought against Private Chany. Colonel in the chair; present is our interpreter, the prosecutor and her brother (Belgians who can only speak Flemish), their interpreter and four of us NCOs from No. 2, a sprightly bit of muslin with a big blue hat, daughter of the jeweller who sold the accused a ring. Here are the persons – voluble Flemings, expansive interpreters, silent prisoner, watchful military police; later on we had to make our evidence into the form of signed depositions given on oath, administered by Captain Cole and all present standing while the witness is sworn. In the corridors outside when we had to retire was a stream of wounded and convalescent men, occasionally a captain or a priest or some of our orderlies. The accused was remanded for trial by court martial.

### Wednesday, 18 August 1915

Colonel is more than pleased with the work of our two stations and is so confident of its ordered working that he proposes to go on leave early in September. I took the opportunity of explaining to him how slender is the margin on which we have achieved a success. We work at continuous and unremitting high pressure with no strength in reserve. Our strain is unrelieved by 'off days' such as the other CCSs have after a general evacuation. Our cycle is continuous without relief – take away a man or two among us and the machine, being so finely adjusted, might smash to pieces for lack of one small but essential unit. NCOs are doing the work of GDOs and of GDOs proper we have but one. I fancy the colonel understands our difficulty – but though he may add to our staff he can't remove our chief and engrossing obstacle, namely the nurses.

### Friday, 20 August 1915

Wasted half the day at the court martial. It is however an intriguing experience to have seen one from beginning to end – though the promulgation of sentence is reserved. The ceremony of taking the oath in turn interspersed with passages from the Army Act is rather impressive. Chany pleaded guilty to the military charge of breaking out of barracks – not guilty to the allegation of larceny, and according to rumours, inference and inductions which seem to pullulate in the ante rooms and corridors of law courts, Chany is likely to get off on the more serious accusations.

It happened to fall to my lot to take the prisoner's rations to him in the dark dirty cell of the Mairie – a tiresome duty having to walk there three or four times a day. I took trouble about him, added small comforts to his meagre allowance and apparently touched the hard heart of this cynical old soldier, with the thin spare face and unsmiling countenance. He begged me last night to accept a few pence to buy a drink at his expense. I refused of course – then with a harsh and firm gesture he seized my hand and kissed it, almost passionately – poor fellow I was touched and sorry for him – what odd little things move the heart.

One of the nurses played battledore and shuttlecock all yesterday afternoon with three wounded officers, who showed agility and endurance. The mobile X-ray car has been at our station much of the day taking plates of three or four of our patients. Only one required anything of the sort but the RAMC lieutenant in charge meant to make the most of it and had a whole day out. He is clearly a most competent man, his human frailty being that he has to repeat every sentence six or eight times. He wants to be emphatic and only achieves being a champion bore – but staff and patients laughed heartily. Anyhow he knows his job thoroughly and has a magnificent equipment – a vast motor car fitted with the most modern equipment – I dare say the thing may have cost a couple of thousand pounds – the gift of the ladies of Cheltenham College. God bless them all.

## Saturday, 21 August 1915

Our horses have been banished. This is a comfort and relief. Acting upon some secular convention, each RAMC officer in a CCS unit has his horse; every three horses enjoy the services of two orderlies or grooms. Five of our fellows therefore since our arrival at Le Havre have been looking after the stable. Occasionally on our marches at Le Havre officers used to ride, but we are not a horsey lot and the waste of time, men, money and good horses has been the subject of comment. A fortnight ago our five men were retransferred to No. 1 station and their place was taken by men sent up to us from the base. We now rejoice to hear that horses too have taken their departure; from a military point of view they were useless and the wastage of men occupied in this kind of duty is great. Horsemen reduced and men saved would form a division – while there is a whole army corps of batmen!

The war saw a reduction, though not quite the demise, in the horse's military role. Many top commanders had served in the cavalry including Sir John French and Sir Douglas Haig; a deep feeling about the nobility of the horse and its prowess in war was embedded in their hearts. Their days of glory as young men were spent in the saddle. On the other hand, during the war, it became clear that a charging horse was no match for machine guns and tanks. Moreover, they needed a lot of fodder and attention. It was pointless for RAMC officers to have horses; many were doctors in private life and had never ridden a horse. However, for the RAMC, horses played a most important part in bringing the wounded to safety over the muddy soil of Flanders. It is estimated that eight million horses died altogether during the war, of which nearly 500,000 were serving Britain. Their sacrifice is recorded in the Animals in War Memorial in Park Lane, London and others around the world, one of them carrying the epitaph 'Most obediently and often most painfully they died – faithful unto death.'

Private Chany grows somewhat lethargic. Confinement in this nasty cell is somnolent, but he has now permission to walk about the passage and get what fresh air can penetrate the little deep-walled yards. Why isn't his sentence promulgated? I am getting tired of my four daily journeys to the town hall, though it increases my acquaintance of the French officials – policemen of various grades – there is also a French prisoner, an engineer soldier, who is serving fifteen days for breaking the nose of a compatriot in a moment of enthusiasm – one of the most amusing little fellows I ever saw in my life, and certainly the best humoured criminal I ever made a friend of. He spends most of the day standing behind a barrier under the great colonnade watching all the movement of the square and holding a levee of numerous admirers, and he has many. He smokes incessantly and is never without a smile. The prison will lose its charm and Hazebrouck a cheery figure when my friend departs a free man, seven days hence, to re-join his unit at Bordeaux.

## Monday, 23 August 1915

Swinging the lead doesn't mean malingering – only shirking one's duties in an amiable way. There is much of it, more among officers than men, which is easily understood – though many men reach us with a confidential note warning us that the man's complaint is not readily diagnosed – this of course is pure malingering which is the logical development of swinging the lead. A man gets battered and concussed by six weeks of shell fire and, if his morale is not strong, the temptation to escape by any available ruse is often irresistible. Desertion pure and simple is growing less common for the police system makes escape a virtual impossibility and the death sentence will then be carried into effect. There are however, many cases of crime being committed in order to get sent down to the base where long terms of military imprisonment are served. So common was this manoeuvre that effort is now made to keep the man with his unit and men who are not actually in the line and who commit serious offences are generally sent to the trenches or else sent to relief camps near the front where they undergo various lengths of field punishment, one feature of which is being fastened in public to a tree or a gun – the modern variant of the village stocks.

It sounds a callous punishment and so it is, for the culprit gets little sympathy from his mates and undergoes mischievous scrutiny by the natives – still the humiliation is an effective deterrent, and there is no savour in his daily task of cleaning latrine buckets. Private Chany left us today for a term of four weeks' field punishment – a dapper well-turned-out old malefactor for whom nobody in the unit feels a spark of affection except myself. He was acquitted on the charge of larceny (lucky man) and on the whole got off pretty easy on the military offence to which he pleaded guilty. I had a few words with him when bidding farewell this morning. I fancy the old cynic is grateful for the trouble I have taken to soften his discomforts during the last ten days – the experience, this peep into the underworld of the army, has been of value.

Field punishment No.1 (or 'crucifixion'), was criticized at home as degrading by trade unionists and other concerned citizens. So, in 1916, the army authorities consulted their French and Italian allies as to their practices; the French did not use it, neither did the Italians. The latter, however, were very tough with errant soldiers, being free and arbitrary with the death penalty, and resorting to an unpleasant regime *'prigione di rigore'* where prisoners' legs were held in irons. Sir Douglas Haig insisted on maintaining No. 1, but the method was standarized to make it less liable to criticism.

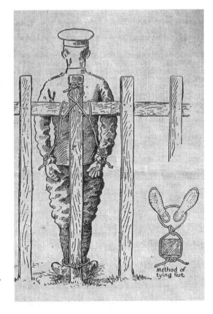

Method of tying feet

**Tuesday, 24 August 1915**

Much speculation about the naval action in the Gulf of Riga. All this retreat from Warsaw and the subsequent capture of great fortresses has caused little comment among us, but the 'battle of Riga' (to rhyme with tiger) is a source of wild conversation. The Paris newspapers haven't arrived and the ambulance train at the moment is six hours overdue. It would suggest a successful *Taube* raid on the main line – ten days ago they succeeded in making an awkward fissure in the railway embankment a few miles to the north.

Earlier in the month, the Germans tried unsuccessfully to destroy the Russian naval forces in the Gulf of Riga and capture this important city, the third in Russia, which had strong German traditions and affinities. The Russian Baltic fleet, with the help of the British Navy, drove off a powerful German flotilla; British submarines played a notable part in the action, one of them severely damaging the German battle cruiser, SMS *Moltke*. Riga remained in Russian hands until September 1917. German defeat and the Russian Revolution created the opportunity for Latvia to declare independence, with Riga as its capital, in 1918. After two decades as an independent nation, it was forcibly absorbed into the Soviet Union but recovered its independence in 1991.

**Thursday, 26 August 1915**

*Des pluies sont tombées en Ecosse* ... so I read in a French weather report. How refreshing it sounds, how I would savour a drenching in some preharvest storm in Fife. Here they are carrying their grain. Ten minutes' walk in any direction takes one into a cornfield where the old men and the gallant Frenchwomen are hard at their farm work.

Talking with men back from leave. They all seem to have had words with slackers they met everywhere at home. I observe the growth of resentment against this desertion of us – I hear threats of what should and will be done after the war, and I doubt not that, though many would forgive, there are some who will carry their threats into effect. We are in many ways impotent here and it is because of strikes at home involving delay of production, combined with just that shortage of men which can convert a defeat into a victory – the extra 20,000 men who might have reinforced us at Neuve Chapelle, but they weren't there. It is now the small margin that is needed, the extra weight to turn the balance, the four or five per cent of voters who win a general election. And all the time we have the maddening knowledge that a million or more healthy young fellows can be spared at home to supplement the old and tired brigade at a shilling a day. The excuse that the country doesn't realise the situation can no longer be pleaded, unless indeed we acknowledge ourselves to be a nation of idiots. The truth is that we have pampered ourselves and each other until public opinion is so anaemic as to tolerate a scandal in the eyes of Europe.

The French are very discreet. Their newspapers are very civil and their statesmen pay us warm compliments. '*Nous ne sommes pas ingrates,*' said the handsome woman who serves me chocolate and omelette – '*nous savons bien ce que vous avez fait,*' said her splendid husband home on leave – but they both intimate politely that it doesn't represent our maximum effort and in this war it is only the maximum that can triumph.


## Friday, 27 August 1915

The colonel showed me his new stretcher equipment by which it is possible to carry the trestle apparatus within the limbs of the stretcher itself. It is a marvel of ingenious contraction of space, strength and convenience, and to carry out the inventors' intention of economy, I have named it the 'Gretcher' – a compendium portmanteau word of Grech and stretcher.


## Saturday, 28 August 1915

Colonel Grech tells me he has taken the stretcher to GHQ at St Omer where it had a friendly reception and underwent severe tests with a selection of heavy men. I urged him to patent it; it is probable that a million stretchers would be ordered, and the colonel should certainly get a royalty for his idea. Staff Sergeant Griggs who made the sample model should share the spoils.

Crawford's encouragement to Colonel Grech to patent his stretcher might have led to disappointment, since at least eighty other stretcher designs appeared during the war.

### Sunday, August 29 1915

Officers' luggage is immensely heavy. I fancy that thirty-five pounds is the limit allowed to the normal regimental officer – but in fact many of the kits weigh up to 200 pounds! We have to toil up to the attic, and, when it is there, the officer sends for it as he wants to find toothpicks or some old number of the *Daily Mail*. We make the officer servants help but some men bring no servant with them and often enough the servant is not to be found when the kit has to be opened.

The mass of luggage is astonishing. One hears of the privation of the trenches but officers come in and, on opening their valise, one will often find three or four pairs of boots, a couple of extra overcoats and two spare uniforms. Lots of men have boxes and bags also. The second feature of these kits is their dirt and disorganisation. One wonders what the servants are for and why the officers tolerate the squalor of their clothes. Clean linen is messed up with old tobacco, fresh notepaper is rammed into jaded boots, and handkerchiefs are used to wrap up open tins of potted meat. There is a general *macédoine* of clothes, knick-knacks, cheap literature and 6in shell cases; rubbish galore, dirt in profusion, vermin always menacing. I have made it my business to disinfect scores of these kits as they are a danger to our clean little community. The officer on departure smells the pungent powders, sneezes, makes enquiries of Corporal Lisgo and then salaams the hygienic precautions of the RAMC and thanks us for our pains.

### Monday, 30 August 1915

A patient came today diagnosed as having trench fever. Have we discovered a new disease? The term has been common among us for a long time and the meaning we attached to it is tolerably clear – but that it should now have received official sanction is surprising. Gastroenteritis and neurasthenia are our polite names for the humours and discomforts of immobile warfare by which men are afflicted – but our cant phrase for malingering is now apparently to be used in a more serious sense.

How disagreeable some officers are. Their nerves of course are awry but as a rule the effect of shock, worry and apprehension upon the rank and file is to produce a somnolent reaction on entering hospital; the man becomes quiescent and relieved, the officer snappish. The man is grateful for attention, the officer vexed because he doesn't get more of it. Why? This generalisation is only based on our experience of numbers far smaller among officers than men, but up to date it is exact.

They are a curious study these officers. Their conversation, so far as it relates to military affairs, is tactical and not strategic, but they talk chiefly about their billets and personal grievances. One never hears a word about the men of the army. I take it that there is now a greater variation in status among officers than ever before. Many of them take pride and pleasure in ordering their servants about with merciless pressure. The officer of old standing is much more modest in his manner, though more touchy about trifles. The staff officer of whom we see many – visitors as well as patients – seems to be a regular tyrant, and the ADCs (I have just had an interview with one of Plumer's) are far more conceited than the field marshals. Officers as a rule are popular among the men, but less so than our journalists are apt to believe. The soldier is cautious when talking to newspaper men and thinks the safest course lies in paying compliments all round.

Coin is getting uncommonly scarce in Hazebrouck. Five franc notes are common and the accumulation of these neat fellows in the Hazebrouck strongboxes must be immense. But one can't get them changed without difficulty. At Bailleul the municipal authorities, acting I suppose with govern-ment sanction, have issued local notes for circulation in the neighbourhood, as low as 50 centimes. Very dirty they get these new *assignats*, but they pro-vide a real convenience in small transactions. The gold exchange is heavily weighted against France. One can get 27.50 francs for an English sovereign. It is, I suppose, a bad sign that this depreciation has gone so far. Nonetheless, Hazebrouck is happy making more profit during a month of wartime than during a year of peace.

How they rob us! But they do so in a most friendly and amiable fashion. Sometimes they go too far. The barber on the town square habitually charged us a franc for having our hair cut, whereas the native paid fifty centimes. Some officers went there and, after tonsure, refused to pay more than the half franc. The man stormed and raged, threatened to sue them – they laid their grievance before the town major who threatened to put the shop out of bounds. That would have spelt ruin to the man and he is now more moderate, but even so a private soldier still pays more than Monsieur Vanook, our local millionaire.

## Wednesday, 1 September 1915

A sick officer came in with the diagnosis GOK – otherwise God Only Knows, the Mont des Cats name for malingering. The colonel has been enquiring into our enormous consumption of milk. I think we have used 350 tins during August, besides 250 litres of fresh milk. Evidently, the QM has reported the matter, hence enquiries and a pretty smart reprimand. We are all glad, for the ridiculous waste of milk and eggs, while experimenting in cake and biscuit making (the afternoon amusement of the nurses), is fast becoming a scandal and we heartily trust it will be stopped. Moreover if eggs, etc. can only be used for the patients, the constant invasion of the kitchen will be lessened. The nurses make themselves an infernal nuisance to the cooks. The well-defined army rule is that the kitchen is the cook's castle and nobody can go in without his express sanction.

> At Mont des Cats there was a monastery of Trappists who speak only when necessary and are discouraged from idle talk. It was a strategically important hill around which much fighting took place. At the time, there were only thirty monks left, many having joined the army. Crawford describes it as 'a tawdry sham gothic place with lots of tiles – now occupied by our convalescent camp with perhaps 700 patients', some of whom were doubtless malingering. The monastery was one of many large buildings in France taken over for military purposes; it was virtually destroyed in 1918, but reconstructed. The monks at various times in their 300 year history have made beer and cheese to support themselves.

## Thursday, 2 September 1915

Ned Talbot came in to see me – generally mistaken for a general – medals, staff lappets and shortness of stature make him look very important. Ned gave me a most depressing account of the Dardanelles and the Russian reports are invariably admissions of retreat. Here we progress a mile or two a month. At home we have strikes and shirks. People in Britain are adjured to make 'sacrifices'. This word is obsolete in France for nothing is spoken of but 'duty' – here is a fundamental difference between our allies and ourselves. General Perceval has come in as a patient.

> Brigadier-General Sir E.M. Perceval was to command the 49th Division at the Battles of Somme (1916) and Passchendaele (1917), two of the largest battles in which Britain participated, each with huge casualties.

I saw a fairly stout man in a tiny go-cart, driving a dog. In justice to the man I must admit that he was a cripple, as a pair of crutches projected from his coach – but even so it strikes one as cruel to harness these nice friendly Flemish dogs to such heavy burdens. Our men who see this for the first time begin by being amused, but merge into indignant when they see that the practice of harnessing dogs to hand carts is so common. For my part, I can't say that the dogs seem to mind, or to suffer from the work. They are all well-nourished, and very talkative. They pull astonishing weights. The Belgian army uses them on machine gun work and the French have them beneath stretcher wheels in the firing line where they do admirable work – but the idea is distasteful to our minds, though I have seen many a horse and donkey at home far worse treated than these dogs.

The military police raided an estaminet with an outhouse chock full of our army equipment – clothes, stores and arms of every description. Thousands of men, apart from troops on the march, pass through here on their way to and from leave or duty. Some of them succumb to the temptation of gambling and liquor, and are ready to sell every rag off their backs to get a few pence more – this is literally true – men strip themselves for the sake of a few glasses of beer. But these pawnshops are a source of another danger – the merchanting of stolen or looted goods. The margin between the *bona fide* souvenir and the ill-gotten loot is often narrow and the prowlers who rob deserted houses and strip the corpse deserve all the severe treatment meted out by the army authorities. There never was a campaign in which there was less of the camp follower than this war. The situation is well in hand. Criminal larceny is rare.

Looting, however, in the technical sense, is not uncommon. Take Ypres, for example. That peaceable and innocent old town is now a mass of ruins; the resident population is reduced from thousands to a little over a hundred. Heavy shells pour in day by day. A man sees a deserted house with its outer wall fallen in; there is perhaps good furniture in the ground floor room, with rain pouring in and the prospect of the whole place being powdered to dust by the next shell. To remove something which belongs to no one – to an owner possibly dead, and to remove an article of which the life in situ may only be an hour more, does not involve a heinous moral offence. It is thus that our dugouts have been furnished, all done openly and, were the owner to appear, the goods would be readily restored. Still it is a pity that conditions make or allow us to act thus in an allied country.

When the authorities catch a man doing deliberate loot, for which no utilitarian excuse can be advanced, they show resentment. A man called

Dufros, connected with the ASC, got hold of a very large church bell and managed to send it home. He was discovered, told to restore the bell, and had to send a special messenger to England to bring it back. There have been several courts martial and I believe one officer at least has been cashiered.

The souvenir craze is more reasonable till it degenerates into the other thing. The ordinary soldier collects badges, buttons, numerals and every kind of oddment. He is fond of a German helmet, captures any foreign rifle or ammunition he can find. He is also fond of rosaries for which he pays quite ridiculous prices. The children ask one in the streets for souvenirs and never get any. A year ago our men used to cut off all their buttons, etc. and distribute them to the enthusiastic French. Nowadays these transports have moderated on either side and nobody but the children ask for things openly. The passion for them is still there and one hears endless talk about souvenirs and souvenir hunting. The souvenirs I have got hold of are interesting to me – chiefly the official papers of our hospital – blank forms I mean, a few concert programmes, postal forms, and by the way, a man gave me a Belgian handkerchief printed with all the accoutrements of the Belgian soldier, and very old fashioned equipment it looks. I have also bought some of the local bank notes circulating in towns close by here, Lille, Roubaix, Rouen and Poperinghe or Bailleul.

> Souvenirs were collected for their historical and nostalgic value; some doubtless also expected that they would have monetary value in future – which was indeed the case, particularly as regards medals. The medals of Robert Porter, Surgeon General of the Second Army, a regular visitor to Crawford's CCS, were sold for £4,200 in 2006 by Dix Noonan Webb.

### Friday, 3 September 1915
Our gas has broken down which causes great trouble. The primus burner in hourly demand and nobody but I knows how to work the tiresome thing.

### Sunday, 5 September 1915
This morning being Sunday, one of our flibbertigibbety nurses turned our ragtime gramophone onto sacred music, and while we were having breakfast it played the hymn 'For those in Peril on the Sea'. The hymn is fine, the setting grandiose – but it is not materially better than many others in the hymnal – yet it has an overpowering effect upon soldiers. I don't quite know

why – but it is unquestionable that few of us in France can hear it and still fewer can sing it without brimming eyes.

> The hymn, with words by William Whiting and music by John B. Dykes, still brings tears to many, particularly those who were alive in the Second World War and recalls the heroic deeds of the sailors who saved their lives. It is specially associated with the navies of Britain and USA. The first verse gives the flavour of the hymn:
>
> *Eternal Father, strong to save,*
> *Whose arm hath bound the restless wave,*
> *Who bidd'st the mighty ocean deep*
> *Its own appointed limits keep;*
> *Oh, hear us when we cry to Thee,*
> *For those in peril on the sea!*

The mystery of the sea, the immobile trench warfare of the Grand Fleet, the privations endured so patiently by our sailors, the terrific proportion of death to wounds – we know all these things, vaguely picture the conditions of naval warfare and conclude that poisonous gasses and liquid fire are as nothing compared with the perils of the deep. If a sailor came into a roomful of soldiers there is an instinctive hush of respect. He has come to us from the unknown and is going back to the unknown. We know that he fights the elements as well as the enemy – we almost look upon him as a superman – not as the jolly Jack Tar, the handy man who appeals to the London crowd. A short acquaintance proves him to be much the same as ourselves, though his outlook on life is controlled by a wider perspective and he is more apt to lapse into the brown study as he sees visions of the blue seas – but still he is a human and lovable creature, for whom we have admiration and respect, and we remember him with emotion when we have that ocean hymn.

I suppose sailors like music as much as we do. Doesn't their band play during the fatiguing business of coaling ships? We have few bands here. One or two units are able to swank with official music, but, the bandsman being usually drafted into the stretcher bearing parties, organised music is rare. All the more common is the unofficial music we raise among ourselves. At old No. 12 we had a band of our own. There was no brass, no string, no organ, but the tin kettles and pennywhistles amplified by mouth organs and speaking trumpets, tooth combs, cymbals, and tom toms and triangle, all directed by the SM who is a capital and most humorous conductor; a real success, nay a triumph, was achieved. What began as a farce ended in high operation. We used to perform just before we went to bed. My contribution was to hum the deep notes through the megaphone and a grand rolling volcano I produced. Yes, it was all a success, and the French cottagers in our neighbourhood used to turn out in scores to hear '*ces Anglais*' sing their hymns. They thought it was a religious service, and it sounded like one. Not only were there the hymns ('Abide with me' sung adorably to this astonishing accompaniment), but some of our favourite songs such as 'All the Birds of the air were a sighing and a sobbin' when they heard of the death of poor cock Robin' or else 'Mowing the meadow' or 'Old soldiers never die, never die, never die' all these songs with skill and restraint have their solemn effects – while our ridiculous band with twenty performers produced a thin stream of ghostlike music – something intangible, something 'umbratilous', the faint echo of beautiful things with a delicate attenuated charm of its own.

We have no band now. At No. 1, they make efforts to revive it and give an occasional concert. No. 2 is of course too small for instrumental music though we sing a bit, especially the kitchen party whom I join now and then to contribute a deep bass. Those who sing well together fight well together. Our music should be more cultivated. Two or three mouth organs in a company are worth five miles a day marching, avoid endless sore feet, such is the invigorating effect of martial music – the swing and the rhythm of marching revive the moment a whistle or mouth organ begins to play. Pace can be immediately increased and some day, God help us, we shall be marched home by civilian bands who will turn out to give us a welcome back.

We hear that our interpreter is leaving us, Vicomte Braga de Souza. He is to take up some appointment on the general staff – this is promotion. We wish him well. At first he did not make too favourable an impression on us, and I am pretty sure that his translations are often inaccurate, but he has always increased his popularity and leaves us with the reputation of being a real sport. It is a pity we can't find officers of our own who can talk French well enough – but the linguistic ignorance of our officers is positively phenomenal.

### Monday, 6 September 1915

The colonel had a start for he was told that his stretcher was already in use by the French RAMC, and has been so for months past. He spent much of yesterday searching French CCSs, and finally discovered a stretcher with four little legs. His mind was relieved – the French apparatus is in no way similar to his own – indeed is to all appearances quite futile.

How I wish I could see something of the country. I have been here two months, I suppose, and, except for one trip to St Omer, I don't think I have ever been a mile away from the town hall. It is tiring this complete immobility, but a necessary evil in our system. *Optat ephippia bos* – while the despatch riders who see the world tell us that their ideal is to sit still in Hazebrouck.

> The full line from the Roman poet Horace is *Optat ephippia bos piger, optat orare caballus* – the lazy ox wants to be dressed up as a horse, while the horse wants to plough.

General Perceval left us this morning. He shook hands with the orderlies and expressed himself honoured by our care. He looks far from well, a nasty lead colour on the cheeks, but he could no longer keep away from the damp farmhouse behind the line where he got his serious chill. An officer and gentleman – dignified in movement and speech and giving 10,000 lessons a day to the young swankers who form the majority of our patients.

## Tuesday, 7 September 1915

I was talking to some men of the Northumberland Fusiliers who marched in yesterday evening and they were congratulating themselves that, though their battalion was exhausted by its march from Watten or thereabouts, not a single man fell out of the ranks. Some of the other men said that a certain proportion, perhaps rather high, had broken down, and that their colonel had threatened that 'an example' would be made of anybody who fell out today during the final lap. It was understood unofficially that he meant a man or two might be shot.

Army boots are largely responsible for these marching difficulties. Sometimes it comes about that a whole unit is served out with new boots the morning of a long route march, or even just before leaving for the front. Sore feet are inevitable and numerous, wounded feet not uncommon. I have seen a man with a hole in his heel almost big enough to carry a marble – then sepsis follows and the danger point is reached. Men ought to be allowed to break in their boots just as their physical training proceeds, by regularised steps – but, in being served with new boots, the old friends have to be surrendered. Were the man allowed to keep the old pair for a fortnight during the modelling of the new ones, how many troubles would be avoided. Our boots are good; there is no doubt of it. At first the quality was low and certain consignments were disgraceful, but for the last few months, the workmanship has been good and the fitting has required attention. Our principle is to average sizes, to be too broad rather than too narrow, and to make the boots for hard and long wear. The French follow another theory.

Their boots are less standardised, a greater choice being thus obtainable and they are designed to afford immediate comfort and ease. They are cheaper than ours on the whole, thinner and fewer nails in the sole and softer leather in the uppers. They are not intended to last for months and months. They wear out quicker, but are more frequently replaced. Complaints are rarer than *chez nous*, and their long distance marching is magnificent – ugly to watch for they trudge along without regard to step or smartness – but they do cover the ground (territorials can do 120 miles a week), and their boot system, marching practice too, is thoroughly justified by results.

## Thursday, 9 September 1915

This morning, I passed a big convoy of refugees, grown up people dragging along amorphous sacks and bundles representing all that remains of their worldly goods. The escort is provided by the local gendarmes, and the procession is headed by a very handsome Belgian soldier who lives next door almost to our station. Just as they got close to their destination I noticed a group of old women on the pavement, ages say 80, 75 and 70, with a concerted movement they rushed forward, pushed past the French police and effusively greeted another party of three old ladies, also aged approximately 70, 75 and 80. Such a pretty *rencontre*, the wise and wizened old faces breaking out into the sunshine and happiness of less tragic days.

It is a pitiful necessity to remove these people from their homes. Some-times it is necessary owing to shelling by the enemy, but when we press forward it is equally necessary for us to clear out the inhabitants. For their part they seem ready to stay within the fire zone as long as they can earn a few francs by selling foodstuffs to the troops. And there is no doubt that it is not only legitimate trading which makes so many reluctant to abandon their houses. The sniper is often victualed by the Franco-Belgian peasant. It has been repeatedly proved that communication with the enemy proceeds from natives living within our lines. Case after case has been established and summary executions are the result. Yet this espionage continues almost unabated, likewise sheltering of German sharp shooters, communications by signals, movements by dogs and pigeons, by telephone, by speaking tube and actually by wireless. What surprises our men is the method adopted by the Germans of getting into touch with these traitors. Were relations opened before the war? It seems almost impossible that these elaborate arrange-ments, which extend from one end of the line to the other, can all have been contrived since trench warfare began. We have nothing to compare with it, and suffer proportionately.

This morning a patient who sleeps in the small ward next to the nurses' sitting room complained of their noisy behaviour about midnight. The parties concerned were the night nurse, a day nurse who had no business out of her lodgings after 9pm, and a RAMC officer attached to headquarters, who crept into our station at nine o'clock and stumbled out after midnight. Accordingly, the patient complained and our MO took the odd course of removing him to the far end of the corridor as if he expects the nurses and their friends to misbehave again tonight. One fears a scandal and that we NCOs and men, who have kept ourselves scrupulously aloof having neither aided nor abetted the malefactors, may find ourselves disagreeably mixed up in the affair.

## Saturday, 11 September 1915

A fresh easterly wind all yesterday and this morning to bring us the ceaseless boom of heavy guns – the shelling which is preparatory to an infantry attack. Is the attack about to begin? The absence of casualties during the last few days means a rush later on when the congestion will be such as to make careful treatment very difficult and hazardous. New ammunition works are being erected just beyond the station barrier – a precise invitation to the *Taubes* to pay us a visit as the neurotic manager of our gasworks sagely observed. The government must have had reasons for choosing Hazebrouck, which prima facie would appear rather near the line for such a purpose. Let us hope that it connotes their perfect confidence in holding our present lines, and an expectation of an early advance.

Spent most of the afternoon finishing off the colonel's office. The walls have been repapered and all the woodwork stained and grained by the expert brush of Sergeant Nunn, and inserting in one of the cupboard panels our initials – his N, my C and Corporal Lisgo's capital L. On the inner door is an E for Evans and a huge G for the colonel himself. Evans wanted an A for Alexander but we all refused to support him.

## Sunday, 12 September 1915

People seem to have been coming in and out of the place all day long. We seem to attract visitors of every 'rank and quality', the odd phrase applied to our soldiers abroad in one of the intercessory prayers.

Rank and quality – I wonder who evolved this gargoyle of a description – how much better if the simple old style 'officers and men'. The distinction between the two is tending in point of fact to reduction, though in practice the new-born officer is just as standoffish as ever was the old pre-war officer –

more so I fancy in some cases where the officer is forever perched upon a precarious dignity. We come into contact with so many who never commanded more than a squad of clerks or accountants five months ago and whose heads are now turned by the importance of their position as sublieutenants. Again there is the man who joined twelve months ago and who has had the luck to secure rapid promotion – he is as supercilious towards brother officers as the fresh subaltern is towards men. Then the third category consists of men who are proud to be 'hail fellow well met' with every private in the street. He doesn't win the respect of the latter or gain the confidence of his fellows. The best type is the man who has been a good many years in the army, and who, owing to the long felt congestion, has failed to secure promotion. A man has just come in with myalgia, Lieutenant Birtles. He is 38 years old and has held a commission for eighteen years. His kind of man knows more than the new captain, as much as most majors. He understands the men and is consistent in attitude, gentle, ferocious or apathetic – a man who can be sized up and who is always true to sample.

I note the unerring intuition and speed with which an officer is assessed by his men. He is watched by a thousand times more closely than he knows. His manners, skill, conversation, kit, tastes, friends and frailties – they are all known, scheduled and docketed. It is seldom that the collective judgment miscarries, though for a time there may be errors of understanding. Officers don't realise how the precise and exact wordings of some remark are repeated and discussed. It is a daily occurrence to note the CO's face. He is looking 'black' – or amused or pleased or puzzled. In the long run, the officer's characteristics are known to a nicety, far more clearly than to his friends and even his relations. There are solemn discussions and conferences held about officers. Very amusing they are where sobriety crosses swords with frivolity while the wit, malice and affection take their share in the tournament. A silver new moon trying to jostle the setting sun.

## Monday, 13 September 1915
Such a wonderful day. How radiant life would be looking on such an afternoon with the yellow corn crops around us and the ochre patches of East Lothian producing good barley and wheat, with the Bass Rock like an elephant wading through a pool, with North Berwick Law imitating, oh so unsuccessfully, the adorable lines of Fujiyama, with the May Island standing watch at one end of the Forth and Inchkeith at the other – and all the sweet babies chattering over their tea, and a beloved and beautiful woman mothering our little world.

Four men have now been sent to the base, too ill to go on working. Two of them have already been discharged from the army. It is a bad business especially taking into account that in three cases the trouble is kidney disease. It is difficult to believe that our conditions can have bred the disease – more likely that careless medical examination before we left failed to detect the disease. Morris, who is seriously ill, was a capital fellow and efficient in ward work – such a man as our unit cannot afford to lose.

## Tuesday, 14 September 1915

Went to St Omer with the station washing. We saw some of the river and canal barges which are used for transport of wounded. They get down to Rouen and Havre and, I believe, also northwards to the coast. They are said to be successful from the medical point of view – but it must be dullish work for the RAMC crews. St Omer is a beautiful town, now aglow with self-importance and the amassing of money, being our general headquarters. I was amazed at the number of officers loafing about the streets – scarcely a French soldier of any description was visible – but ours are there in hundreds, largely staff men, but I noticed pretty nearly every unit represented, though of rank and file few were to be seen. There is a huge depot of the ASC and stacks of cars are parked in different squares and open spaces. By the *jardin publique* there must be almost 400, many of which have stood there for weeks and have never once moved their position. The drivers and mechanics have nothing to do but keep the engines clean and spend much of their time gambling. Can one be surprised? But it was the loafing officers who filled me with astonishment. What can they be doing? How do they all come there? I quite understand that hundreds of officers have staff billets – the refuge and ideal of the *fainéant soldat* – but there were groups of officers, tens and twelves who weren't staff men at all, hanging about and gossiping for all the world as though we were at peace. I suppose it would be difficult to stop this waste.

The St Omer military police are very drastic in keeping men up to the scratch in the matter of belts, puttees and all the unessentials of good soldiering – one is expected to be as smart as though one were at Aldershot. I doubt if French is responsible for he isn't over particular about such things – probably it is the town commandant who makes his police show this activity. Next to the officers, military police are the most noticeable figures in the town. Hazebrouck too is being smartened up a bit. Our town major (English by name from Shropshire) has given instructions that we are to be more scrupulous in our costume, and latterly some of our men have been appre-hended for not wearing puttees. Our police have just come here from Ypres and our old lot have gone there. Ypres is a looting centre and our new force likes to be as severe to the putteeless man as they used to be to the looter.

## Thursday, 16 September 1915

The colonel showed me his latest stretcher. A few days ago a new stretcher was served out to us officially, to be used for sitting up gas cases. The disadvantages of this stretcher are so numerous and so grave as to make the whole apparatus worthless. The additional weight is large, the lateral projections prevent the thing being put into many ambulance cars, the man cannot be carried when sitting up, and finally the balance being wrong, the whole thing would topple over backwards if the patient gave a deep cough. And this is the last addition to our official equipment. The colonel saw it and wondered. In ten minutes he devised the alternative and within a couple of hours the new model was made – better in every way – the man can be carried, weight added is negligible, no interference with traction etc. It is extraordinary that the authorities should have issued the other, which one hopes may shortly be replaced by Gretcher No. 2.

I had an amusing and novel experience this afternoon. The x-ray van paid us a visit – the staff went away to tea leaving the officer here – Captain Lang as he now is, and as garrulous as ever. A patient came in with a bad foot. Lang insisted on putting him through the rays, but mechanics were absent and I was accordingly jammed into the engine room for twenty minutes with instructions how to extinguish a conflagration if one should occur. I was there all alone, kept having fire alarms and got fearfully hot – however nothing untoward occurred, and Lang chattered and gibbered congratulations.

## Friday, 17 September 1915

Two of our men left us today. Private Drummond, our aged and dissolute Scot, Private Scarbrook, a young and potentially distinguished ditto, Drummond to the base, Scarbrook to become instructor in petard and grenade throwing. But what an amusing old soul is Jock Drummond. He gave us the slip on the way to the station where I had to hand him over to the transport authorities, and it was only by luck that I detected him through hearing his shrill fruity voice raised in argument with a group of RE men at the post office. We beat the buildings, got him out and worked him into the Rouen train. Somehow he was full of whisky, where procured I can't imagine, for he had none starting. Finally I discovered a sober ASC man (a pawky body from Glasgow), and placed him in charge of Jock, to make sure the man duly reached his destination. Old Jock tittered with beery pride, shook hands with everyone within reach and by now should be at his headquarters.

Scarbrook is a Scot recruited somewhere in Mile End – suffering from a terrific hernia, recommended for stripes and a Distinguished Service Medal, two good conduct badges, a wayward tongue and at times a well-oiled throat – a chest simply covered with the arms and achievements of his regiment, an affair ten inches across and at least eight deep. This was inflicted in Hong Kong, he said. The contract price was a guinea, but as the tattooist failed to turn up at the last appointment when the supporters of the shield were to be put in, Jock junior only paid him a florin. Wit, courage and devilry form the character of this entertaining person.

## Saturday, 18 September 1915

The commandant of No. 21 ambulance train refused to take an officer's luggage this afternoon. He said there was no room, that officers were only entitled to thirty-five or forty pounds in addition to their kit, etc. The stuff belonged to a Major Martin – in addition to a large valise, he had a large square box, various odds and ends and an armchair folded up in canvas; ultimately, after a long wrangle, the OC train consented to take it, protesting that such a baggage should be sent by goods train – he is quite right.

## Sunday, 19 September 1915

A long French convoy passed this afternoon. There seems to be a large transposition in process. I must say the French convoys compare very un-favourably with our own. What is good in the French army is very good – what is not good falls into the lowest category of efficiency.

Yet take for example the *Garde des Voies de Communication*. We laugh at them and externally they don't seem to deserve anything else. They are the most aged, ragged and untidy troops in France, dressed anyhow, armed anyhow and loafing about bridges and railway crossings as though they were half asleep. On further investigation, however, one comes to find that the GVC, as these grand papas are termed, work long hours, get no credit and short leave, have to live in makeshift huts along the line and none the less perform their arduous duties with much efficiency and no complaints. France owes a great debt to these venerable *poilus*, for the railway lines have been guarded by their unremitting vigilance. I have seen so much of them and so often that I now detect what at first sight is not noticed – how keenly they are watching the passers-by from beneath their bushy eyebrows.

60

The local commandant of the GVC, Captain Petit-Jean, is no longer young, having snow white hair and moustaches – but he has the self-confidence of fifteen, the vivacity of twenty-five, the figure of thirty, and, also medals, an immense variety of costume, and a *ratelier* which gleams in the sunshine like the polished corners of the temple. He returns a salute from *'un de ces Anglais'* with the ceremony he would himself use in addressing General Joffre. I should like to sponge a tea off Captain Littlejohn – but I am unlucky in these efforts. The dean, the mayor, the abbé, the head of the French Red Cross, and Vanook the millionaire – all these people would interest me as studies *chez eux* – but I don't despair. Meanwhile, I get entertainment from my washerwoman and others in the humbler walks of Hazebrouck.

## Monday, 20 September 1915

And very good fun they are too – what better company could one ask than that of three old sports who spent the whole day here emptying the cesspool in our court yard? Such spirits and animation over their foul job of bailing out muck with small buckets, from 6.15am till 5pm. Every now and then one of them would slip out for a chopin of beer, returning to his work with fresh zest and always a merry joke or gesture. At home one would expect (and encounter) grumpiness or discontent – but here the gay philosophy of France, tempered by the solid virtues of Flanders, confer a distinction, and nearly always an attraction to people and even to duties which we would look on with aversion or disgust.

Miss McCarthy came today, the nurse inspector. She did not content herself with her proper duties of looking into the nurses and nurses' system but went through the kitchen and made complaints and actually inspected the latrines, as if she could form any judgement when the place was in an impossible condition.

Great troop movements these last few days. The 27th and Canadians coming in. French troops going both north and south – is the long promised attack going to begin? Yesterday we could not evacuate our patients as no less than three ambulance trains passed through Hazebrouck without stopping – no room for our cases. It appears that the Germans took it into their heads to shell some of our trenches with a number of casualties as a result. There has been much heavy firing on our part for ten days or more.

The troop movements were in preparation for the joint Anglo-French battles of Loos and Artois.

## Tuesday, 21 September 1915

The nurses are chattering like magpies this morning and buzzing aimlessly around like bluebottles. They cannot be still for a moment. They are worried, some with sheer panic, others through imbecility; in the midst of their agitation who should stroll in but Mother McCarthy in her grey bonnet. Tumult and confusion. But the old lady asked the way to the colonel's room. What passed we don't know, but Evans went in for a moment with a despatch, and he says that Mother McCarthy was standing with her back to the mantelpiece, apparently cornered, and the colonel was smiling that ominous smile which shows all his gleaming back teeth. Who knows what passed? Evans' inference, combined with the colonel's vexation yesterday that his men should be messed about by an inspector of nurses, leads us to hope that Mother McCarthy got a good telling off and that she actually came here to make amends and to persuade the colonel to refrain from sending in a complaint to the DMS.

## Wednesday, 22 September 1915

Stiff and tired today. I might say very stiff. I got a chill at No. 1, then slept badly and failed to get warm until I swung the lead in a pasture field about half a mile off – where I lay alternately on my back, face and side with a warm sun doing me all the good in the world. But I must be careful for muscular rheumatism which threatens is paralysis to me.

Mother McCarthy's visit hasn't chastened the nurses unless indeed it is true, as rumoured, that two or three of them are under notice to leave. They make the most of their remaining days of dominion and spaciousness. One of them stayed until midnight, though expected to be gone by nine.

Whatever the conduct of nurses here, the public wanted stories of their heroism – on this day *The Times* reported that an English nurse in Paris, Mary Davies, deliberately made herself a guinea pig, injecting herself with a culture to induce gas gangrene. She then went to the doctor who was experimenting on a quinine based cure, which he successfully gave her, as soon as the symptoms appeared. She was saved and the treatment was implemented in the American Ambulance.

# III

# 25 September 1915 to 2 January 1916

*Der Leichenfeld von Loos – morale of wounded men – Hazebrouck groans under British occupation – dental red tape – visit of an august personage – hospital crisis – lice, flees and scabies – Churchill's speech horrifies – inspection trip with General Porter – boot problem and foot problem – French cartoons and posters – French replaced by Haig – Crawford granted leave.*

On 25 September the British joined the French in the Loos-Artois offensive before they were fully equipped to do so; their preference was for the spring of 1916. The British element in the campaign failed because there were insufficient troops and weaponry to follow through early surprise and success; moreover, the German machine guns decimated the British soldiers so ruthlessly that the Germans refrained from the slaughter, in a moment of apparent humanity, and dubbed the battle *Der Leichenfeld von Loos* (the corpse field of Loos). British casualties were 60,000. Blame was heaped on Sir John French and his command of the British armies in France was taken over by Sir Douglas Haig.

In October, after much delay and disagreement between (and within) the allies, a campaign was started to relieve Serbia; had it started in January, it might have been successful. Instead, many British troops got bogged down in the region of Salonica, unable to make progress and unable to withdraw, for fear of losing 'the sneaks of Romania and Greece' as potential allies and of unleashing Bulgarian adventurism. The British and allied soldiers suffered many casualties in inconsequential skirmishes, as well as much disease. Around the same time the final arrangements were made to withdraw from the Dardanelles after nearly a year's effort; the actual withdrawal was miraculously accomplished in December without loss, but the total British and French casualties of this failed campaign were 141,000; particularly large losses (relative to their populations) were suffered by Australian and New Zealand forces.

One consequence of the Dardanelles disaster was that Winston Churchill gave up his diminished ministerial appointment, Chancellor of the Duchy of Lancaster, and sought a command in France. Sir John French treated him to the *vie de château* and wanted to give him command of a brigade, but there was much criticism of influential people being parachuted into high positions; he had to settle for a battalion, the 6th Scottish Fusiliers, where he made a notable contribution.

To add to woes of the Western Front, Salonica and Dardanelles, a campaign in Mesopotamia went badly wrong when a British-Indian force found itself besieged in Kut Al Amara on 8 December, from which they could only escape nearly five months later with heavy losses.

One piece of good news for Crawford was that his wife Connie was expecting a child at the end of the year and this enabled Crawford to go on special leave in early January.

## Saturday, 25 September 1915

All night long incessant cannonade in the direction of Armentières. This afternoon orders arrived from the DMS to evacuate all possible movables. This we were busied on from 12pm till 1pm when a steady drenching rain began – all against us. We can get no confirmation of the story told us yesterday afternoon by one of our patients, a young blood on the staff of somebody or other, that we had driven the critical wedge between Lille and Armentières. Let us hope it may still prove true, but the young man's powers of observation and analysis were rather discounted by his announcement that behind the front line of German trenches there was little for us to fear!

The ignorance of officers, and above all their hopelessly unprofessional way of looking at things offers a sad contrast to the attitude of the enemy. From all accounts we receive of the young German officers who are made prisoners of war (I mean of men who joined since the war began), it would appear that the newest subaltern is serious over his work – haughty perhaps, or brutal or ignorant – but he takes himself very earnestly never forgets he is an officer and loses no chance of self-improvement in captivity even when sick. Everything in fact is subordinated to the central and dominating ideal of efficiency. How different with us. How small is the percentage of young officers who really seem thorough and who concentrate every ounce of their energy and every minute of their time upon the supreme necessity. One can't blame them. They reflect the crass vacillation of our rulers. I remember months ago in London walking down Bond Street and counting the officers in uniform; then I walked along Piccadilly and counted afresh. I can't recall the figure I got to, but it was immense, sixty or seventy I think, and the authorities have had to take severe action about night clubs, and neglect of duty. The pity of it all is that, if these brave fellows were better trained and could more fully grasp the science of war, fortune would often have smiled more brightly upon our arms.

## Sunday, 26 September 1915

Late last night our orders to evacuate remaining officers were cancelled. Four officers aided by two nurses were engaged between 8.30pm and 9.15pm in a drunken sprawl on the staircase. At 4am, we were called up to admit a patient and as we came downstairs a strange visitor furtively sneaked off the premises. This is the state of things in our CCS! I feel much embarrassed. I do not know what I should reply to the colonel if, in the event of a scandal ensuing, he were to ask me if I thought I had acted in a friendly manner towards him in refraining from speaking out. What could I say? If Lord Kitchener had entered our place at midday today and found five officers being plied with drink by two nurses, two of the officers being quite the worse for liquor, our colonel would have been relieved of his command within the week. And yet it is not my business to enter complaints. The army is the army, my rank is negligible and technically I have no access to the colonel, who in turn has no technical right to receive a report from me. But on broad grounds it is impossible to tolerate this condition of things much longer – after all one does owe a duty to oneself. I am doing my best to stimulate the courage of our very hesitating sergeant.

Perhaps things will solve themselves by a movement. Reports coming in today only agree in the statement that the Gordons and another Scottish regiment have suffered terribly – but the French are believed to have made progress below Lille, and at one time it was again reported that Lille had actually been retaken.

## Monday, 27 September 1915

The French report is clear and decisive – if such an action could be repeated ten days running we should have won our final and definitive victory by Michaelmas. As regards ourselves we have suffered heavy losses, probably 25,000 casualties, and the material gains seem relatively small. Still we have probably prevented the enemy from reinforcing himself on the Souchez line and perhaps we may have drawn German troops from the Lens district.

British casualties amounted to 60,000 by the time the battle was over.

### Wednesday, 29 September 1915

At No. 1 theatre all day. Attended eleven operations, nearly all shrapnel and gunshot wounds. In one case the piece of shrapnel which had caused serious trouble turned out to be a piece of a cartridge clip! And in another case a bullet, when extracted, looked suspiciously like one of our own. Most of the operations were performed by Professor Kay (an RAMC Major). I fancy he is a great Glasgow surgeon. He has great merits, but, for a certain class of wound, Dawson runs him very close. Operation after operation with no time even to swab the floor before the next patient is on the table.

### Thursday, 30 September 1915

Again at No. 1. The colonel has detailed me for duty there. The work during the last week has been heavy, and in Gray's absence they have found themselves unable to keep the theatre in proper condition. So I remain on the staff of No. 2, but attached to No. 1.

Great conveys have been rolling in to one hospital or another at all hours of the day – heavily loaded trains pass constantly up the line. And all the men are so happy and cheerful – one actually hears the wounded men croaking out choruses – they are conscious, or feel it, of our impending victory. It is true they have fallen by the way, but they have taken their share and bring back endless stories of the amazing speed with which the German bolted. And to these men the relief of leaving the front honourably wounded is inconceivable after months and months of killing, anxiety and fatigue. Their frank joy at the luxury of the plain hot soup we give them, at sitting down without restraint, at being beyond the range of gunfire – all this produces a delirious relaxation which makes these heroes quite childlike. Their obedience to our orders is touching, their gratitude unforgettable and, above all, one will remember the gay and hilarious talk of these shattered men. But what a spectacle! The rainy weather churned the surface into a glutinous slush – the mud dried on them, and it is no uncommon thing to see men who are almost white with the dust which has powdered over the encrusted clay.

We read in our home newspapers of men telling their interviewers that they are longing to be back in France for another shot at the Germans. Their real sentiments are quite different. They feel no personal desire for vengeance against Germans; at least the sentiment isn't very deeply seated. The man who has been at the front, in the trenches for a few months, longs for his release. A wound, even when severe, is the messenger of freedom. I have never yet met a man wounded or unwounded who wants to return to the trenches or indeed who even says he does. They are much too wise and too plucky to romance on such a theme for those who know, even if they may talk big to people at home. They loathe the actual fighting except for moments of exhilarating success, and ninety-nine per cent of our soldiers pray that they may never see a trench again. They are so naïve, so genuine and so sincere in their conversation that there can be no mistaking the sentiment of the army as a whole, that is of those who have learned the truth by the cruelty of their experiences. But, as for escaping the burden by cowardly methods, it is reprobated by all. There have been isolated cases of self-inflicted wounds, and there has also been malingering, and straggling which has merged into desertion. There must be weaklings in every army, especially in such an army as ours where many men were forced by pressure and cajolery to recruit quite against their desires. But the courage and morale of the troops is as a whole superb.

## Monday, 4 October 1915

Leo Kennedy turned up – his battalion came to grief – not indeed that the casualties were as severe as is usual with a badly hammered unit, but the leadership seems to have been thoroughly weak and vacillating. How common this is – the amateur officer is our cardinal danger, and how can we avoid it with our civilianised traditions?

> Captain Leo Kennedy of the Scots Guards, Crawford's first cousin, won a MC. After the war, he was a reporter for *The Times* and author of several books, including *Salisbury (1830–1903) Portrait of a Statesman*, a biography of the late nineteenth century Conservative Prime Minister.

## Tuesday, 5 October 1915

Six months in the army! I should like an hour to summarise some impressions, but I am rushed from morning till night, and have no time except about 7.10pm to 7.30pm when I can swing the lead – too tired when in bed to write as I used to do. The fact is I am worked hard and continuously now that I have charge of the two theatres; the officers' gives me little trouble, and, although for the last few days operations have been infrequent, I know I am doing good work at No. 1 and, as such, I am satisfied. I have reorganised the whole practice and have redistributed the duties of all but Major Kay, the head surgeon, and moreover I have got the place into apple-pie order; at least I shall have done so in a few days more. At the officers' the work continues to increase and the pressure on our little staff, which is quite outnumbered by the officers' servants, grows really serious – in fact I don't think it can go on – for men will work hard and willingly under men even if incompetent, but they will not work under women who never cease from nagging and recrimination. Where the women are incompetent into the bargain as well, the average soldier comes near to downing tools.

Does the average soldier exist in the new army? I rather question it for he still retains enough of the old civilian perspective to introduce a far greater variety than ever existed among the old regulars. Today an elderly looking private, Brookes, came in, badly crippled with rheumatism. The sergeant major greeted him with, 'well, my son, what is the matter with you?' He told his ailment, and in the course of examination for our records announced that his age was 61; today in fact his birthday. Our paternal SM (aged about 38) congratulated him, asked how long he had been in the army – the man is in the special navvy battalion of the RE. Well, he has been in the army one month. 'I have three sons at the front and I thought it my duty to come out and help them. When I enlisted I dyed my hair and moustache and gave my age as 47. They took me on for the special battalion and I think that in a week or too I shall be ready to do my bit again.' Courageous as the 'average' soldier is I doubt if such indomitable pluck and determination is to be found very often – such a gallant old fellow, so modest and unaffected, almost apologising for his advanced age, while we stood round in genuine admiration.

### Wednesday, 6 October 1915

Several men have told me that, though continuously in the trenches for the last six months, they have never fired one shot out of their rifles. One man told me that he hadn't fired except once when a friend gave him his rifle to take a sporting shot at a *Taube*.

### Thursday, 7 October 1915

I see I am confirmed as lance corporal. No power short of a field court martial can take my rank from me. Moreover, my pay is increased by five francs a day. A lance corporal I have always thought sounded a very absurd rank, but I no longer take this view. An L/C is an NCO and as such can give orders to all privates. There is a great prestige added by the single stripe, in some ways more accrues to it in the eyes of the private than to the more exalted symbol of the sergeant, for the L/C is the next and nearest to the private, and to become the lance corporal is the first and immediate ambition of those who desire promotion. I should like to end the war as a sergeant, I confess.

## Saturday, 9 October 1915

At a very long and distressing operation, I can't understand how the man stood the pain which must have been terrific. After a bit, during the worst of the probing and sewing, Major Kay happened to ask a question which brought an answer about pigeons. The man, Beardsall, it appears, is a pigeon fancier and he began to tell us about his pigeons. He became quite eloquent in rather a rambling style. He has tippler pigeons. 'Do they topple?' asked Kay? 'No, tipplers don't tipple'. No, says Kay, 'I asked if they topple'. 'Not very often', replied Beardsall, 'they sometimes do'. He talked a lot about his birds, and boasted a good deal. All the while, Major Kay was putting stitches through him – conversation almost made the patient calm, it certainly reduced his suffering.

## Monday, 11 October 1915

Paid my two francs towards the 'extras' at the sergeant's mess where I eat at No. 1. All NCOs go there and all the privates eat together next door, I fear in squalor, discomfort and confusion. We on the other hand fare well. The cook is not brilliant, but he can roast a joint, makes good potatoes and passable puddings – we buy extra vegetables, bread and a few other luxuries from our common fund. We have a servant of our own, Tom Footitt, the famous Paris clown. When war broke out he joined the Foreign Legion with many other young Britons then living in Paris. After six months of the trenches he was transferred to the RAMC, and is a fund of amusement to us all. He is more French than English and works like a slave. Harry Hill and Stanley were two others who served in the Legion and were subsequently transferred (without asking their views or permission) to the British Army – all three found their way to our unit.

Tom Footitt was the son of George Footitt, an English clown who was very successful in Paris in the late 19th century. George's best known routine was knocking about a Cuban clown, Chocolat. Tom joined his father as a clown before the war and he also acted in early films.

Urgent orders have been arriving for us to send to the nearest railhead (Caestre) all the fighting equipment of men who have passed through our station en route to the base. They leave their rifles, pouches, cartridges, etc.

in our pack stores. During the recent fighting much equipment was lost and efforts are being made to supply the shortage. The Durhams lost masses of stuff and one Yorkshire regiment lost half its kits – the men simply threw them into the ditches before the action began. Sometimes, when there is an experienced soldier in command, all the men's packs are collected before a severe action or charge and are left behind in proper custody. Other COs seem to think that men can or will make a bayonet charge carrying 6olbs strapped over their shoulders. They can't and they won't, the result being a tremendous loss of valuable stuff all of which is regrettable. Today we are emptying our station, apparently by order of the DMS, which means that another rush of work may be expected.

## Tuesday, 12 October 1915

The boys are pouring back to the Petit Séminaire, holidays having ended. Where they will be housed I can't think, as we occupy most of the buildings. They are a pinched thin-lipped wizened lot of boys, all too old looking for their tender years, and many of them with contracted eyes caused by excessive study. They are severely kept in hand – but that is the method of dealing with embryo priests the world over. They may neither receive nor send a letter without its being examined by one of the authorities – neither is a boy allowed to have a visit even from his parents without somebody in authority being in the room.

On the whole the priests in authority have behaved in a very friendly way towards us. We must be a serious nuisance to them yet they have readily acquiesced in the way we have taken possession of their building, except for their own apartments in the cloister and one or two dormitories. But they watch us all day long. They seem to think we mean to appropriate the stores and linen cupboards – they jealously guard a wooden bench twenty feet long and when anything is moved they complain to the colonel who, being an RC himself, has no scruple in telling them off handsomely.

Hazebrouck must sometimes groan under our occupation, for we have taken control of the town – we settle the public house hours, we police the streets, we now manage the drainage and sanitation. Some weeks ago two breweries at Strazeele were closed down because they insisted on brewing their liquor with dirty water, and at least one brewery in Hazebrouck has been shut in the same way. The fact is that in these little frontier towns the municipal authorities cannot cope with the problems arising from the presence of our troops – perhaps a thousand permanent ones, and during movement of the forces running up to 5,000 and 10,000 during the twenty-four hours. It is essential for health, safety and propriety that our town major should exercise complete power under such conditions, and up to now matters have always been managed with tact. Captain English, our town major, has been promoted to Béthune; his successor does not seem to understand his status quite so well.

The colonel said to me that, had it not been for the German counter attacks which were repelled with disastrous loss to the enemy, the battle of Loos would have resembled Neuve Chapelle – a great victory as announced to the world but in reality a costly and dangerous fiasco. Our casualties gigantic, our net gains negligible. The subsequent struggle, when the Germans tried to retake their lost ground at Loos has redeemed it from a serious failure – but it required six months preparation to begin afresh after Neuve Chapelle. Shall we be ready again before Easter? All the expected movement, anticipated day by day during the last week, seems again postponed and we all fear that the new Balkan venture may, indeed must, divert troops badly needed on our front here.

I find myself walking about Hazebrouck quite unconscious of being abroad. Every sight, and sometimes I feel almost every face in the town is so familiar to me that I feel in a degree more at home than in London itself. I have been here four months without spending a night away from the place. Never since my schooldays began have I been immobile so long, and during the last fifteen or twenty years it has been exceptional for me to stay for a fortnight at home without an intermission. So France is no longer 'abroad' to me – at least I feel terribly at home here.

### Saturday, 16 October 1915

Corporal Fitzgerald got very well oiled last night, offered to fight everybody and finally came to blows with Abram of Wigan – knocked out two of his sham teeth (and private property too, not government property, as Abram complained). However, Ainsworth of Haigh was called in to help his friend, and, between them, Fitzgerald was mastered and strapped onto a stretcher. He spent the night in close arrest under the charge of Captain Robinson of Nelson – so Lancashire has had its say in the tragedy of this irascible Irish cockney.

Crawford saw himself as a Lancashire man (he was for eighteen years the MP for Chorley), and a Scot; his home was at Haigh Hall, he controlled the Wigan Coal & Iron Company and participated in many local charities. Ainsworth was one of three comrades from No. 12 CCS to attend his funeral in 1940.

71

## Monday, 18 October 1915

Tinnitus case, otherwise dull day cleansing theatre and sterilising. General Mitford left No. 2 today and gave twenty francs for the mess of the staff. Unfortunately we no longer have a mess – we are elbowed out of our own room by the officers' servants who completely outnumber us and our boys pick up their meals in kitchen, pantry or dispensary as best they can. This is a pity – at one time when we averaged ten or twelve servants we could maintain equality of ratio, but now that we have twenty and twenty-five visitors we are snowed under and our own unit is dispersed. We no longer meet these men at mealtime when six weeks ago we used to have enjoyable banter and many tall stories. However, twenty francs is a handsome tip, and as we have two other generals in the place (or is it three?) we expect to grow rich. Several men have had quite a lot of money – these are the nursing orderlies who do most for patients, though many others who slave equally hard go unrewarded. This, I suppose, is always the way with gratuities – the right man is often overlooked or indeed his work prevents his being seen or acknowledged. I have had no tips lately.

## Wednesday, 20 October 1915

Bad dental cases. Why are these operations so much more distressing than a big surgical one? They are usually more noisy with a special type of messiness.

## Friday, 22 October 1915

Spent much of the day at No. 2 as Corporal Lisgo has gone on leave and work there is consequently at high pressure owing to the loss of one man, so slender is the margin on which we work. Things continue much as usual, the duties are heavier – officers much the same type; two nights ago three of them took a bottle of whiskey from the dining room table up to their bedroom where they started playing poker. Private Court pursued the whiskey, took it away much to their annoyance. Today, General Hoskyns, a patient, complained that our brand of champagne was not to his liking! What are we coming to?

Our new matron (MacCrae) doesn't make friends. She is harsh in voice and without a gleam of humour. Moreover, she takes furtive methods of obtaining information. It is always considered unpardonable for nurses to cross-examine one man about another. This she did, asking Hyde about me. Hyde, who is a schoolmaster of good standing, works under me in No. 1 theatre. MacCrae came in the other afternoon while I was out. She knows me quite well; we have talked together a dozen times. Here is the conversation between her and Hyde. Sister Andrews present.

MacCrae: 'Is it Corporal Crawford who works here?' Hyde: 'Yes, sister'.
MacCrae 'It is Lord Crawford is it not?' Hyde: 'Yes, sister'.
MacCrae: 'Do you like him?' Hyde – silence – reads a book in his hand.
MacCrae: 'What sort of man is he?' Hyde still silent.
MacCrae: 'It isn't unreasonable to ask. I merely want to know something about him.' Hyde – persistent silence – still reads though he looks up to show that he heard her remark.

MacCrae suddenly to Hyde, 'Are you a painter?' Hyde: 'I will answer your question when you have answered mine. Are you a kitchen maid?'

MacCrae: 'That is a most impertinent thing to say – most impertinent.' Hyde: 'I have made it a rule never to be impertinent unless the person in question has been impertinent to me first'.

MacCrae left forthwith, followed by Andrews who, as Hyde said, 'for the first time in our acquaintance seemed quite pleased with me.'

## Saturday, 23 October 1915

O'Grady, our dental surgeon, tells me that in August he applied for cement of a good quality for stopping teeth – that officially supplied being not only bad in quality, but almost dangerous. On 9 October, he received the stuff with a portentous document from the Privy Council signed by Almeric Fitzroy: 'Synthetic cement, value 13/6d.' Such red tape in one medical department, while shocking waste runs riot in others, makes one wonder. I continue to get delightful accounts of Connie and the children at Balcarres. Bless all their hearts. They seem so happy and busy.

Sir Almeric Fitzroy was Clerk to the Privy Council and author of its history. Balcarres was Crawford's Scottish home in Fife.

## Wednesday, 27 October 1915

Since the early hours of this morning, we have been scrubbing, washing, decorating, titivating the Maison Warein in expectation of a visit of an august personage. We were told that General Plumer was to come, but we know and see so much of generals that we were left unmoved. In the afternoon, however, when we were told the King was to come, interest was shown and also some energy among our tired men. He was due at 4.15pm; tea was prepared by the nurses, ring led by the new matron, who busied themselves with erecting palm trees in new green flower pots. Bouquets galore, ugly linoleum and table cloths, bustle, rehearsals of curtseying in the hall, etc. All I saw of King George was a motor car of superb design, flying past our front door at forty miles an hour. Some say they saw General Joffre, others that the Prince of Wales was with the King and that French too was an occupant. There must have been three cars with cyclists as escort. 'Well I am disappointed,' said Bully Beef to Major Kay who had been putting her through a course of curtseying – showing her how to draw back her stout and somewhat rheumatic right leg – '. . . to think of the lovely home-made scones we had got ready for him.'

### Thursday, 28 October 1915

This evening I made her chuckle by saying, 'Never mind, sister, this is some consolation for not having the King here – in fact I expect it will give you even more entertainment' – as a German prisoner was brought in suffering from a broken scalp. Lieutenant Buchholz fell with his *Taube* into our lives. I don't think he was wounded, but is badly contused and thoroughly shaken by the misadventure. One heard mutterings of indignation at the care bestowed on him compared with the smaller formalities and precautions taken with our own officers. 'Five men to get out a stretcher' – 'Dammed if I will cook for a German', quoth the cook. I try to inculcate the other view. We can heap coals of fire on this man's head by good treatment. Every prisoner who returns to Germany having suffered kindly and sympathetic incarceration here will contribute to the huge reaction which is to shake Germany later on. To such men it will prove useless to say we are devilish and inhuman. Their treatment here will give the lie to such a charge and their own experiences will greatly modify the false opinions of their friends and relatives – alas that we have so few Germans to spread our own propaganda.

### Friday, 29 October 1915

Buchholz gives some trouble. His wound isn't serious, but, being a prisoner, he has to be watched. We have formed relays of batmen to do sentry duty and a man with fixed bayonet is always by the bed – but behind the screen, so the sisters insist, although the bayonet gleams and towers over it. Where there is a guard, there also should be found a corporal and at three o'clock this morning I find myself sitting in the dispensary, cold and shivering, but ready to rouse the sleepers at my feet who have already done their turns. The fellows on the floor slumber peacefully. Dixon, RFA, standing by the bed is eating a gigantic piece of cake, I write my diary, with three or four hours of candlelight and silence before me. But it is very chilly.

My memory goes back to a post house in Siberia somewhere by the Chinese frontier. I can't remember its name but it meant watermelons or some such thing. Conditions are different but the temperature or the position of the candles as I write, or else some undefined trifle recalled the place to my memory – and fifteen years have passed. But I won't moralise – instead I will see that Lieutenant Buchholz has not shaken off his bandages and that Gunner Dixon does not sleep.

It is 7pm. Except for fifty minutes devoted to meals and their digestion, I have been incessantly on duty, now for sixteen hours and very tired. Buchholz was evacuated today, happily, for he gave us a lot of work. I practically had to carry him from the ambulance to the train. Poor beast – he could have walked alone with ease, but this semblance of weakness, with his head all bandaged up solaced our prisoner. The people on the railway platform behaved with great restraint – likewise our men, on and about the train. Buchholz too was quiet and dignified in a most distressing situation, behaving in a way which appealed to me. I could not help contrasting him with some of our own patients in hospital with their weak faces and vacillating manners. Though young Buchholz is only seventeen, he had a professional and business-like air, lacking in many of our officers of ten years' service.

## Saturday, 30 October 1915
Colonel Sprot of Stravithie came to pay me a visit. He is commandant of the St Omer line of communication – rather an important post. He also has to look after German prisoners en route for England, and he says that, whereas the officers always complain of their food, etc., the men seem delighted to scrub floors or to do any vile job allotted to them.

> Col. Alexander Sprot of Stravithie was a Fife neighbour of Crawford. After the war he had a moment of glory when he defeated the former Prime Minister, Herbert Asquith, in the 1918 election to become MP for East Fife, which Asquith had represented for over thirty years.

## Sunday, 31 October 1915
First day of our hospital crisis. At 6am I found an officer from the HQ staff in bed in ward No. 2. He came in latish last night without any kit, without any warning to staff, and he wasn't entered in the A and D book. This was the climax. The officer has already misbehaved himself in a scandalous fashion

and I reported the affair to Sergeant Nunn, who reports to the SM – who reports to the colonel, and I was cross-examined. The colonel was greatly shocked and surprised. He interviewed some of our men and was confirmed in the shock he had received from myself. There will be developments. We owe something to ourselves at No. 2 station. Many of us could not afford to be associated with any public scandal. We have long been living on the edge of a volcano. Drink, gambling, disregard of hospital rules, and other things as well – all this was giving us our evil reputation and the time has at last come when we should assert ourselves.

Indeed, Nunn, who is a diffident person, has in my opinion been far too tolerant of irregularities. Matters should have been reported weeks ago. Had our unit contained some ill affected or vindictive person we might have been pilloried in the press, discussed in Parliament, made the centre of an ugly scandal – the hospital would have been closed, the colonel *Stellenbosched* and the staff discredited. I had hoped that the new matron would have improved matters. She has contented herself with changing un-essentials. Her mind turns to green flower pots, shining brass and bees waxed floors. Of fundamentals, she is totally ignorant. She is hopeless as a reformer, too blind and too tactless also. A crisis, therefore, has to be brought about and I am glad that it should have been directly owing to somebody not belonging to our own unit.

## Monday, 1 November 1915

Second day of the crisis. At 10.30pm, Evans, Bunn, the night orderly, and I, were summoned to the DMS office where we were separately examined by General Porter. He is much grieved, very angry too that a member of his personal staff should have so grossly disregarded discipline and propriety. One at least of our nurses will disappear. There should be a clean sweep. I told the colonel today that, had it not been for the women, none of these scandals would have occurred – for there would have been no inducement for these nocturnal visits and we ourselves would have stopped the gambling and liquor. But our establishment is ruled by women and terrific has been their failure. I reminded the colonel that four months or more ago when he projected No. 2, I warned him, from the experience of officers' hospitals at home, that he would find this class of patient difficult to control and that they would give an immense amount of extra and needless work to the staff. He differed from me on the ground that, here in France, they would be under military and not civilian control. How wrong his forecast was, how correct was mine. He sees it now. He means to rectify matters.

## Tuesday, 2 November 1915

Mother McCarthy was here tonight. She too, like our matron, only saw trifles when she paid her last visit, and left in total ignorance of all that mattered. I note much resentment among our men at the serious mess the sisters have got us into. Another thing impresses me a good deal, namely the paucity of the colonel's information compared with our full knowledge. He seems fondly to believe that there have been one or two irregularities, but has no idea how frequent and how varied they really are. How much the underworld knows – how little is the knowledge of our rulers!

This has been a long busy and very tiring day for me, drenched several times, and doing extra work with two of our men still absent on leave.

## Wednesday, 3 November 1915

Bully Beef in tears most of the morning. Remorse is setting in that, while personally dissociated from scandal, she tolerated it in others where she ought to have acted with promptitude and firmness. Yet I dare say she was frightened of the sharp tongues of those she should have rebuked. RE Railway Corps beginning to take over sections of our railway. They are dressed in blue with leather belts and yellow stripes – they also have a wonderful gabardine for rainy weather making them look like the crew of a steam trawler.

## Thursday, 4 November 1915

Busy day. Cameron of Lochiel here, rather a fine fellow who would look well in his kilt on his moor.

> Col. Donald Cameron of Lochiel, 25th chief of Clan Cameron, raised a battalion of Cameron Highlanders in August 1914. He himself led a charge through a storm of fire at the recent battle of Loos and was invalided back to UK; he was awarded a Conspicuous Gallantry Medal. The courage of the Camerons (they were 'fiercer than fierceness itself') and their loyalty to their chief is summed up in their marching song:
>
> > *Oh, proudly they walk, but each Cameron knows*
> > *He may tread on the heather no more,*
> > *But boldly he follows his chief to the field*
> > *Where his laurels were gathered before.*

## Saturday, 6 November 1915

There was a serious accident at the hand grenade school, a rifle bomb bursting prematurely. Several officers and men were killed. Twelve wounded officers came to us and No. 1 also received several patients. I was in the operating theatre until five o'clock this morning. Two of the abdominal cases were of the utmost gravity. Very tired this morning from last night's effort. The labour of clearing up the theatre after major operations is heavy.

The ambulance train brought down over 100 cases of frozen feet, alas, how early the winter is setting in – this large number coming in so suddenly rather indicates that we were unprepared for the emergency. The CO of the train got so tired of waiting for our officers that he left without taking their luggage. It lay disconsolate, two tons of it, on the platform. It is high time that the rule about officers' luggage was enforced.

## Tuesday, 9 November 1915

I received a tip of fifty centimes for holding an officer's horse in the street – one of these men who come into Hazebrouck shopping. We are holding our ground. Our offensive has stopped. The number of wounded is trifling, though there is a lamentable increase in sick cases owing to the bad weather.

New regulation by the town major that all must be in barrack or billet by 8.30pm, instead of 9pm. Tiresome, for it upsets our evening routine in a very awkward fashion and doesn't seem to effect any useful purpose, unless indeed it proves true that fresh and onerous restrictions on the sale of liquor are to be imposed. As it is we live under pretty stringent regulations. Hours are already much limited, beer is very thin, spirits are forbidden – but as every house and cottage is a potential estaminet there is little obstacle to those who mean to get the stuff. I question whether these drastic byelaws are really effective, except as regards the shy man (and we are few) who doesn't like to ask for a rum.

## Wednesday, 10 November 1915

Corporal Lisgo is 40 today and to celebrate the event he chose his dinner and tea. We all overate ourselves and behaved much like schoolboys – an easy day.

## Thursday, 11 November 1915

Only one evacuation to the base today! A record! Captain Davidson, on leaving this afternoon, said he had greatly benefited by his stay and paid us the doubtful compliment (though it came from his heart) of saying that the place was more like a club than a hospital.

## Friday, 12 November 1915

An easy day only ten patients being moved – a contrast to last week. For the first time for a couple of months I had two hours off this afternoon and lay on the floor with the greatest happiness in Evans' room. Disturbed in the midst of my slumbers by soft snoring beside me and realised that Private Court likewise was in repose, dreaming sweetly of his Mary (Stratford on Avon).

## Saturday, 13 November 1915

Lance Corporal Nicholson is leaving us for the base – not owing to illness of a definite character so much as worry arising from the constant friction between himself and the SM who nags as badly as the women. I regret his loss. He is invaluable to the unit and in some ways almost irreplaceable.

New regulations for the patients have just been posted in the wards. Among them is an explicit prohibition of drinking liquor in the bedrooms! Significant that such an order should be necessary. It is also forbidden to give tips to the orderlies – a consolation to mean officers and no deterrent to those who are grateful for the infinite trouble expended on them. I don't think any of the orderlies have made fortunes from the largesse of the patients, but one way and another an appreciable number of five franc notes have been circulated. In a busy week one or two of the men have had three and even four of these commodities, and well have the tips been deserved. At present, I hold fifty francs for our unit as a whole, but we don't know how to spend the money as, having no mess of our own, we have no collective needs. I see how unevenly the practice of giving tips works. At No. 1 there is, of course, no tipping but our men get many presents, often something of value, in the form of souvenirs. Here all souvenirs go as compliments to the nurses. There must be a dozen large shell cases in the house and our orderlies have to keep them polished.

## Monday, 15 November 1915

All our blankets went to No. 1 to be disinfected; high time too, for we were getting over verminous. The louse is a curious animal which deserves study. It is believed that he can burrow through a serge jacket, otherwise it is difficult to explain how a chance louse, picked up while carrying a patient or in an ambulance car, can get around – of necessity via neck or wrist, without being detected en route. Anyhow he gets in and propagates his species with enthusiasm. Perhaps the best way to slay the pest is to expose the infected article of clothing to frost – in this cold weather such a course is easy – a night out of doors will free any shirt of the infliction. Where the louse thrives the flea is absent, and vice versa. The louse has no guile, no power of evasion, deception or initiative like the bug, and so far as I can see he has no natural enemy. Mankind persecutes him, but only in self-defence and his power of resistance, owing to the fertility of the tribe, is great. Moreover, no ordinary squeeze of the fingers will slay him – he requires a serious pressure and then explodes with a little pop. He is sluggish in movement, immobile when detecting danger. He looks like an aeroplane resting on the ground and also bears a curious resemblance to the thresh engine where the high pressure temperature works such havoc among his race.

He is one of the three curses of the British army. The chief curse is well known to us all. The louse occupies the second place. I allot the third to scabies, the skin disease which we all catch in turn, the RAMC I mean – infection from such troubles is inevitable from carrying or washing patients. It is damnable infliction tickling one to merriment, then irritating to the point of torture and finally, if unchecked, scabies will prevent sleep, injure digestion, destroy temper and finally land the victim in a lunatic asylum. Madness indeed is the ultimate outcome of this disease.

The worst of scabies is that, though one can't avoid catching it, the ignorance of the disease lets it grow needlessly serious. If grappled with at once it can be cured in forty-eight hours. The compound of zinc ointment and sulphur – the simplest recipe imaginable – has never failed to kill the parasite at the outset: yet so ignorant is the army of the method of attacking the disease that thousands of men have to leave their units suffering from advanced stages of the illness. Time, money, efficiency all thrown away and needless distress tolerated from crass ignorance. I blame the regimental doctors. An army order on the subject would very likely result in preventing the loss of say 500 or even 750 fighting men every week – but any orders are often devoted to routine matters that are of no account in fighting the Germans!

The army's 'chief curse' is doubtless VD, which was responsible for more hospitalization than any other illness in the war.

### Wednesday, 17 November 1915

Churchill's speech fills me with amazement and horror. The speech of a traitor and a cad for he admits having resigned his place in the government because his personal ambition was thwarted, and his attack on Kitchener, a few days after he has left and cannot reply, is bound to provoke embittered controversy, bound therefore to weaken the prestige of the government and thus to impair the unity on which our fighting powers must rest.

And we are to have him in France. I suppose he will try to boss French as he tried to boss Fisher. I am sorry for French, still more for the grave effects his impulsive nature may exercise on our campaign. The average soldier reposes confidence in French, though he is not looked upon as a genius and is thought to lack initiative. They adore Joffre – they fear Kitchener as field marshal – but the idea of a politician fresh from defeat in council coming over here to retrieve a damaged reputation is abhorrent. Yet our newspapers pay Churchill compliments for a speech at once mean, vindictive and dangerous to the state. As for Asquith, that he should have allowed the attack on Kitchener to go unanswered fills me with distress, but I suppose his nerve has long since been washed away in champagne.

These political manoeuvres puzzle and annoy the soldier. He hates and abominates war – fine fighter as he is – but he longs to be back in Blightly, passionately to be home again. It is not unnatural for him to assume that these House of Commons shindies, like the industrial strikes, weaken us over here. Lloyd George has told us that Britain is not doing her utmost, and the betrayal eats into our souls.

> Kitchener had left a few days previously to report on potential evacuation of the Dardanelles, his cabinet colleagues hoping that thereby he could be eased out of office as War Minister. Winston Churchill was forced to resign as Chancellor of the Duchy of Lancaster and take the blame for the Dardanelles disaster. It was the lowest point of his career and he then sought to rejoin the army. He was given the command of the 6th battalion of the Royal Scots Fusiliers. At first resentful of his being imposed on them, they were soon won over by his magnetic and original personality – in his first speech to them he urged them to declare war on the louse.

## Thursday, 18 November 1915

Busy all day, and no evacuation train. Among recent curiosities (a) milk has been boiled in the theatre and (b) instruments have been sterilised in the kitchen, I don't know which affronts me most. Rumour that a hospital ship has been torpedoed at Folkestone. This doesn't strike me as improbable as the Germans have just alleged that these ships carry munitions, so that have made an *a priori* excuse.

Full reports of the reply made by Asquith to Churchill show that the attack on Kitchener was unanswered. Is there no answer? How hopeless the outlook is and yet somehow one hopes that internal and technical difficulties may shortly injure the Germans beyond remedy.

Captain O. Stanley here. Derby's brother, I suppose, a noisy patient with an endless kit.

## Monday, 22 November 1915

We got our new issue of clothing today. I drew a new jacket and trousers together with a serviceable cardigan, waistcoat and the new model cap – soft, clothy, heavy and warm. We have been talking about nothing else all day. Our pleasure is like that afforded to schoolgirls by a gift of fashionable clothes. My cap (or the angle at which it is worn) causes great amusement.

Overcoats we have not received and the issue of boots and socks is postponed till tomorrow. The motor transport men have got good leather and fleece coats. Their job is cold, especially as they have to sleep in their motors which are arctic and often enough very wet and dirty too. The quartermaster has been most obstructive about issuing the new ration to these men. Obstruction, however, is the duty of the quartermaster. He is the treasury clerk of the army, who raises objections to all expenditure. The task does not inure to his popularity. To refuse is invidious and liable to misrepresentation, yet as I tell the old boy when he declines our requests, he and his colleagues in the army are the chief bulwark between Britain and bankruptcy.

But even so the waste is portentous. The matron thinks nothing of sending the three ton lorry to carry a parcel weighing a few ounces from one hospital to the other – the cost in petrol alone is a shilling. Heaven knows what the cost must be of the joy rides of young staff officers who come here to spend the afternoon in grand cars, with ASC men in waiting. I read Lord St Davids' opinions on a certain class of influential officers with interest.

Lord St Davids, former Liberal MP, was ennobled in 1908. On 16 November he alleged indolence, favouritism, frivolity and incompetence against the British Army GHQ in France. Its staff was five or six times the size of the French GHQ, though the French Army was much larger; high born ladies had visited the front, with no obvious military purpose. He was shot down by several outraged correspondents in *The Times* and was forced into a partial withdrawal in the House of Lords.

## Tuesday, 23 November 1915

Now we have a thaw which will produce its own crop of pulmonary troubles – on the whole however the army is standing the health strain wonderfully. Frozen feet have been frequent.

## Wednesday, 24 November 1915

Another visit from General Plumer. He has a pleasant plum coloured face modelled on the structure of a parroquet. What we want are generals with the faces of tigers or vultures or alligators – something that can fight. The rumour goes the round that tomorrow is some great festival when it is considered legitimate for all the young men (especially foreign soldiers) to kiss all the young women. I asked a mature *poilu* at the station about it and he assured me that, since the war began, all such levities have ceased. As far as Hazebrouck is concerned, there appears to be nothing in the way of amusement or entertainment, private or public. There is greater confidence than was the case a short time ago, but festivities of all kinds are a taboo. The very idea of proposing a cinema would produce a revolt among people to whom the war is a serious reality.

## Thursday, 25 November 1915

First snow. The winter campaign has been going on for nearly a month, but the piercing cold brings it home to us. Many cases of frostbite – the station was covered with poor fellows hobbling along to the ambulance train.

It occurred to me suddenly, when in the office of the railway military police where I have many friends, that a sprig of mistletoe hanging from the lamp heralded Xmas. A month today! It is unbelievable. Little did I ever expect to spend this Christmas in Hazebrouck. But we must make up our minds to do so. We make no progress. We have violent bombardments of various sectors of the German lines every few days – the Germans make very little reply – but no movement follows and there appears to be little motive except to fire off the ammunition which our politicians tell us is all important. The danger is always more clear to my mind that the effort to secure men is not commensurate with the successful increase of ammunition. An army of men normally supplied with ammunition would have been sufficient to keep Bulgaria quiet and also to enlist Greek and Romanian help – but it is to guns and their provender that all eyes have been turned for six months past. Another 40,000 men would have converted Loos from a tragedy to a triumph – likewise at Neuve Chapelle, likewise perhaps at Salonica, but we are always too late with the men notwithstanding the spurt in munitions. Drank tea this evening with my washerwoman whose beverage, like her laundry, is without compare in Hazebrouck. Her husband is working at the new ammunition factory which has been established beyond the railway in the quarter known as the *nouveau monde*. French and English are working there side by side – there must be seventy or more of our people (all soldiers) and they get on very well with the French artisans. He described to me a new implement being turned out – it is a kind of track in which six or eight rifles are fastened, ordinary rifles, which can be fired quickly like a Maxim. The idea, he says, is borrowed from the Germans.

## Saturday, 27 November 1915

My feet ache – all the ball of the foot is bruised by our infernal cobble stones, curved upwards and rounded which makes walking at night when streets are pitch dark (and very wet) a suite of blows beneath the boot.

> Robert Graves, one of the finest of war poets, writing about his service in the Welsh Division in *Goodbye To All That*, refers to the difficulty of walking on cobble stones and he recounts 'when a staff officer came by in a Rolls Royce and cursed us for our bad march discipline, I felt like throwing something at him'. His contempt for staff officers is echoed by Crawford and his comrades.

## Sunday, 28 November 1915

Major Roberts RFA (staff) left us today; he has attracted our notice as being proprietor of the biggest kit we have ever handled. It weighs little under a quarter of a ton – five great lumps of vanity. He is *bel homme*, knows it. He is a tyrant, but thinks himself modest. He carries a primus stove 'to the trenches' to sterilise his water and to cook his Benger. Even in hospital he has every kind of extra meal which his servant has to prepare at all hours of the day and night. He departed from us as a stretcher case – but on the railway platform he changed his mind and walked briskly to the ambulance train, glancing from time to time at the immaculate crease in his trousers. His servant goes with him to Boulogne. Thence he returns to his unit when he will get his leave papers signed and will follow Roberts to England. Meanwhile, Roberts will have been to the WO and Nicholson (the servant) will re-join the major in retirement. So an able-bodied man is to be withdrawn from the front to promote the comfort of an idle and conceited man.

It is such things which make us smile when we read the violent attacks made on Lord St Davids who criticises GHQ. We have no experience of Sir John French's entourage, but our knowledge of other staff officers is enough to depress. We have had them as patients and as visitors. We may be unlucky in the type which finds its way to Hazebrouck.

But for vanity, ignorance and self-indulgence some of them can safely defy competition. The French so often tell us how they regret the incompetence of our officers. Soldiers are incomparable, their leaders too often hopeless and irremediable failures.

One is struck by the literature in the officers' valises. A certain number of them have a drill book, a few, two or three per cent perhaps have other books on military subjects. The remainder of the literature is novels or magazines. No sign of any effort to learn French. The Flemings in this part of France are quick to learn English and it is almost unnecessary for us to talk French. We can shop quite well in our own tongue.

But when one has to discuss things that matter, to talk of politics, business strategy, then the insularity of our officers is deplored. Reliance is placed on the interpreters whose character is often as suspect as their English. The French don't exactly resent the general assumption that English has got to be talked to and by our officers, but they politely regret that effort is never made to learn French. Even officers whose positions make a working knowledge of French essential, those, for instance, engaged in directing railway traffic, blunder along because they can't understand a word spoken by a French railway guard. Our soldiers are amazed at the prevalence of brilliant linguists among the Germans.

## Tuesday, 30 November 1915

General Porter took me on a visit to establishments under his control. At Poperinghe we saw two astonishing divisional bath establishments. At one of them, 800 men are bathed and re-clothed every day. Forty or fifty Belgian women are employed washing and mending the underclothes. The happiness of the men when in their tubs is splendid. The idea is that every man shall have a bath and fresh supply of underclothing every ten days or so – but it is naturally impossible to carry this into effect always.

From Poperinghe we went to a FA two or three miles further on – a shocking, desolate place. Indeed in Hazebrouck we live a life of incessant picnic compared with the horrible conditions prevailing in the field – no water except on the ground, bad food or rather good food badly cooked – wretched accommodation – transport bad, all amenities of life deficient – post irregular; the poor fellows are far worse off than those in the trenches in many essentials – but so plucky and persevering, though of course all genuine interest in their work is atrophied by acute discomfort and suffering.

We visited a small French CCS which was loading an AT while we were there. The equipment of the biggish French hospital is sadly deficient. They keep sending to our theatre for instruments, even for common operations like tracheotomy, and whenever the civilians get a chance they get our surgeons to treat them in preference to the French. I fancy that French surgery reaches a degree of brilliancy and daring to which we do not aspire, but that on average the whole French RAMC is infinitely lower than ours.

I record a few striking things General Porter told me.

(a) The enlarged experience of shrapnel, sterilisation and antiseptics have given the surgeons the confidence to perform previously impossible operations. The percentage of those recovering from severe abdominal wounds has now risen to sixty-eight.

(b) The handling of the wounded has been revolutionised by the advent of motor ambulances. He made the first application for motors. The demand was fought on financial grounds, but his case was unanswerable and now the old-fashioned horse ambulance is only used far up the line where cars can't go owing to roughness of the ground. There must be thousands of the motor ambulance cars now – well equipped and skilfully handled by ASC men – doing magnificent work.

(c) The steady improvement of the ambulance trains has also helped the wounded. Besides wards for sick and wounded, these trains have dispensaries, pack stores, kitchens, quartermaster stores and operating theatres – the train in short is a microcosm of a base hospital, with office, nurse billets, officer lodging and mess, isolation wards and so forth. They travel so slowly and the time occupied by loading patients is so long that comfort is necessary from one end of the train to the other. There is difficulty in moving them (they are of an enormous length), and others claim use of the line. One quite understands that each group fights for its own interest – still somebody should insist upon better regulation of the service.

(d) The Belgian population is so much impressed by the immunity of our troops from typhoid that thousands have been converted to our system of inoculation. Twelve months ago every other house was infected, mortality was high with consequent danger to our troops. A movement arose among the civilians to be inoculated. By now upwards of 40,000 have been treated and the illness is practically defunct. This is credited to our example and propaganda – for we have nobody who can talk Flemish and the local people are by nature suspicious. The firmness of our RAMC in insisting upon inoculation, notwithstanding the hostility of cranks and fanatics, will prove an essential factor in our ultimate victory.

## Wednesday, 1 December 1915

Crowds round the cheap tobacco shops – hustling and jostling in the rather staid and phlegmatic fashion of the Low Countries. Tobacco has run out during the last week or two – the commoner brands, for much of the tobacco growing districts are in German hands, and the government has also been unable to maintain the manufacture at a normal level. So the Hazebrouckois smoker has found himself dismayed by notices on the tobacco shop windows '*Plus de Tabac*'. He has had to contain his pipe in patience. Today the new supplies were sent in by the government agents and the thrifty Hazebrouckois laid in immoderate stocks. A fresh shortage is threatened – when my own cigarettes fail towards the end of the week, I smoke the French Maryland cigarette with satisfaction: three a penny and the nice green package enriched by a tricolour *affiche* '*Vive la France.*'

## Thursday, 2 December 1915

No. 1 has many trench feet still coming in notwithstanding a complete thaw. Even a couple of degrees of frost can knock a man out if he is standing in deep water. Many cases come from the reserve trenches, which in some ways are more dangerous than the front line. The German artillery hesitates to aim shells of large calibre at our front line for fear they may fall short and injure their own troops. Their efforts are therefore directed against our reserve trenches where life is spent dodging German shells without the chance of firing a shot in reply.

## Friday, 3 December 1915

Cases of trench feet and frozen feet keep pouring in, likewise men suffering from trench fever (pyrexia). How many new complaints have sprung from this vile war! The treatment of frozen feet is still tentative. Much disagreement as to the best methods and at No. 1 Beale is using two or three different styles – the cotton wool cure and the foot drill system being the two best. The latter consists in alternate immersion of the foot in hot and cold water. Massage gives poor results as the surface of the foot is too friable to permit much friction. For gassing also no satisfactory treatment has yet been devised – at any rate there is much variety in the methods of grappling with the dangerous symptoms. A bad crossing in a hospital ship, producing violent nausea, has proved most salutary, but alas ordinary vomiting, which can be easily stimulated, gives insignificant success. Whereas, therefore, medicine hasn't done much to meet the new ailments, surgery has made striking progress, although it must be admitted that the wounds present no special features of novelty.

The colonel has had an elaborate chart prepared by Dawson to show the weekly consumption of alcohol. It is a most misleading document for the averages of consumption are derived from the total number of consumers – some of whom may be here only for a single meal. Figures prove anything and these show a miraculously small imbibing faculty. No account is taken of red and white wine or stout – nor is the liquor brought into the house from shops in the town included. The return in short is inaccurate from half a dozen aspects. Major Kay, who I need hardly say is blissfully ignorant of the state of things, was trying to show the colonel the fallacies of the return, but the colonel refused to be convinced, though he got pretty testy at Kay's argument. The first six weeks of the return were made *ex-post facto* and based wholly on guesswork. A teetotaller for instance was entered as being on champagne diet. Bully Beef, not a born mathematician, cooks these figures week by week and at the outset had to cook returns for a period of six weeks. The colonel, however, is pleased and well satisfied of our sobriety. Bless him. They say at No. 1 that he is about to give birth to a new thing in stretchers.

With his scientific bent, Crawford was always interested in statistics. Later, he became President of the Manchester Statistical Society.

## Monday, 6 December 1915

Wet weather again and the boot problem begins to exercise the mind. The boot problem is correlative to the foot problem. Quite apart from frostbite there are maladies of the feet which cause much trouble, from chilblains and bruising to mummification and cramp. The big gumboots served out to men in the advanced trenches are all very well in their way. John Redmond seems to think that, when the men are relieved, they leave their successors nice clean and dry gumboots. Too often the boots are coated with mud inside and out – the men have to put them on hastily, and a few degrees of frost will cause trouble forthwith. The feet also swell a good deal in the elastic India rubber and there is trouble when they put their hard leather boots on again. In some units men even in the advanced trenches have to strip their feet for an hour every few days. It is cold and the men rub their feet with their hands which does them good – their socks dry and their boots at least get drier. Boracic powder is doled out, but in spite of all precautions the conditions cause much distress. Up till now very few new boots seem to have been issued – we can get none whatever. Old boots resoled can be had and many people prefer them to the unused article.

> John Redmond, leader of the Irish MPs in Westminster, was a fervent believer in achieving Home Rule for Ireland, by constitutional means, within the British Empire. He took a great interest in the welfare of the troops, many of whom were Irish.

### Tuesday, 7 December 1915
Yesterday a smart young officer in a lofty dogcart drove a spanking pair of polo ponies tandem past our gate – it is all an unbelievable combination in this time of war. Why are such things allowed? The French territorials mounting guard close by us watched it as one would look at a good turn at a circus. How often we heard the natives say 'English soldiers bons, English officers no bons', a saddening reflection when one hears it so frequently on their lips. It is only too true that from one cause and another, the impression left by our officers upon our allies is unfavourable.

### Wednesday, 8 December 1915
The news of our defeat on the Tigris is hard to bear – it has made a big impression on our men. There is something mysterious about the land of the Garden of Eden and we felt that there at least a campaign was being conducted with some forethought. But we are still hopeful. A good woman from whom I buy odds and ends, Veuve d'Assonville (three sons at the front), said to me today when talking of the situation in a melancholy tone,

*'Pour moi, je retiens toujours la confiance en St Antoine de Padoue'* – *'et vous avez bien raison, Madame'*, I replied; what less could I say, what more? Yet I feel that we must not rely overmuch upon second class saints.

> St Anthony was the saint to invoke to recover what has been lost. There had been an over-ambitious attempt to capture Baghdad, enabling the much underestimated Turks to lay siege to 8,000 British-Indian troops at Kut Al Amara; most were to die a hideous death when the siege ended the following April. The Mesopotamian campaign was undertaken to secure the oil fields, vital for the fleet, but the attempt on Baghdad was unnecessary for that aim.

## Thursday, 9 December 1915

GHQ has issued orders that all kits are to be inventoried. This is impossible unless the staff of the pack store is trebled and its space doubled. The notice is issued by the DMS, who disapproves of it, and Colonel Grech is determined to fight it as best he can. The scheme is so impracticable that it must break down in practice. One asks oneself why GHQ sends out a fiat without making the smallest enquiry as to the need for action or the possibility of carrying its orders into effect. Some smart young major on the general staff must have done this – thoughtlessly and without the smallest regard for the waste of time and energy required. It is alas so easy to publish instructions which occupy six or eight lines of foolscap – yet so difficult to fulfil the order.

> The order was revoked, see 17 December.

Sikh troops passing in a long Indian file, mules carrying light guns, evidently a mountain battery in this the flattest of countries. Doubtless they are to find their way to the uplands of the Balkan peninsula. How they shiver these Indian troops in the bleak winter of northern France. It is not the actual cold, for in point of fact the weather is again warm and muggy – but it is the constant exposure to wet which causes them so much suffering. All these Indian troops wear mackintosh hoods to their overcoats, very much like the French model. I have always thought it an excellent arrangement and wonder why it isn't adopted for us. The rain streams off our close fitting caps and down our necks. The new winter service caps are an improvement on our old flat-topped headgear – they are warmer and have good flaps for the ears and the upper part of the neck. But they seem to retain moisture, and after a certain amount of drenching they pour off steady streams of water onto one's shoulders and collar. Our overcoats too are made of very permeable cloth. Oilskins should be more widely used. They are cheap, light to carry, small to pack, warm to wear and quite rainproof.

## Saturday, 11 December 1915

Frozen rabbit has arrived. According to the quartermaster the siding at Caestre must be pretty well loaded up with the stuff and he urges us to eat them swiftly lest they decay. Somehow I have a prejudice against the article but Goode, the cook, says he can fake it up so as to be indistinguishable from chicken. Long may he prosper. With quite inadequate equipment he feeds seventy of us every day – his kitchen is about ten feet by eight feet, and his range is what I see in the six or eight room houses of Hazebrouck.

Connie sends me a long letter from aunt Jeanie retailing various conversations which leave an impression of disquiet and anxiety at home. Here we are less subject to these fits of melancholy. We see and feel our own danger on our own front and we quickly have brought home to us the immediate results of a German bombardment or of ten degrees of frost. But we hear none of the domestic dissensions except through newspapers, though men back home on leave and occasional letters give more personal narratives. Moreover, the average man especially in these short dark days, finds little opportunity of studying the press. I am not surprised at the growing vigour of criticism at home.

Indecision and complacency are too great, confidence that we shall muddle through is still too deep seated. This must surely be the first war in which the Treasury has abdicated all functions of parsimony and retrenchment, yet we constantly find essentials lacking, both in men and munitions with plenty of extravagance elsewhere – but it is the craven fear of the domestic future which dogs the footsteps and haunts the ambitions of our statesmen at home. What a contrast with France. Here they go through a periodical crisis, but the offending minister is fired out forthwith – no needless parley. If he hedges or if he is incompetent, or if his activity is open to doubt, out he goes and a successor is installed in a day or two. The calm immovable determination of the French public is so unchallengeable that no minister can survive suspicion for twenty-four hours.

## Sunday, 12 December 1915

A very quiet day. One of the ambulance cars backing into our courtyard to evacuate patients succeeded in knocking down one half of our great yard doors – a thing twelve feet or fifteen feet high. This caused us great amusement

91

except indeed to Sergeant Nunn who scented a new job forthwith. The colonel too witnessed the catastrophe from the office window, hastened down and poured imprecations on the driver. It is seldom that they make a mistake; in fact the ambulance drivers are very skilled indeed and work their cars with the utmost speed and balance over shockingly bad roads.

The SM's conversation is very egoistic, and therefore boring – but tonight I got him to deal with impersonal matters. He told me about the malingerers and shirkers at No. 1. At present there are 400 patients or so, the bulk of whom are medical cases. He says there are thirty or forty confirmed shirkers, men who refuse to drop a cigarette end into the rubbish tins beside their hands and who decline to tidy their blankets or clean their cots. What can be done with them? As a rule, they are put into bed again and limited to a milk diet. This kind goeth not forth save only by prayer and by fasting. The remedy as a rule proves efficacious but he says his difficulties are great and incessant.

At the foot parade today, a man confessed that his extremities had not been washed since he left England twelve weeks ago. It seems to me that besides rebuking (and cleansing) the man, it would have been well to report his MO to his commanding officer.

## Monday, 13 December 1915

Cold again. Bully Beef left us early on leave. We expect, however, that she won't come back again, though she bade us expect her on the twenty-third. A new nurse has come, gigantic in stature with a deep bass voice and slow gesture; very Scots in accent and deliberate in all her ways. Name as yet unknown, but shaping well. We have great hopes of her as she has the same technical qualifications as Alexander, we feel that she may be the long desired substitute. Sergeant Tidy left for leave yesterday. When will my turn come?

## Tuesday, 14 December 1915

Craig is her name. We have had a very quiet day again and she occupies herself by keeping her eyes open and saying little. But she has already made one or two observations which count. To Nunn she said, 'Yes, I know Sister MacCrae (the matron). I knew her at No. 14 general hospital. I had nothing to do with her there for we were in different departments, but I know her quite well.' This was eloquent. To a very youthful officer who asked for whiskey and soda, she gave an emphatic refusal, and added, 'In my opinion, you ought to be on a milk diet' – a double-edged remark which we all thought very neat.

## Wednesday, 15 December 1915

Today, a most wonderful cartoon in the *Echo de Paris* by Abel Faivre showing all degrees and ranks of the French population crowding into the Bank of France with their subscriptions. There are also some capital posters. I wish I could get copies of them. Three in particular struck my fancy. One represents a typical group of French soldiers, young and old, *poilus* and *jeunesse*, dressed anyhow and trudging off to the front. One waves an adieu to his wife and children, reminding her to do her best '*pour la Victoire et pour le Retour*'. Another represents a sentry at some bank glancing at the crowd behind him '*Eux aussi, ils font leur devoir*', as they pay in their money. The last issued poster shows the Gallic *coq de France* bending down out of the golden coin, and pecking vivaciously at a prostrate German. Forain has drawn a splendid poster for the French Red Cross inviting money for the prisoners of war. It is simply the pathetic figure of a French prisoner writing on his knee. It is suggested in a vague way that the man is shivering with cold, he begs for boots, for clothing – a very arresting design. There are others, all of them so intimate in their appeal, and I need hardly add drawn and printed with all the French genius for illustrated posters. How I should like to see the exhibition of the Raemaekers cartoons in London. For mordant satire, he must surely be unapproachable.

French artists contributed greatly to the war effort. Most banks had their own posters to encourage subscription to each new war loan. Louis Raemaekers, a Dutch cartoonist of German origin, was particularly savage in his anti-German cartoons. The Fine Art Society put on a big exhibition of his work in London in 1915 and the publication of his cartoons included a plug from the Prime Minister; the cartoons were widely syndicated in USA, where they strongly influenced opinion against Germany and towards entering the war.

## Thursday, 16 December 1915

Most of the morning made unbearable by the *vidange* – our cesspools in the courtyard being sucked dry by a machine worked by the ASC. I am bound to say these men do their work with great thoroughness, as indeed all of the sanitary duties of the army are carried out – altogether admirable. The greatest care has been devoted to the prophylactic measures. I met a RAMC colonel in Le Havre in June who told me that, being unfit for active service in the field, he had obtained a roving commission to kill flies. Le Havre itself was within his jurisdiction. He was confident of being able to reduce the

DOWNING STREET,

WHITEHALL, S.W.

MR. RAEMAEKERS' powerful work gives form and colour to the menace which the Allies are averting from the liberty, the civilisation and the humanity of the future. He shows us our enemies as they appear to the unbiassed eyes of a neutral, and wherever his pictures are seen determination will be strengthened to tolerate no end of the war save the final overthrow of the Prussian military power.

*Signed* H. H. ASQUITH

*Asquith's preface to Raemaekers book* (Internet)

number of disease carriers by many hundred millions. Practically the whole of the drainage of Le Havre is now managed by our sanitary police. Here in Hazebrouck our sanitary squads keep the town clean and it is the same in all the big villages of the neighbourhood. Without such precautions the whole thing would come to grief in a week or two. In combination with inoculation,

1. (*Left*) Private D.L. Crawford, 57840, RAMC, his hair 'a bit *coupé en brosse*' [p. 36]. He was attached to No. 12 Casualty Clearing Station (CCS) in Flanders.

2. (*Right*) The 27th Earl of Crawford & Balcarres, a leading figure in politics, industry and the arts.

3. An MP for 18 years before the war, he was Conservative Chief Whip.

4. Crawford was Chairman of Wigan Coal and Iron Company, a diversified family business that employed over 10,000 people [p. 193].

5. One of Crawford's jobs was carrying the wounded to and from the hospital trains [p. 117].

6. Operating theatres were often in makeshift places; Crawford was intensely proud of one that he set up in a lace factory in Hazebrouck, a centre of the Flemish textile industry [p. 23].

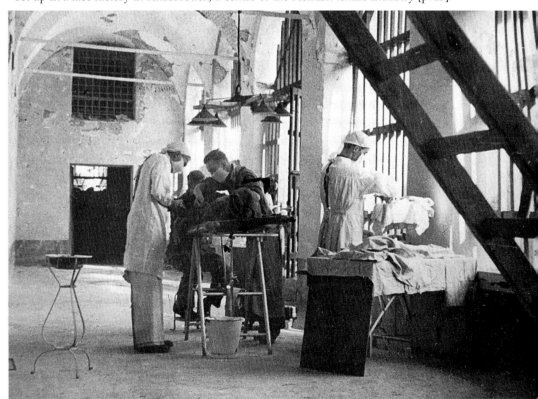

7 & 8. 'Red Beard', Crawford's father, the
26th Earl, scientist, collector, philatelist
and pioneer in the distribution of
electricity in London. An astronomer, he
led an expedition to Cadiz in 1870 to
observe a solar corona. His munificence
ensured the future of the Royal
Observatory Edinburgh.

9. Crawford was a founder of the Art Fund,
through which he presented a painting by
Ugolino to the National Gallery.

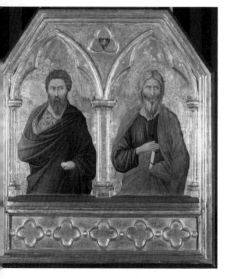

LORD LINDSAY, M.P., F.R.S., P.R.A.S.

REPRODUCED BY PERMISSION FROM "VANITY FAIR"

MAY, 1878

10. Crawford enlisted in the RAMC after the disastrous Battle of Neuve Chapelle, 'a costly and dangerous fiasco' [p. 71]; the government was blamed for shell shortages in *The Times*; at the same time, the Dardanelles campaign was unravelling.

11. (*Left*) Comrades in arms in 1914, Lord Fisher, First Sea Lord, and Winston Churchill, First Lord of the Admiralty, fell out over the Dardanelles in 1915, leading to a 'cabinet crisis in England' [p. 6]. Both resigned their posts and the Liberal Prime Minister Asquith had to accept a coalition with the Conservatives.

12. (*Right*) The dynamic Churchill was replaced by the languid A.J. Balfour, who summoned Crawford from France as he 'wants me to become Civil Lord of the Admiralty' [p. 8]. He thought Crawford's refusal to be a minister indefensible.

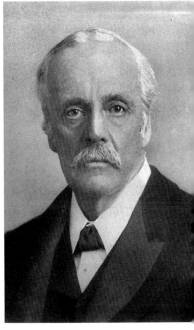

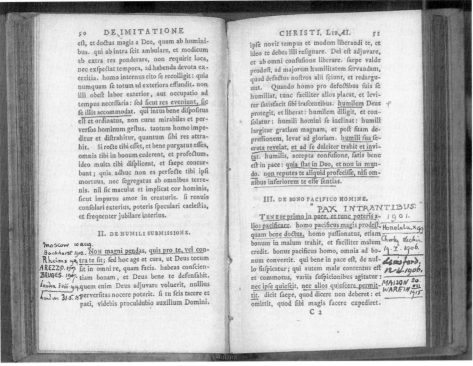

13. Regular reading of St Thomas à Kempis' *Imitation of Christ* inspired Crawford. After rejecting Balfour's offer of ministerial office [p. 9], Crawford took comfort in the words of St Thomas in *de humili submissione*.

14. His diary was written with limited time, light and space at his disposal; he was often interrupted by comrades or the call of duty or enemy action.

15. From an early age, Crawford played a major role in Britain's leading museums, such as the Victoria & Albert. He has been called 'The Uncrowned King of British Art' [p. 197].

16. Grande Place, with its 'steep pitched irregular roofs' [p. 132]. The *Epi de Blé* contravened regulations and was closed by the 'tiresome and fussy' Town Major – with the result that it became a 'house of evil repute' [p. 115]. Hazebrouck was Crawford's base for over a year.

53. - HAZEBROUCK. - La Grand' Place

17. An officer in the front row chats to a nurse rather than face the camera. Some officers were 'unwise in their zealous attentions towards the nurses' [p. 24].

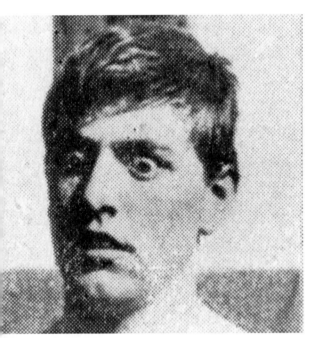

18. 'How many new complaints have sprung from this vile war!' Especially puzzling was shell shock, which some of the men called 'GOK – otherwise God Only Knows' [p. 49].

19. The louse was 'one of the three curses of the British army' [p. 80]; it caused trench fever, a sort of flu, which afflicted a quarter of British troops.

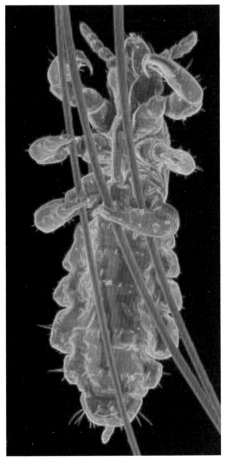

**Entanglements**

"COME ON, BERT, IT'S SAFER IN THE TRENCHES"

*Bruce Bairnsfather*
*with apologies to*
*Raphaël Kirchner*

20. Trench foot and other foot ailments were common. One man had 'a hole in his heel almost big enough to carry a marble' [p. 54].

21. The sight of 1,200 VD cases shocked Crawford at a hospital in Le Havre. Catching the disease was 'a breach of contract towards our King and country' [p. 5].

22. 'The handling of the wounded has been revolutionised by motor ambulances ... the old fashioned horse ambulance is only used far up the line where cars can't go' [p. 86].

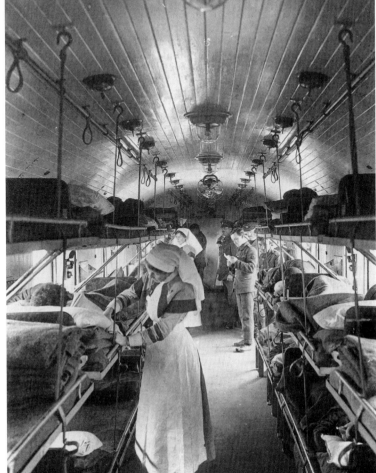

23. New hospital trains were 'a microcosm of a base hospital' [p. 86].

24. Barges helped the wounded on their way through France's network of canals – 'dullish work for the RAMC crews' [p. 58].

25. The wounded were given limited treatment in the trenches. The RAMC developed an efficient system of evacuation to casualty clearing stations and hospitals [p. xxxiv].

26. CCSs were often in tents, ready to move within 24 hours. This one was depicted by Crawford's fellow clan member, Sir Daryl Lindsay, an Australian artist and museum curator, whose family had first left Scotland more than two centuries ago.

27. The *Petit Séminaire St François* was requisitioned for No. 12 CCS. 'We must be a serious nuisance to them, yet they have readily acquiesced in the way we have taken possession of their building' [p. 70].

28. Hazebrouck was fortunate in the energetic leadership of Abbé Lemire, who was mayor, deputy and priest, here seen in battered Ypres nearby. The locals 'saluted him as though he were a King or Pope' [p. 41].

CAMPAGNE DE 1914-1915
*Visite aux ruines d'Ypres du député l'abbé Lemire d'Hazebrouck.*
The Abbé Lemire, deputy of Hazebrouck, visiting the ruins of Ypres.

29. The Australians were rowdy, casual and undisciplined. 'They slouch about anyhow' [p. 147] and despised fussy military rules. The locals were 'disgusted' by their conduct, but they were great fighters.

30. The Cloth Hall in the 'peaceable and innocent old town' of Ypres was deliberately set on fire [p. 50]. The Australians, whose conduct had so disgusted the locals, redeemed themselves in the Battle of Hazebrouck, before their triumphant entry into Ypres.

31. *Taubes* spied and dropped bombs on Hazebrouck. 'Our anti-aircraft guns peppered' them [p. 126], usually without success.

32. 'Lieutenant Buchholz fell with his *Taube* into our lives' [p. 74]. Crawford was put in charge of the prisoner.

33. 'Montenegro follows Serbia into the fist of the Teuton' [p. 119]. The exiled King Nicholas is seen here with Sir Douglas Haig, C-in-C of the British Expeditionary Force.

34. 'Kut has surrendered. Another ten days and the Grand Duke would have saved the situation' [p.164].

35. 'Today, a most wonderful cartoon in the *Echo de Paris* by Abel Faivre showing all degrees and ranks of the French population crowding into the Bank of France with their subscriptions' to bonds which were being issued to finance the war effort [p. 93]. Crawford was a keen reader of the French newspapers and was later to be offered a commission to liaise with the Maison de la Presse in Paris.

L'ARMÉE DES CIVILS

36 & 37. Crawford liked the posters produced by leading French artists – 'I wish I could get copies of them' [p. 93]. One that he particularly liked was borrowed by an American charity, the Lafayette Fund, which was set up to help French soldiers. It was accused of violating American neutrality. Another poster echoed General Pétain's battle cry at the Battle of Verdun *'Courage, on les aura'*.

– *N'oublie pas de souscrire…pour la Victoire !...et le retour !*

THE LA FAYETTE FUND IS SENDING
COMFORT KITS TO THESE SOLDIERS WHICH
THEIR FAMILIES CANNOT PROVIDE.

*On les aura !*

2ᵉ EMPRUNT
DE
LA DÉFENSE NATIONALE

*Souscrivez*

38. They may not all have had a very military bearing and some of them were 'aged, ragged and untidy' [p. 60], but France owed a great debt to the 'venerable' *poilus* who guarded the railway system.

39. Crawford marvelled at how 'quick and accurate' the mobile laboratory was at analyzing blood and tracing infectious disease [p. 149].

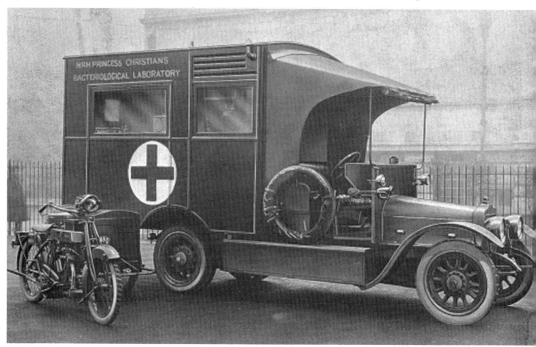

40. Dentistry is 'the pariah of medical science' in the BEF in France. 'The ownership of teeth is apparently looked upon as a luxury in the British Army' [p. 135]. The dental profession got a fillip when Sir Douglas Haig needed treatment.

41. 'Sick and wounded horses are doctored by clever vets belonging to the Army Veterinary Corps. It sounds a dull job, but ideal for the horsey man' [p. 161].

POUR TON PAYS TU LE FERAS
ET POUR TON BIEN PAREILLEMENT

10

S. S. d'Etat du Service de Santé M.P.A.O. n° 27

42. The RAMC's insistence upon inoculation, 'notwithstanding the hostility of cranks and fanatics, will prove an essential factor in our ultimate victory' [p. 87]. French soldiers were encouraged to be inoculated by posters which appealed to their patriotism and self-interest.

43. The Kaiser believed in brutality as evidence of strength. Crawford was shocked at the 'sad spectacle of refugees' [p. 16].

44. The execution of the British nurse, Edith Cavell, despite saving many German, as well as allied, lives, was the subject of world-wide condemnation. Institutions and streets were named after her, including at Arques, the RAMC's dental headquarters [p. 161].

45 & 46. Religious and cultural buildings were targeted, such as the cathedral at Rheims and the library at Louvain. The bombing of St Apollinaire at Ravenna was 'typical and symptomatic of their desire to hurt, to intimidate and to smash' [p. 128].

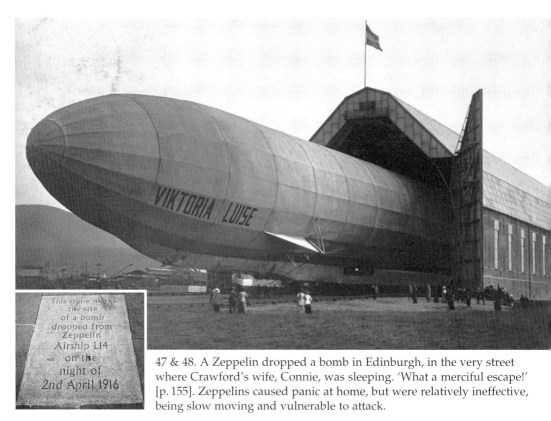

47 & 48. A Zeppelin dropped a bomb in Edinburgh, in the very street where Crawford's wife, Connie, was sleeping. 'What a merciful escape!' [p. 155]. Zeppelins caused panic at home, but were relatively ineffective, being slow moving and vulnerable to attack.

*This stone marks the site of a bomb dropped from Zeppelin Airship L14 on the night of 2nd April 1916*

49. President Wilson was outraged by the attack on SS *Sussex* with its American casualties. 'I was surprised at the effect of the torpedo . . . How she ever regained port seems a mystery' [p. 162].

0. Unlimited submarine warfare helped bring America into the war – an important contribution to the allied victory. The Kaiser not only lost a few teeth, but also his empire and his crown.

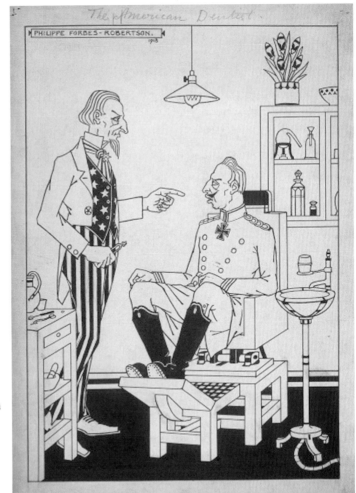

51. Voluntary help to the war effort was enormous. Two spinsters of Southfields sent out a novel wishing luck 'to the Tommy or Reggie who receives this book' [p. 171]. Stoke Newington's gift of an ambulance was blessed by the Bishop of London.

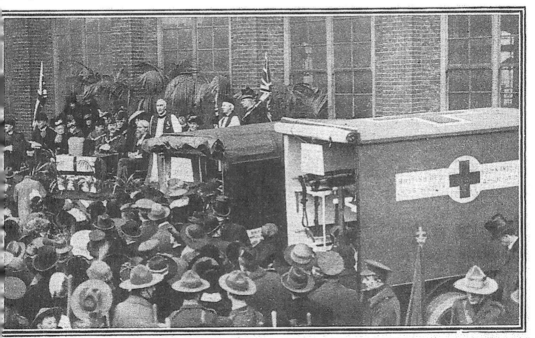

THE CHURCH'S BLESSING IN A GREAT CAUSE.

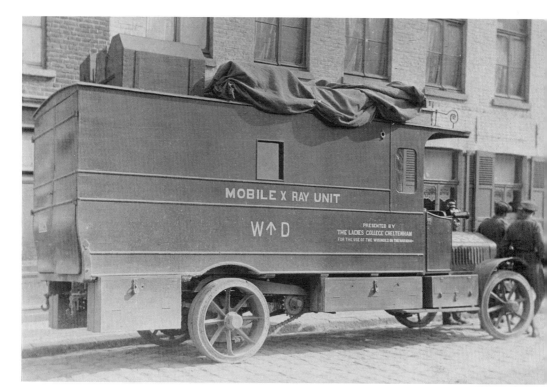

52 & 53. The 'garrulous' Captain Lang's X-Ray machine was provided by the ladies of Cheltenham College. 'God bless them all' [p. 42] wrote Crawford, who once was 'jammed into the engine room for 20 minutes ... and got fearfully hot' [p. 59]. The radiographers had protective clothing.

54. 'Parcels from Connie and the children' arrived with food, linen and crockery [p. 7]; she ran a convalescent home for wounded soldiers at their Scottish home (seen here holding her daughter Mary). Part of the *Bibliotheca Lindesiana* is behind the group.

55. Indians endured many casualties and much illness on the Western Front. 'How they shiver, these Indian troops in the bleak winter of Northern France ... the constant exposure to wet causes them much suffering' [p. 90].

56. 'There was a tree felling competition between lumbermen of the various allies. Vast quantities of timber are used in trench warfare, but it is difficult to believe that we need to import foresters to France. Our men seemed to be having a cushy time' [p. 174].

57. Lord Kitchener, the War Minisiter, leaves a destroyer to board the SS *Hampshire*, shortly to be blown up by a mine. The news 'caused us stupefaction' [p. 179]. The ensuing cabinet reconstruction led to Crawford returning to London as Minister of Agriculture.

they have succeeded in eradicating typhoid, typhus and in reducing to a very small minimum all the normal infectious diseases which can be carried by vermin or by dirt.

Great incinerators are at work everywhere, and though the French smiled superciliously at the outset, they now appreciate what is being done and constantly apply to the ASC and RAMC for help. Seldom can such help be given for the care of our own military units taxes the efforts of the staff to the utmost, and there must be some limit to the number of men employed on such jobs, though the sanitary condition of our troops and the areas they occupy is a primary consideration to the GHQ. One officer is devoting his whole time to analysis of foodstuffs – not with a view to testing its qualities, but in order to make the best possible distribution of nutritive material.

### Friday, 17 December 1915

Some days ago we were ordered to make inventories of all officers' kits passing through our hands. We complained, the colonel complained, our DMS did the same, and most of the RAMC units concerned followed suit. We now get an explanation and a withdrawal of the order, by GHQ. It transpires that the order was only intended to refer to deceased officers' kits – but they forgot to insert the word 'deceased'. What folly! A new poster appeared today, an appeal by the *Bureau des renseignements des familles dispersées* – which traces the lost and vanished, restoring many to their homes and relations, though alas many of the requests for information can never be answered. It represents an oldish man with his two grandchildren, their parents being *dispersés*. Such a sad grave old face and such wan timid young ones. How bravely the French carry their mourning, and though working on ridiculously small sums, how effective are these patriotic agencies.

The news of Sir John French's resignation would have produced a panic six months ago. Immediately after the battle of Loos, it would have caused dismay. This morning it was read with equanimity. The general feeling is that he has done his part, that he must be completely worn out, and then no plan or initiative could any longer be expected of him. There has been nothing inspiring about his leadership, no personal note or intimate touch which could interest, still less endear him, to the army. He was cautious, prudent, anxious for the welfare of his men, painstaking in the extreme and also reluctant to acquiesce in the severe measures necessary from time to time. The spirit which once brought him to the verge of being a fine cavalry leader has vanished, and the general impression he has left upon the mind of the rank and file is that of an oldish and retiring man. The strain of these

last few months must have been quite terrific. Nobody without a dominating force and personality at 45 could expect to be full of vitality and impact twenty years later. As to his successor, Sir Douglas Haig, time will show. His experience is great and he has more of the hatchet face than Sir John French.

He is popular with soldiers particularly with NCOs. There are many stories of his friendship and good feeling towards them.

## Saturday, 18 December 1915

The ambulance train was very late today. We stood waiting on the bleak and exposed railway platform over an hour. A very long train drew slowly through and from the faces massed at each window we quickly saw that it was a big force of drafts for the line. As they passed through the station we were greeted with shouts of welcome, snatches of song and cries of 'are we downhearted?' – followed by that odious chorus of 'No'. We watched the procession with sad reflections of those who are no longer gay in approaching the crisis of war. Some minutes later the troop train backed on to the platform next to where we were expecting the ambulance. The carriage windows were still crowded as before with noisy travellers. Gradually the shouting and chaffing subsided. Those who had the front view slowly realised who were the occupants of the platform – why so many men had arms in slings and heads bound up – why others had both feet swathed in white cotton boots, why so many RAMC men were standing there, why there was a long row of tenanted stretchers. All this they gradually realised. The men further back inside the carriages came to understand it too and almost suddenly this whole trainload of new soldiers, 1,200 of them or more, was startled into silence, complete, tense and respectful. For the first time these men were in presence of the real thing.

## Monday, 20 December 1915

I see the newspapers are inviting hospitable and trusting people at home to give Christmas entertainment to lonely soldiers. I confess that, when lonely, the soldier is apt to fall into temptation and I fear me there may be lapses from virtue which will shock the charitably minded. The lonely soldier is scarcer than the newspapers might lead one to think, but he exists out here if not at home. I came across one the other day, lost rather than lonely, a hungry infantry man from Lancashire.

Lisgo and I were in a restaurant and we noticed a half starved fellow in front of us with a cup of coffee. He asked us what he would have to pay – twenty-five centimes the landlady told us, but she added, as she saw a look of dismay on the man's countenance, *pour lui je le ferai 20 centimes car il a l'air tellement fatigué*. I pushed across some cakes we had ordered, the adorable knick-knacks of pastry in which Hazebrouck excels. He ate with vigour, recovered some of his spirits, and finally observed that it was his first decent meal for four days. He had been on leave, a terrible crossing each way which had punished him badly. He had meditated suicide but no means offered themselves and while thinking over the matter had a fresh attack of nausea. No more leave for him. He had only been on the sea three times and on each occasion landed more dead than alive. And to crown his misfortunes on getting back to France he found himself at Hazebrouck instead of at Poperinghe. He went on to Poperinghe. They sent him to Bailleul. There he got lost in finding his unit which had moved and they sent him to St Omer. Then he got back to Hazebrouck where we saw him – a melancholy, shy and perhaps rather a stupid man who, without a sixpence in his pocket, had been wandering all over the countryside, sleeping in railway sheds, eating stale beef and biscuit served out at reinforcement billets, and gradually becoming more and more obsessed by the fear of being mistaken for a deserter.

## Wednesday, 22 December 1915

The news of Livio's death touches me closely – he was one of the most powerful intellects I ever knew, but so diffident in manner and so self–disparaging that he always did himself an injustice. He died at Padua while in training. The name recalls to me the gay times of my happy and irresponsible youth when I spent a joyous week in its colonnades celebrating the tercentenary of Galileo. I was then an undergraduate – representing the Oxford Union at the festivities, and had a *succès fou* with the Italian students. How gloomy these colonnades must have seemed to Aunt Ada during the last week of Livio's life.

> Livio Caetani was Crawford's first cousin, the son of his aunt, Ada Bootle-Wilbraham, and Onorato, Duke of Sermoneta. Livio's brother, Gelasio, was a mining engineer with the Italian army; he blew up an Austrian fort on top of Col di Lana in the Dolomites. Later he restored Ninfa, a town abandoned because of plague, near Latina, creating one of the world's great gardens, and was Italian ambassador to the United States.

## Thursday, 23 December 1915

Suvla Bay evacuated, Anzac evacuated and without loss, the Serbian relief party safe back in Salonica, our Baghdad expedition fighting a rear guard action as far as Kut El Amara – surely the British, taking Mons and Antwerp into account as well, have established an unrivalled reputation for successful retreat. And a fine test it is of military valour and skill. But we retreat where we want to advance or else we are stationary – when we do advance, we come to a standstill before the true objective is achieved. How gloomy and disheartened we should be. What a nervous panicky Christmas will be spent at home and how much curtailed all the festivities will be. I can hear people saying that good cheer would be indecent, considering all the poor fellows in France.

And we ourselves? Men back from leave and hospitals are hurrying back to the line because they don't want to miss Xmas. The post and parcels office have been working day and night for a week past, so terrific is the mass of presents to be distributed. The shops of Hazebrouck are crammed with every kind of Xmas card, present, decoration, foodstuffs, all for our troops, all being snapped up as soon as the shops open. Our cooks are beginning work every morning at two o'clock. The competition for turkeys and geese has run the price up to an absurd figure. All hospitals are gay with bunting flags and so forth, the big receiving room at No. 1 being like a Christmas tree. Never have I seen Xmas preparations proceed with such vigour and thoroughness. There is no sign of depression here. Anxiety is there, but for Xmas at any rate there is to be oblivion. There will be no truce in the front line, that is to say none of that absurd fraternising which did so much harm last year – but I doubt if the Germans will go out of their way to make a serious attack, their last effort having been pretty costly, and we are not very likely to begin it.

> 'Absurd fraternising' refers to a truce at Christmas in 1914 between British and German soldiers, in which up to 100,000 troops met one another, sang hymns together, exchanged gifts and collected their dead from each others' lines – much to the consternation of the GHQ on each side. In fact, there were spasmodic Christmas truces in 1915 on the front line.

### Sunday, 26 December 1915

We ate freely and on the whole imbibed with discretion: but owing to lack of caution on the part of two of our staff, there was no roast beef – our boasted *pièce de résistance*. Alas and alas, how irresistible is the temptation, how fatal the results. No. 1 was pandemonium; 500 patients I should think and a high proportion anxious to make the festival hideous, though they were controlled with a pretty firm hand – but even so there were lapses both among the patients and the staff, the higher grades of which did not distinguish themselves. Were the liquor facilities such as they have normally been at home, the army as an entity would be pretty well incapacitated.

## Monday, 27 December 1915

Tons of parcels have reached us and tons more, posted too late at home, will doubtless pour in for the next fortnight. One looks with dismay upon the broken and shapeless lumps which arrive. The SM of the post office tells me that here are now 5,000 bags of parcels lying at Folkestone awaiting transport and escort which the Admiralty cannot supply! The Post Office accommodation is limited, labour is scarce, tonnage is needed for more important goods, and generally speaking the authorities are not over anxious to encourage great generosity at home. Were the postal rates reduced, the increased work could not be encompassed. The postage on a small cake or pudding equals the cost of the article, and the smaller the parcel the higher the rate. This is a hardship on those who can least afford the high postage tax, but I think on the whole the authorities are justified. Unlimited facilities would simply snow us up. As it is, the Post Office staff has to call upon the RAMC and other units for the loan of motor wagons.

And the amount of time and energy wasted owing to defective packing and addresses! Good people at home wrap up parcels as though they needed transit to the next street – thin paper, cotton instead of string, goods which perish in a few hours, lamentably insufficient addresses. In fact, there ought to be demonstrations (with exhibits) of how to pack parcels for the front. Sack loads are returned every day to the General Post Office in London – rotten fish, fruit, pastry, pulverised tobacco, crushed bottles from which the liquid has drenched other people's goods, every sort of rubbish which was worthless at the outset of its career and even so never finds its destination. The GPO will not open and distribute the contents of parcels from which addresses have vanished, but they do not object to the CO giving away the parcels sent to deceased soldiers, though the CO must himself take the responsibility. Our postal service at Hazebrouck is admirable and a great credit to the REs who control it. As regards men in the front line, delay is of course common, but the RE staff cannot be blamed for that.

Every day at the railway station I see huge barrows loaded with parcels for French prisoners in Germany. All of them are carefully sewn up in canvas or cotton coverings, neatly packed and clearly addressed. The German regulations are very stringent on the subject and, if not followed, the consignment is pinched. A special sort of bread is baked to send to Germany, rolls which appear to pass twice through the oven, hard enough to last for a month and scarcely susceptible to damp. The prisoners soak them in coffee or soup or whatever they have to drink. Fancy having to send bread to

Germany! We may be sure the Germans don't have to send any to their compatriots locked up in Britain.

## Tuesday, 28 December 1915

At the station today notices are posted up recommending those who send parcels to Germany to employ wax instead of lead for the seals. The reason is not far to seek. Ten pounds is the limit of weight. The brother of the woman who now supplies me with a bath (our old bath place having been monopolised by the tiresome RFC people, who permanently booked the place every evening between five and eight, my only free time) is a prisoner in Germany; he was in the customs and was captured early in the war. She tells me that he acknowledges every parcel she has sent – but that every halfpenny she has sent by *mandat postale* has gone astray. Her weekly parcel consists of four pounds of bread, butter in a sealed tin, jam, preserved fruit, an article or two of clothing and a *Paris d'épice*. This week she is sending forty sous in the parcel and awaits anxiously his reply as to its safe arrival. I am sceptical; for one may presume all parcels are examined.

The *poilu* was much in evidence at the railway station this morning. The more I observe the *poilu*, I mean the elderly territorial, the fewer signs of military training can I detect. He holds himself badly, marches, dresses, stands, salutes anyhow, and generally behaves like a middle-aged citizen unexpectedly clothed in uniform. His clothes never fit, his uniform is all odds and ends, his equipment is seemingly improvised in his own parlour, and he carries half a dozen types of firearm. No half dozen men belonging to the same unit are dressed alike. Yet he has great qualities and has deserved well of *La Patrie*.

## Thursday, 30 December 1915

Xmas has made us return to the discussion long since abandoned as quixotic or interminable, as to when the war will end '*après la guerre finit*' as runs the only French song we know, and we only know these first four words of it. And we discussed moreover the allied problem – namely the length of time required to get a million men home and what proportion of that million, in the event of victory, would be required for an army of occupation. Our talk ended abruptly as we realised its absurdity, more abruptly indeed than our earlier discussions a few months ago – but that we should have reverted to the subject at all marks a certain revival of confidence which has been growing for the last ten days – for no apparent or tangible reason: but then it is based on the vague belief of those back from the line that our position grows more secure and more menacing every day.

## Friday, 31 December 1915

We are following the domestic crisis about the unmarried shirker with greater interest than has been evinced on any political question at home since the spring. The AS would mercilessly force the recusant to join the army – not indeed to become a combatant on foreign soil but to do the menial work of the army at home. There are plenty of latrines in Blighty.

## Saturday, 1 January 1916

The news has reached me this morning that Lady Omega has arrived at Balcarres. God bless her and her mother too. I hope to get leave on Monday morning.

> Lady Omega is the nickname given to Crawford's and Connie's 8th (and presumed last) child, Barbara, born on 31 December.

## Sunday, 2 January 1916

Unfortunately there is a peculiar high (or low) tide at Boulogne on the third, fourth and fifth of this month and the boat train only gets to Boulogne an hour after the morning boat has left. Thanks to Dawson, I am forewarned, and, thanks to the colonel, forearmed. He has got me a special movement order, so that I can depart tonight and make certain of catching the packet tomorrow morning.

> As Crawford was about to go on leave, John Glubb, a wounded 18 year old infantryman, was admitted to the CCS. Glubb records in his diary tipping a RAMC corporal sixpence for carrying his bag. Later he learned that the corporal was Lord Crawford and observed 'I don't suppose that I shall ever again have the chance to give a sixpenny tip to an earl'. He later commanded the Arab Legion (precursor of the Royal Jordanian Army) from 1939 to 1956 when he was dismissed by King Hussein who wanted to disassociate himself from perceived British influence. Glubb's jaw was shattered on the Western Front. Arabs nicknamed him Abu Hunaik ('father of the jaw') and he was also familiarly known as Glubb Pasha.

# IV

# 2 to 12 January 1916

## A week's leave in Scotland

Finally, nine months after joining up, Crawford got his first leave. It was a special leave by virtue of the imminent arrival of another child. He went to Balcarres, his home in Fife, and spent eight days with his wife, their new baby daughter, Barbara, and the rest of his children.

Crawford felt that leave was unfairly allocated. His colonel had four leaves in 1915, but 'only a dozen of our men have now been home. Nobody is entitled to leave, but there is an understanding that, after three months abroad, the men shall be allowed home in rota if the work of the unit permits their absence. Yet I have come across scores of men who have been here twelve months and have had no leave, while lots of others who have only been here six months have been to England twice or oftener ... all want to get home, many passionately desire it, and it is vexatious to see fellows get away twice before others get away at all.' He himself was upset that he had not been able to get any assurance to within six weeks of when his turn would come.

There was bitterness among the rank and file at the inequality shown in the matter of leave. Officers got leave every three months 'with mathematical regularity'. For NCOs and the rank and file there was believed to be favouritism in the allocation of leave; the chances were better if you were on good terms with the sergeant major or quartermaster. On allegations of bribery in the allocation of leave, Crawford commented, 'These I do not credit in general and, as regards ourselves, I readily contradict in particular – but that the charge should be brought is significant and distasteful'.

He praised No. 15 CCS where leave is settled by ballot, 'with the proviso that no two men out of the same ward should go home the same day. The result has been that everybody is well satisfied, there has been no recrimination, and the leave is going like clockwork. The men know approximately when they can expect leave, which is a real comfort and advantage'.

Crawford was particularly critical of those politicians who seem to flit freely between parliament and military service, obtaining leave whenever they want, and who 'get high rank, but seem to spend more time at home than in the field. How does it come about that these frauds are allowed to retain their commissions? They must be drawing salaries and costing the country money, but their military value is nil, and in a sense they may always be a potential danger, for, when in France, they must have some authority and their inexperience might involve us in serious trouble.' F.E. Smith, the Solicitor General (later, as Lord Birkenhead, Lord Chancellor), and Winston Churchill were cited as specimens of this category.

Crawford's account of his short leave is presented as a series of sketches, highlighting episodes on the two day journey from Hazebrouck to Fife and back again rather than a daily account of life as in the rest of the diary.

**Hazebrouck Station**. *Laetus exitus*. 8pm. 'Corporal Lord Crawford,' said the RE clerk in the railway transport officer's room, reading from a paper in his hand. 'Here is his movement order. Where is he?' 'Oh thanks, I will take it,' I replied. 'But who are you?' 'I am Corporal Crawford.' 'Are you Lord Crawford too?' 'Yes', I answered, 'but in Hazebrouck I am generally known as corporal'.

*'Laetus exitus'* is a reference to a phrase from Thomas à Kempis – see note on page 113.

So I sat me down on one of the rare benches which offer hospitality on the railway platform. I have been here with patients every day for months past, but never before have I sat down. I found that the whole perspective of the place changed. No ambulance train, no crowd of wounded men, no stretchers, and being seated, the scale of the place seemed to grow as I looked towards the roof from my low level. Station officials, French and British, seeing my kitbag and haversack, came to congratulate me on getting leave – much handshaking and good wishes for the New Year from our police and detectives and felicitations from my French colleagues and acquaintances.

**The train to Calais.** Third class carriage, well lighted, clean and warm. Notices posted on the walls '*Taisez-vous. Méfiez vous. Les oreilles ennemies vous*

TAISEZ-VOUS!
MÉFIEZ-VOUS!
LES OREILLES ENNEMIES
VOUS ÉCOUTENT

Prescription de la Circulaire du Ministre de la Guerre
en date du 28 octobre 1915.

*écoutent*'. It is a well-timed lesson for the French penchant for loud conversation in public places – and, therefore, for espionage as well. We read the warning, scrutinised one another, felt reassured and then began to talk.

> The injunction against careless talk was propagated through posters, but in other ways as well, for example as a decorative message on dishes and plates.

An RFA man going back to duty after a sojourn at Arques ... a giant from a 75-battery ... a well-dressed civilian ... a French infantry man recently sent home from hospital at Berlin, one of the *grands blessés*, and a prisoner of war since August 1914. The greatest chatterbox I ever met! He could not raise his right arm and his thigh had been badly smashed. Spirits inextinguishable, though sorry that his physical condition involved his becoming a *réformé*. 'And what is Germany like today, are they hungry?' 'I wouldn't say so, but our 60-year-old guards did not have enough to eat. In the mornings they would beg us for some of our (normally black) bread or ask us to buy some of the white bread that we had been sent from home. I pitied these wretched civilians dressed in uniform and we sometimes gave them a present of some food.'

'I would never have pitied them,' interposed the French artillery man, 'as far as I am concerned they are Boches – that is enough for me, more than enough ...' followed by an eruption of expletives as he described various scenes of horror in his own experience. The civilian in the far corner agreed. The denunciations became redundant and I switched off the conversation to something or other which led us to cock fighting. What can the subject sequence have been?

Yes, he was an amateur of cock fighting, this artilleryman, though more interested in breeding the animals than in matching them … wondered if I could bring him back a good cock from England, a little one, well spurred … had bought birds in England, Germany, Russia and even from Japan. Lots of words and phrases I could not understand, nor could our fellow travellers. So while his eloquence exuberated, I lapsed into silence. But the 75-battery man was too tactful to pursue a topic which he saw was beyond our ken, and, after a moment of recuperation, began to sing an English song. 'Frederick taught me,' he said. Frederick was in a Highland regiment, was billeted in his brother's house at Armentières, was a great favourite with the family, after twelve months was beginning to talk a word or two of French, was teaching them to talk English, to sing English, probably to imbibe too, though *de la manière écossaise*. Frederick was going to tour in France with the family after the war and in return was to arrange a visit to Scotland and England for his good friends. 'He's a good bloke this Frederick – perhaps you know him?', and with that he raised his great carcase on to the bench, stretched himself out, sang a line or two of the English song, and presently dropped off to sleep.

**The train to Boulogne.** At Calais we had to change. I lost my companions and fell in with three French infantry men, a sailor from a submarine and three young Belgian recruits, the latter in the smart well-cut uniforms with which the new Belgian army is being equipped. Poor Belgium! We are promised a New Heaven and a New Earth – shall there not also be a New Hell for the assassins who have desolated that fair country? Meanwhile at least there are new uniforms and a new army to begin with. Why do our men feel so deeply, with such genuine conviction, for Belgium as a nation while disliking the Belgian as an individual? Such, alas, is our frame of mind and these three young fellows did nothing to dispel it. How they groused, complained and boasted! To hear them speak one would think that they alone had to stand in two feet of slimy trench water – that there were no German gas cylinders or whizzbangs or machine guns except on their front. I asked myself if our brave fellows were enjoying their picnic. The man from the submarine was silent, but his eyes talked. 'And is there no snow on the Vosges mountains?' murmured the French infantryman in front of me. They gradually reduced us all to silence for their manner was insistent, their pronunciation broad, and their voices loud, interesting all the same. They denounced their sergeants for cruelty, their quartermaster for corruption and their officers for rapacity. 'Look at my badge,' said one of them pointing to the little enamel circle in his cap – 'were my captain to see it tomorrow, he would say, 'Look at this badge, my friend … oh but it's broken' and pop it into his pocket.'

**Boulogne station.** Monday, 3 January 1916 1am. I stumbled across a bombardier and a trooper in the Scots Greys who had got no passes. They asked me where I was going and how to escape the fate of those who get stranded at such places, namely internment in one of the vile reinforcement billets. Like myself, these men had got in front of the ordinary leave train and consequently could show no document to justify their presence at Boulogne. I told them I meant to work my way to the soldiers' home, but the idea didn't appeal to them and we parted. The station was dark and few people were about except military police. Many of them are recent enlistments from the constabulary at home and combine civilian with military discipline, exaggerating both and making the law odious in our eyes. I walked up to the barrier, showed no papers except my railway pass, and asked in a cold voice where I should find the NCO in charge of the soldiers' home. 'Not here just now', replied the policeman on duty. I wearily trudged past the barrier, chucked my kit upon the adjacent bench and sat down. I watched some officers carrying their own luggage, which amused me immensely, they were so clumsy and awkward. After ten minutes a man employed at the soldiers' home arrived. In a leisurely way, I attached myself to his suite and half a dozen of us were marched out of the station. The police were eluded.

**The soldiers' home.** 2am. Church Army, YMCA, Salvation Army, societies, clubs, collective and individual generosity – all vie with each other in meeting the needs of soldiers abroad. The soldiers' home is a godsend to lost and honest men. The one in question seems to be a big abandoned warehouse, several stories high, facing one of the quays. The handful of us was put into an apartment with blankets on the floor. 'You needn't be afraid', said our cicerone, 'We take great trouble to keep them clean'.

**The soldiers' home.** 3am. I tossed about for an hour. Rats scurried past us, winds whistled through a cavern in the floor and vanished up a cavern in the ceiling, whence were hanging two huge ropes and a wheel half hidden. Something like one of Piranesi's gruesome prisons. Why could I not sleep? Was it the *Imaginatio Locorum et Mutatio* which St Thomas à Kempis says has led so many astray? No, alas, for furtive movements on my person indicated otherwise; I caught and crushed on the floor the fleetest louse that ever plagued me – turned over uneasily and before long must have been asleep. I woke at 7am, the latest hour for months and months past, washed and shaved in the courtyard, ate some breakfast and sallied forth.

**The quay at Boulogne.** Here were the Royal Engineers opposite our leave boat, loading and unloading the mails, helped by ASC men looking a century old and by odds and ends who must have belonged to the Navvies Battalion and have been fired for senility. All were busied with the distribution of our letters and parcels – managed most admirably too. I came across the artilleryman and the dragoon whom I saw last night. How had they fared? Why they found an empty railway train and slept in a first class carriage. It was 'Top 'ole, Top 'ole', but they hadn't been able to arrange that they should be called, overslept themselves and had only just arrived, fearing they might have missed the boat. However, there were delays. Men were marched down to the quay by a spruce young sergeant of the Northumberland Fusiliers – a martinet with a Welsh accent. New army, new manners, and he did small credit to his famous unit. We were harassed by him for some little time. At last, the moment came for us to be marched aboard. From sheer love of bossing, the swanker took us by a circuitous route.

**The leave boat.** At last! The boat was crowded with officers of whom quite half seemed to have staff appointments, all of them doubtless mentioned in despatches. Of rank and file there were not very many for, I fancy, the Poperinghe-Hazebrouck train must be met by a boat later in the day. Wind! Most of us were on the upper deck, clinging to rails, ropes, chimney stacks and one another. Most of us survived. We talked in a rambling inconsequent way to keep up our spirits, feeling all the time that a hideous and humiliating doom was impending. Somebody propounded a riddle – is it not adroit? 'If the DADRT meets the DADMS, which of them salutes the RTO?'

The acronyms represent Deputy Assistant Director Railway Traffic – Deputy Assistant Director Medical Services – Rail Transportation Officer.

Somebody whistled a tune, then somebody collapsed and for a moment panic ensued – but we pulled ourselves together, getting more green every minute. Most of us managed to get through the ordeal and when I discerned the white cliffs emerging from a cloudy haze, much closer than I expected, I called out 'Blighty.' And from that moment all fears of seasickness vanished.

Our escorting destroyer drew to one side and we passed along the anti-submarine netting which protects the harbour. A few minutes more, beating about while another packet left the port, and we were alongside the quay. Blighty again!

**Folkestone Pier.** How familiar it all seemed. The Kent policemen, the railway guards, the congestion of trains and the quality of the tea we bought at the buffet, the staleness and cost of the bun, above all the dignified and leisurely delay of an hour.

**The train.** We steamed up that hill – people in the streets and looking from their windows waved their hands to us – it is the furlough-man back from the front, and, day by day, the friendly inhabitants of Folkestone offer their greetings to the familiar train. Our carriage wasn't very full. It was very quiet and sober. The RE sergeant major smoked half a cigar (to take away the taste of the bun) and then slept. The Belgian soldier opposite me asked advice. He was going to Bournemouth on leave where his parents were living. '*Quel pays*', he exclaimed looking out. Could anything be more peaceful, more remote from war? A glorious sunshine gilding the beautiful landscape with its unmistakeable air of *bienséance* – agriculture 'as usual' – well-furnished stock yards, farms with the appearance of ordered comfort and prosperity dating from Georgian times – no sentries on the line, no bridges guarded, no GVC, no soldiers, not even a duty armlet – no ruins to be seen, above all no thunder of the guns *Quel pays – Quel pays*, indeed!

**Victoria Station.** We trooped out on to the platform rather shy and bewildered, wondering if our friends would be there to meet us. The officers were all scrupulously clean – not so the rank and file – we felt dirtier than we were. Towards the end of the platform was gathered a big crowd behind a strong barrier. Our friends waiting for us! We scanned their faces eagerly; they looked at us, and looked us up and down. What were they saying? 'Ah, a Gordon Highlander … a Red Cross man … one of the new sheepskin coats … a German helmet tied to his belt … a staff officer' and so forth. Then we understood that they were mere sightseers who had come down to Victoria Station to see the sight of the afternoon. It made us still more shy. We merged into the crowd outside, took our various roads to home and family. We asked ourselves (at least I did) if crowds assemble to witness the leave takings when we go back to our work abroad – if London finds our farewells as attractive as our arrival.

109

**The night sleeper.** To Fife by the 11.45pm from Kings Cross.

**Balcarres.** Tuesday, 4 January 1916. Found all the family, including Connie and Lady Omega, in great spirits – colds in the head prevalent, but otherwise all well, including James who has been in somewhat poor health.

Eight days later ...

**Victoria station.** Wednesday, 12 January 1916 9.15am. Crowds again, but happily no one is allowed through the barriers unless escorted by a soldier. A quiet crowd – so were the crowds last night at Kirkcaldy and Edinburgh. Now and then the laughter of strained merriment, dim cheering as one train after another left the bay – farewells throttled in sobs of those who stayed to see the train actually steam out. Most of our relatives left before the final departure. How wise.

**London to Folkestone.** Quiet station, quiet train. We spoke very little and felt very much – read papers, looked out of window. Some hospitable man, a KOYLI, produced a whisky bottle. One or two men just moistened their lips from politeness, but wanted neither sustenance nor mirth. As the stations flickered past my eyes became accustomed to the recurrent picture posters issued by the parliamentary recruiting committee, the only true and fearless presentment of our fundamental need. These pictures on the hoardings which began to be issued fifteen months ago, have been correct throughout, have never minimised our necessities, and have consistently appealed to patriotism and duty. The committee is criticised for the tone and substance of its pictorial cries – but how favourably do they compare with the political stargazers who cannot reveal their real views, or else are unwilling to publish the hard facts of our parlous situation.

**Folkestone Pier.** Three trains had preceded ours. On reaching the pier we beheld the big turbine steamer making her way out to sea, her decks seething with brown figures – we were too late. Visions of the detention camps crossed our minds. After we had been standing about silently for an hour, a fresh young naval officer came down, talked to the RTO, and said, 'Well, we'd better have the gunboat', and went to the signalling office at the end of the quay. A dirty coal-black packet with two funnels, her number painted in huge white figures on the captain's tar sheet. We supposed she was a French gunboat, 40-years-old, dismantled long ago as obsolete, and now reverting to her former calling. Though unarmed, she had the unmistakeable *tournure* of the man of war. Moreover some of our sailors were on board and the commander (wearing what we call a cap comforter and looking twice as old and obsolete as his craft) was certainly a naval officer. I suppose 600 of us were crowded onto No. 6028 – but she did her duty by us and we paid our tribute to Mother Ocean.

**Lady Angela Forbes.** A troop hut pinched from its original duty of housing soldiers and converted into a buffet for men reaching Boulogne docks. We formed up into a gigantic battalion, having caught up the 1,500 men who had travelled before us, and patiently worked our way through the refreshment hut, bought French rolls stuffed with minced ham and drank very welcome bowls of tea. We were still reserved, not to say taciturn. The food warmed us up and we began to be reconciled to our return. We were all grateful to Lady Angela Forbes after whom the hut is named. She was impersonated by a grave lady of 65 who was assisted by a sweet little ladies-maid of 19, soberly dressed in black.

Lady Angela Forbes was one of the most enterprising of aristocratic ladies who went to help the troops in France. She started a canteen for soldiers at Boulogne station, meeting every train of wounded as it arrived. It was a great success and others soon followed. They were known as Angelinas and run mainly by her friends and relatives. Near one of her canteens, in 1917, a riot took place at which a clergyman heard her say 'damn' and she was said to have washed her hair in the canteen; so she was ordered to leave France because of 'unseemly conduct'. The authorities were not keen on freelance activities run by those who spurned red tape. In her memoirs she referred to 'wangling in army bakeries' and 'borrowing a lorry from Transport'. It did not help that her dislike of the C-in-C, Sir Douglas Haig, had been made well known. She protested at her removal from France and was defended in the House of Lords by Lord Wemyss and Lord Ribblesdale, who were, or had been, her lovers.

**The rest camp.** As we emerged the police shepherded us back into our marching formation. Certain units going in the direction of Béthune were withdrawn. The rest of us tried to meet our doom with fortitude, for we were to spend the night in the rest camp. I was with two men of the eleventh motor ambulance convoy who live next to us at Hazebrouck. We grew desperate. A very callow officer passed. One of the two men boldly said to him, 'But sir, we are in the Second Army, ought we not to take the train on to Hazebrouck at once?' 'Yes', said the second lieutenant, taken by surprise and impressed by the tone of authority with which the question was put. 'Yes, you had better fall out'. We did so. We legged it for a distance lest we should be recaptured. We got to the station, dumped our kits and found we had a couple of hours on our hands.

**Boulogne.** What need be said about the town beyond that it was peopled with our soldiers, being an important transport and hospital centre – but one is always amazed afresh by the quantities of soldiers who find occupation away from the front. Whenever one goes it is the same thing, Rouen, Calais, Paris, Le Havre. Herein lies a good deal of the wastage of men and high cost of our enterprise.

**In the train again.** Being irrevocably on the way back to duty, our tongues were unloosened. Before our carriage filled up, I had a rapid narrative from Private Lewis of the Army Service Corps. He had had the greatest difficulty in getting his leave – promised one day, withdrawn the next and for three or four weeks he was hanging about on tenterhooks as he proposed to be married during his holiday. He explained that the mechanical transport men who earn six shillings a day are subject to jealousy and malice from their ordinary sergeants who receive a much lower scale of pay, and the life is bullied out of these highly paid privates. Anyhow he was cruelly messed about, but got home at last where he found that a sum of £70 which he had remitted to his credit at home, four shillings a day for twelve months or more, had been spent, every penny of it, by his family. They too had been doing their bit! He could hardly raise enough to pay for the long-delayed wedding, fifty shillings for the licence, ten shillings for the service (in Cardiff, I think). The poor girl was nearly wild with anxiety and disappointment (two photographs produced), and to crown all he had overstayed his leave by twenty-four hours. Then the RFA man opposite me took his boots off and scratched his heels with such violence that I asked for a peep. It was our old friend scabies, so bad as to have got right down to his feet – I gave him the usual advice, he was impressed, promised to take the necessary steps, and asked me fifty questions about patent medicines on which he has been accustomed to waste his money.

**Our next leave.** The talk got general. When will it come again? Will it be leave next time or a return to Blighty for good? Some said one thing, some another. A Seaforth sergeant gave the war another twelve months. Somebody else thought we should finish in the spring. 'Or by July ...' 'or by October' said other voices. Finally someone announced with pontifical solemnity that we might all agree in admitting that the first seven years of the war would be the most disagreeable. Gradually, as station followed station, we got back to the quick professional style of talk interspersed with the rapid humour of the average soldier. We were 'back to the army again' – ready to be reabsorbed into the enthralling horrors of war, anxious to do our utmost to hasten its conclusion, and animated by the optimism of action which alone can give us confidence, keep us free from care, and ultimately herald us to victory. *Laetus exitus* – perhaps *Laetus redditus* too!

Crawford was adapting a phrase from Thomas à Kempis – *Laetus exitus tristem saepe redditum parit* [A joyful departure often begets a sad return].

# V

# 12 January to 23 March 1916

*Officious military police – clothing reform – NCOs and men will win the war, not officers – follies of GHQ – gathering troops – Crawford proposed as RAMC quartermaster . . . and Viceroy of India – contradictory routine orders – attack on Ravenna's cathedral and other atrocities – carnage at Verdun – dentistry the pariah of medical services – French press attitudes – British government confusion over conscription – French courage and endurance.*

Lack of co-ordination between the allies was coming to be recognised as a serious problem, so a major conference was held in December 1915 in Chantilly to agree plans for simultaneous attacks by France, Britain, Russia and Italy, which had joined the allies in the previous May. The Anglo-French strategy was to carry out a great joint attack on the German positions in the region of the River Somme. Each of the allies had greatly added to their resources of men and materiel during the previous year; they were in a better position to try and drive the Germans back out of France, despite the strength of the German trenches, many dug deep into the ground and virtually beyond bombardment. Britain had introduced conscription in January, which replaced a flagging system of voluntary recruitment.

The German strategy on the other hand, as determined by the Kaiser, also in December, was to deliver an enormous blow on a potentially weak point in the French line and one which would be catastrophic to lose, from a military and psychological point of view. The potentially weak point was the Verdun salient and its network of forts which had been established since 1871 with the aim of preventing any possibility of a German invasion in future. Germans attacked with massive firepower in February; the ensuing battle lasted until November. The combined casualties were 1,000,000, but the French positions were held.

While the French were conducting their heroic defence of Verdun, the British were making preparations for the forthcoming offensive on the Somme; it inevitably had to be postponed because of the situation at Verdun, but was essential to take pressure from the French. Though the British sector was relatively quiescent, there were regular minor skirmishes with many casualties for Crawford and his comrades to treat.

A surprising development for Crawford was the proposal to get him appointed Viceroy of India, promoted by some of his political associates; the change from his humble role in Hazebrouck to the grand lifestyle of the King's representative in India would indeed have been remarkable. Nothing came of the proposal.

## Wednesday, 12 January 1916

Back to the army again, as the old saying goes, after eight days' absence at home. It has been a happy and a satisfactory time to me, watching our goodly and growing family, and seeing Connie recovering her health and spirits so well.

And Hazebrouck? The lime trees in the Rue Nationale have been trimmed, the grove in front of the great church is being pleached. There is frost in the air. The greatest event since my departure has been the visit of two mischievous *Taubes* which dropped bombs a couple of hundred yards from our hospital, and also fired one onto the railway line, just beyond an ambulance train where Lisgo was evacuating some of our patients. Considering the tremendous height from which these aeroplanes were operating, it must be conceded that their aim was wonderful; their shell fell within 100yds of the centre of the station. Of domestic affairs the threat to despatch the ambulance train without waiting for our negligent and time wasting officers has been accomplished. The other day they insisted on eating lunch while the cars waited. On reaching the station, the train had gone – serve them right.

## Thursday, 13 January 1916

While having a superheated hot bath, I had a long talk with a corporal of the military police, my neighbour in cleanliness and an old casual acquaintance. He is much distressed at the disrepute into which the Hazebrouck force is falling owing to the assiduity of the sergeant of police in stimulating weighty crime sheets. The town major likewise, the tiresome and fussy Captain Cantley, worries his subordinate officials with trifling and insignificant cases – clothing for instance, he taking the line adopted by the military police at St Omer, in thinking that men from the line should devote the care to their uniforms expected on the square at Aldershot.

As regards breach of the licensing laws, some French people get tremendously punished and others again incur the lightest penalty. The licensee of the Epi de Blé, a biggish public house in the square, was convicted of selling spirits in defiance of some regulation. The place has been closed for six months, Captain Cantley's sentence being upheld by the French commission to whom an appeal was taken. What is the result? The place has become a house of evil repute instead of a pub which could always be controlled by the police. A similar offence about the same time entailed a closing order for a few weeks. It seems to me that we are not entitled to play fast and loose with the property and livelihood of our allies. We should punish our own men who disobey the law, but to ruin French trades people only produces bad blood and probably is a direct incitement to many of them to pay us out by espionage.

### Friday, 14 January 1916

I find that during my leave the colonel has been active in the matter of clothing reform. We have been gradually accumulating articles outside our official equipment – overcoats, British warms, the short coat favoured by the RFA, riding breeches and light mackintoshes. All are now taboo. We are to revert to the styles which were originally served out to us and all these smart and showy superfluities are to be handed into the pack store. I suppose he is right: but though the new order doesn't affect me in the least, my uniform being wholly orthodox, I have often wished to have a light Burberry – something rainproof without the huge weight of our regular overcoats which absorb water like a sponge. The bulk of these illegal articles were bought by our fellows from patients, who themselves came back from the line with bigger wardrobes than they could carry to the base. A glass or two of beer would buy one a good garment. Leather jackets by the way have been forbidden as well – it is believed that the quartermaster has fur jackets for us, but they remain concealed in his recesses.

We have just got rid of an exceptionally tiresome and ill-behaved officer, which sets me again thinking how serious is the danger involved by the new type of newly joined officers. Early in the war, AJB looking at a casualty list with fifty officers in it, said that if such a rate continued we should be simply impotent to command any new armies we might raise. Since then our casualty lists have sometimes included two or three hundred officers and yet we get along somehow. But is not the basis of our military troubles to be found in ill-trained leaders, not in the generals alone, but in the rank and file of commissioned officers? I have come across scores, I might say hundreds, who are utterly incompetent to lead men, to inspire confidence or respect, to enforce discipline, to behave even as gentlemen.

This war is going to be won by the NCOs and men, not by the commissioned ranks. It is only in the RAMC where officers as a whole are more experienced than before the war. We have been able to enlist the services of the most highly trained civilians, while the combatant forces have had to draw upon wholly inexperienced men. This is our good fortune in the RAMC, compensating perhaps for some of the disasters caused by the inherent defects of newly joined officers elsewhere.

### Saturday, 15 January 1916

Excellent news of Connie and the children. Trimmed our vines, disinfected our blankets, ate lots of sardines. Broke my watch glass again, sixth time in six months, ordered four medals of Joan of Arc by Frémiet. Very beautiful things.

Emmanuel Frémiet's sculpture of Joan of Arc is in the Place des Pyramides, Paris and has been reproduced in many forms and places.

### Sunday, 16 January 1916

We have now to unload from the ambulance train on its return from Remy siding. As the train doesn't draw up on the platform we have to walk out along the rails – getting patients out is difficult, and with stretcher cases decidedly dangerous – for when it is dark one stumbles over points, wires and so forth and trains pass us, jamb us up and generally make the job burdensome to all concerned.

For folly and tactlessness commend me to GHQ. They have just issued as a order to be communicated to troops, the reprint of a lengthy leading article which appeared in the *New York Tribune* on 28 October 1915. The article is clear and has its good points – but it is based on the irremediable optimism which has haunted our path throughout and contains the following sentence; 'The decisive part of the war so far as the battlefield is concerned is now over for Germany!' The three months which have elapsed since this observation have marked the final cataclysm of Serbia and Montenegro, our defeats in Mesopotamia and our withdrawal from the Gallipoli peninsula, where we have not left a single man, according to Asquith's boast – though he forgot to add a reference to 50,000 corpses. One wonders what may have been the object of GHQ in circulating this document. Is it to hearten the troops, to educate us, to be cynical and sarcastic at our expense?

> The headline of the article implied imminent German surrender, but its content makes clear that victory would take a year or two and would be due to the superior economic resources of Germany's opponents – comparing the situation with the American Civil War. Crawford was very critical of the optimistic and dishonest spin regularly put on bad news by the political and military authorities. The same feeling was expressed bitterly by his dining club companion Rudyard Kipling, who had lost his son recently at Loos.
>
> *If any question why we died*
> *Tell them because our fathers lied*

### Germany Is Beaten.

If there were needed any evidence of the actual as contrasted with the apparent condition of the European struggle, it could be found without difficulty in the statements of German public men, German newspapers and German people. After fifteen months of strife, after conquests, victories, triumphs, unequalled since the Napoleonic era, who is it that is talking of peace?

Take the public statements of German statesmen, take the comments of the press, is there any mistaking the fact that in all, at some point, the word peace crops up. "Victorious peace," or some other be-adjectived peace, it is, to be sure, but peace. Travellers returning from Germany recently agree that the only real qualification to German confidence is found in the apprehension of a protracted war. Peace now means victory—but next year?

Now, we in the United States have in our own experience a very admirable standard of measurement for German military success. In our Civil War the victors were over long months and years the vanquished. Defeat, disappointment, blundering stretch all the way from First Bull Run to Chickamauga. Compare German with Confederate successes, and, with proper allowance for the difference in size, the essential fact is the same.

Bathed with an RFC man who told me that last week we accounted for no less than six German aeroplanes. Can this be true? For Haig has vouchsafed us nothing but bad news about our airmen, yet my informant was a sober slow thinking individual who seemed quite certain of his facts. Why is the RFC unpopular? Are we jealous of their high pay and of their beautifully tailored costume, of their waists, their caps, their short jackets, and of the swank which these assets seem to produce? No unit 'keeps itself to itself' more than the RFC and I must admit that they consort as little as possible with the *vulgus* of the British Army. The corps is fashionable – all are heroes in the eyes of the novelty-loving public, yet the percentage who actually do the flying is quite small.

Some RFC pilots saw aerial duels with their German peers as sporting encounters, in the spirit of mediaeval chivalry; it was not much appreciated by the average soldier enduring horrific blows from the German enemy. Crawford was not impressed when RFC men spent a whole morning as a guard of honour for two downed German pilots (see 24 May 1916).

## Thursday, 20 January 1916

We still discuss the problems arising when peace is declared. Today's papers give no concrete encouragement to such hopes. Montenegro follows Serbia into the fist of the Teuton and has declared a separate peace. Can one blame the old King for saving his country from the fate of Belgium even at the cost of bitter humiliation? The Italian papers however seem to indicate, and not obscurely, that the German Crown Princess of Montenegro has induced her husband to use his influence against the true interests and desires of the nation on the whole. It is awkward for Italy that Cattaro harbour is now a secure base for the Austrian fleet. Italy, I suspect, will have to reply to the doubts which must be aroused all over the peninsula at the slow rate of progress achieved on land since the spring. Cadorna writes frank despatches, but his army moves wondrously slow.

Montenegro, a kingdom only since 1910, was absorbed in Yugoslavia in 1918, but secured its independence in 2006. General Luigi Cadorna was chief of staff when Italy joined the war against the Central Powers, having received secret territorial promises at the Treaty of London in 1915. He was a brutal leader, freely applying the death penalty to errant soldiers, but lost several battles, notably Caporetto. His successor, Armando Diaz, contributed to the final defeat of Austria-Hungary in 1918, at the Battle of Vittorio Veneto.

## Friday, 21 January 1916

The colonel tells me he has at last devised a 'fool-proof' stretcher leg – after many experiments and after keeping a couple of our men on the job for the best part of six months. Let us hope it may succeed and earn him a well-deserved honour – shall we say KCB?

## Sunday, 23 January 1916

Much movement of troops lately in both directions, today it is said that the Germans have effected a disastrous explosion beneath our lines near Hill 60, and that the Suffolks have suffered severely. I fear the report is true. We knew that the enemy had countermined us and several efforts were made to take their line of trenches – would it not have been feasible to withdraw altogether from the dangerous zone? For the time we are still getting few wounded cases and many medical. All the stations in the town are pretty well crowded out and we have now re-erected our marquees which will accommodate an extra 200 or 300 cases in the event of emergency (which seems not unexpected). It is four months since Loos and we have a new C-in-C who may make the mistake of being in a hurry to assert his personality. All the same one hopes that a new offensive may not be unduly delayed, though I suppose we must await the fresh equipment of the Russians.

## Monday, 24 January 1916

The colonel asked me this evening if I should like to be a quartermaster in the RAMC and indicated that if I so desired the matter could be arranged. I told him that I would much prefer to continue in the scientific work of the operating theatre, work which interests me enormously and which for a man of my age seems more suitable than a quartermastership – for the latter is a post which should be reserved for old and experienced soldiers, upon whom it is the greatest compliment to confer commissioned rank, and a reward for long and faithful service in the army. Of course the quartermastership is the only commission in the RAMC which can be given to a man who is not qualified as doctor, so I must remain an NCO so long as I am in the RAMC, unless the WO were to give commissions for administrative work at home, for which there has hitherto been no occasion. I wish however that there were more chances of being useful in the theatre, not that I want more men to be wounded – heaven forbid – but I wish that we occupied a position where wounded men are treated instead of our present station which is more convenient for sick and convalescent men.

## Tuesday, 25 January 1916

Anniversary of our wedding – how I wish I were at home! I feel that after the war it will be supreme happiness to exist at home, to have one's mind and body free from care. Evans and I were on the station and watched the vulcanisation of old motor tyres, an industry carried on by a squad of engineers and ASC men. The work is done upon a huge mobile truck – one of the longest I ever saw. The old rubber is placed under pressure and emerges in a more business-like condition. We also saw a French armoured train pass through carrying two howitzer guns, I should think of 12-inch diameter – odd shaped monsters which had a look of the heavy naval gun as well. I never saw so mixed and happy-go-lucky looking men as the gun crews, who seemed to be drawn from all sorts of units and dressed in the most varied costume.

## Wednesday, 26 January 1916

Medical cases still predominate. Bully Beef and the fussy matron still brow-beat the men and dislike one another in private, though for purposes of offence they are combined and inseparable. Bully however has had a nasty knock. She constantly has bottles of bismuth cum soda made up for the patients. She brings back the empty bottles to be refilled, but in point of fact there is always a dose or two left in the bottle. These dregs are pure bismuth – showing that she gives the medicine without shaking the bottle. So the patients have been having the soda without bismuth, and if she gave them the final dose she might poison one or two. She has been confronted with the bottles showing the bismuth sediment but is much too ignorant to be ashamed. Nonetheless it is pretty serious to have such ill-trained women in hospital; fancy they can drug patients whenever they chose.

The sergeant major tells me he is determined to apply for a temporary commission (which means retirement at the end of the war). He is fed up. How many are in a like case! The fact is we are beginning to get stale. Some got stale three months ago – with others three or even six months will elapse before staleness sets in – but that the majority of us are discontented, admits of no doubt. I am sorry about this as we have a real good lot of fellows, who would work well if they were less messed about and if they were more convinced of the value of their efforts. Some day circumstances may permit or encourage me to tell the colonel something about his unit – years hence I mean. How surprised he will be, poor man.

## Thursday, 27 January 1916

We are spring cleaning. The theatre is stacked with rugs, furniture, up-holstery and so forth from the dining room – plants likewise. We have an assortment of lodging house palms, the leaves of which have been cleaned with fresh milk! Could anything be more disgraceful when milk would be a godsend to scores of patients who are ill but not ill enough to justify such a diet, and here we are using it to wipe the dust off the commonest and most vulgar of dirty plants? But the ways of the nurses are inscrutable. The waste they cause is unbelievable. Bicarbonate of soda is drawn from the dispensary to bake buns, iodine and permanganate of potash are used for staining chairs and tables, triangular bandages and lint for polishing furniture, ether for cleaning table cloths – there is no limit to their folly and bad temper.

## Friday, 28 January 1916

I tried on one of the new steel helmets being served out to our men, an adaptation from the French model – but a good deal influenced by the sun helmets used by our Indian and African troops. On the whole I should think the French *casquette* most serviceable though it has a rib down the centre which must encourage the penetration of bullets – ours being smooth all round throw the shot off. It is a valuable safeguard against shrapnel splinters and all indirect missiles – but very uncomfortable, wearisome to the head and, during the summer, will get terribly hot. Officers constantly carry breast plates – thin sheets of steel covered with a closely woven grey or brown cloth – when I say carry them, I mean keep them in their valises – for I have never seen one showing any sign of wearing. What a singular thing this atavism. The Italians, I believe, are armoured *cap à pied* and use spears. Knuckle-dusters and trench daggers together with wire cutters are now a normal feature of first line equipment.

Much speculation in our unit as to changes and promotions expected shortly. Quartermaster Sergeant Wootton is now certain of a commission. Sergeant Major Deans is pleased and flattered by the reception given him by the colonel this morning when he made his application for help – he too expects to be an officer soon. Two such promotions involve much consequent changes and Nunn hopes and believes he will get some decent billet at No. 1. Lisgo our corporal at No. 2 would become sergeant dispenser and head NCO. I presumably would become a full corporal, which I don't want at all, and a fresh lance corporal would be required as well as a man to replace Nunn. All these matters are discussed closely as our comfort depends so largely on forthcoming changes. Our work has been greatly increased of late and we are nervous lest further burdens are to be placed on our shoulders.

The staff sergeant of No. 50 told me that out of sixty patients admitted with scabies no less than fifty were returned to duty next day – the diagnosis having been altogether wrong – the men were suffering from lice big and small, from eczema or other skin complaints. Major Barrett, the skin specialist attached to the Second Army, was called in and agreed that these men hadn't got scabies at all. I hope he made a good row about it. But how ignorant some of these regular RAMC men are! There are now 200 scabies cases at No. 50. There have been over 300 – it is one of the great curses of the army.

## Sunday, 30 January 1916

I believe a lot of time expired territorials are returning home with their papers marked 'fit but unwilling' What a reflection and what chance will a man have who in future has to show his discharge paper marked with such a biting record. This is a serious but not unforeseen flaw in the Territorial Act. The problem of drafts for existing units out here becomes more crucial every day. There are many famous regiments which are almost on the point of extinction. It is of course a pity to break up fresh units at home for conversion into drafts, discouraging alike to officers and men who have laboured hard to give a personality and character to their unit – but I believe the course is justified – in other words that it is preferable to distribute a new battalion, which has not seen foreign service, rather than allow some historic regiment to be decimated in action and then treated as a depot for other units.

It means difficulties in any case. What is to become of the officers in some new battalion thus dispersed? The officers! They are the pivot alike of failure and success. How many failures have I seen – abject irremediable failures. I feel instinctively that the junior German officer is a very different personage – arrogant, robust, self-assertive, confident in his mission and in his cause. He is a bully, with the combination of force and obscenity which is a ruling characteristic of modern Germany – but he has force, he has impetus, he can strike and he can drive. He is a power, emulating his seniors in all that counts in hard war, and, even if he be loathed by the subordinates, whom he treats like slaves, he can and does do things of which too many of our men are quite incapable. The attacks made by the Germans on the French front during these last few days have been astonishing and they must have been largely executed by young and untried men.

### Monday, 31 January 1916
Cold bleak and disagreeable day. Several men kicked by horses. What a lot of these accidents we have.

### Tuesday, 1 February 1916
January gone, December gone, November passed. Have we ended our winter? For our own comfort, let us hope so – but it also means that ever since Loos we have been reduced to the war of immobility. We missed a summer campaign – our autumn campaign was a costly failure, we have now missed a winter campaign and must await the next few weeks of spring, even if not longer delayed, for our next forward pressure.

How tremendous is the German power – how well warned and forearmed they are by our ministerial cries of pain and exhortation as to our tactical schemes. Time after time I hear of cases where infantry officers have discouraged our artillery because the stream of German whizzbangs involves serious injury to their men, whereas our artillery is speculative unless there is an organised searching of every square on the enemy's map. Yes, the Boche is well prepared and may make a terrific onslaught upon us before our spring offensive begins.

> Whizzbangs were shells that travelled so fast that the whizz on arrival was heard before the report of the gun itself.

### Thursday, 3 February 1916

Connie sent me a friendly letter from George Curzon, who says that he had pressed for me to succeed Lord Hardinge as Viceroy in India, and at one time that it appeared probable I should be chosen. I take it as a real compliment on the part of George. I don't speculate as to whether I could have done the job even if invited, eight young children – how could one exile oneself for so many years, but I am bound to say it would have provided a very piquant contrast – the squalor and discomforts of Hazebrouck followed by the spacious glories of the east – let me think no more about it. Fred Thesiger will be a sound, safe and cautious administrator at a moment when precisely those qualities will be most valuable.

> Thesiger, later Lord Chelmsford, had been governor general of Queensland and of New South Wales. To have received the recommendation of Lord Curzon, a former Viceroy of India, was certainly a great compliment. Curzon played many important roles in government, including Foreign Secretary (1919–1924), but, despite his great talents, his career was hampered by his grandeur, vanity and arrogance. A contemporary of Curzon's at Balliol College, Oxford imagines him extolling his own superiority in this rhyme (though some thought that he composed it himself)
>
> > *My name is George Nathaniel Curzon,*
> > *I am a most superior person.*
> > *My cheeks are pink, my hair is sleek,*
> > *I dine at Blenheim twice a week.*

A capital report from WHH of the year's working – a good dividend and a comforting balance for 1916. If this year is a tolerable success, I hope to break the back of death duties.

> W.H. Hewlett was a director of Wigan Coal & Iron Company. Controlled by Crawford, it provided his main income. Originally a colliery business,

it diversified into iron, steel and engineering. It was the largest employer in Wigan. Staff exceeded 10,000 at one time. On the death of his father in 1913, Crawford owed death duties of £107,000, which was gradually paid off from income and from the sale of property, books, stamp collections and pictures. His father had been a magnificent spender, travelling the South Seas on his huge steam yacht, *Valhalla*, with various scientists and a crew of sixty-five, and a great collector. He employed four personal librarians at home. After his death, expenditure had to be curbed.

Success in larger matters, where is it to be found? How critical and how instructive the next few weeks will be. The more I think of it and the more I learn from men back from the line, the more emphatic my opinion that our danger lies in officers who lack personality and training. Eighteen months will develop a good soldier, a very passable NCO – but the period is all too short to instil even the elements of leadership and control into the ordinary middle class fellows who hold the commissions – and moreover I come across hundreds who have neither the character nor the decision to be competent officers even if they had twenty years training – the flabby, easy going temperament of young men brought up in affluence, with never a struggle or effort to their credit – men for whom everything has been done in the past and consequently find themselves helpless to act in the modern conditions of war. It is all too pitiful, too tragic. These subordinate officers have no impact, exercise no influence on their men, and are quite unable to enforce discipline. 'Now sergeant major', said one of them at Loos. 'you will take charge of the company. I shall be by your side – you know better than I do' – the warrant officer led the men to a distinguished success – the self-abnegation of this modest subaltern deserves to be recorded, but alas the new army officer doesn't like to be in the background and they often arouse panic among the men by their wild and dangerous notions.

The men themselves are splendid. They take very little advantage of their ignorant and childish officers, though of course discipline in the line is to a measurable extent maintained by the military police who adopt a very drastic attitude towards a man suspected of desertion. The men see the danger of their officers, see all their puerile and fantastic nonsense, but from a sense of loyalty to the army as a whole there is seldom any serious insubordination. I imagine that the new officers are about as bad as the old officers of the original expeditionary force were good, but it seems to me that the new men are of a different breed – having none of the ingredients needed to mould the leader of men. Before long, I expect to reach the conclusion that in future commissions should only be given to those who have passed a certain period in the ranks.

## Friday, 4 February 1916
Crocuses and snowdrops in the front garden of a little villa in the Rue de Merville – they gave me no satisfaction, only making me long more than ever to be at home. What tires one most is the lack of solitude. One is never alone for five minutes – we are all inveterate chatterboxes. If I sit down to write a letter in the dispensary, the door opens every two minutes and even now, while Corporal Evans beside me sees me writing a diary, his patter and his innocent questions are ceaseless. I go out every night at 8pm till 8.20pm or so to sup at the neighbouring confectioner – there at least, even if I talk or am talked to, I get a change of environment, but the asset of silence is lost to us.

## Saturday, 5 February 1916
A *Taube* came over us at dinner time, shining like a diamond in the clear sky. Our guns peppered it at all ranges and throughout its radius – but my impression is that many of them must have burst a quarter of a mile away from the *Taube* . Another kind of bird has been much in evidence today, the Cheshire bantam battalion which has recently come out – such an odd looking lot of gnomes but I dare say they will make good fighters.

> Bantam battalions were composed of recruits shorter than 5ft 3in, the Army's minimum height requirement. Many were exceptional fighters, often miners by background, who resented being excluded from recruitment because of their short stature. They often came in for ribaldry, not always friendly. The French greeted them as *Petits piccininy soldats*! The first bantam battalion, the 15th Cheshire, was known as 'Bigland's Birkenhead Bantams' after Alfred Bigland MP who promoted the idea of such battalions in the face of some scepticism.

## Sunday, 6 February 1916
GHQ again! This time it is Douglas Haig, who through Macready, Lieutenant General and Adjutant General, issues a fresh routine order about officers' kits. It is numbered 1387 and supersedes number 709 and 1217. A more obscure contradictory and slipslop document it would be hard to evolve, and what is clear in it is evidently based (like its precious predecessors) upon the guesswork of ignorant men. There must be forty or fifty thousand officers in France and at home connected with the BEF, and it would have been

worthwhile to consult practical people who have daily and hourly knowledge of the questions involved. Not so. Some idiot at GHQ draws up a code of impossible rules, wasteful of time and trouble, ineffective in their object and liable moreover to cause confusion and perhaps loss. Another idiot gives the new code his imprimatur, and then somebody else promulgates them for the army as a whole. What I ask myself is whether similar follies are being committed in other and more important routine orders. It is obvious that Macready can't be to blame, for he can know nothing of the subject – but it is equally clear that he is a man who cannot assess his subordinates and lacks the selective judgement essential to the AG.

> As Adjutant General, Macready was responsible for administration and infrastructure of the British forces in France; in view of his function, he was popularly known as Make-Ready.

Alas one hears similar criticism of officers from the second lieutenant upwards. The army must be a poor school, for seemingly these stupid blunders are of daily occurrence. It is our unprofessionalism which is so mordantly contrasted with the keen and alert temperament of the sailors. There is still a fatal atmosphere of taking things easy, of trusting to luck and tradition. I see officers (and men too) who I feel instinctively have never yet fought. They have been in action, and they may have behaved pluckily too, but they have never put out the whole strength of the true fighting man because they don't know what supreme effort means. The average soldier comes from a different stock and even if his experience of strife has hitherto been limited to industrial troubles, he knows from the struggle for his livelihood what sustained and self-devoting effort really is. Nobody is less apt to make inductions and generalisations than the AS on military matters, but once he gets hold of an idea he is prone to abide by his opinions. At present he judges his officers as individuals, but when he comes to realise that collectively they are much the same as individually, there will be a serious danger of disaffection. Another two or three months may pass without the idea taking root in his mind for he is still hoping the best from our spring offensive – but if we have another Neuve Chapelle, which God forbid, I fear a critical situation may arise.

### Wednesday, 9 February 1916
A neat little operation on Lieutenant Potts who got a bullet into his thigh eight months ago. Today, it was removed from his shin bone. Sister Alexander cut all the lean off our bacon this morning to give to the poor patients

(who moreover had two eggs apiece as well). We had to be content with the fat.

It appears to me that the Zeppelin raids at home have produced a panic. The press teems with denunciations of the government and provincial mayors are sending telegrams of dismay and rebuke to the authorities; could anything be better calculated to stimulate the Boches to further excursions? Here we read with surprise this outburst of indignation and timidity. Here one knows how insignificant a fraction of our womenkind have suffered at home compared with the slaughters in France. It is a pity that they lose their heads at home, thus distracting their attention from far more important issues on the continent.

> Zeppelins were rigid airships (or dirigibles) named after their inventor, Count Zeppelin. The first one flew in 1900 and the early models were used for passenger transport. From 1915 they launched bombing raids over Britain, causing considerable alarm and outrage because of civilian casualties, with little impact on the war as a whole. They were slow movers, difficult to control in bad weather and vulnerable to incendiary ammunition. Their menace was mainly psychological. In the 1920s they had success as airliners, especially across the Atlantic, until fixed wing aeroplanes took their place.

### Monday, 14 February 1916
Very busy day – no evacuation – also we had to enforce the new GHQ rule about putting kits into sacks. We made our hall look like a rag and bone shop or a potato merchant's. Major Kay so much annoyed that he told us to use no more sacks until further orders. In the ASC workshop at the back of our place, highly skilled artisans are employed under Corporal Patterson in making souvenirs out of shell cases – they even get unused cases sent them for the purpose, the explosive having been removed. Their work however is admirable – but can one believe or conceive such folly?

### Wednesday, 16 February 1916
St Apollinare injured by Austrian airmen! It gives me a frisson of horror, repels me much more deeply than the outrages at Louvain and Rheims. To think of that great gaunt monument, standing isolated in the grey clay marshes, being bombed by the southern Boche! It is the most brutal ineptitude yet committed. But it is typical and symptomatic of their desire to hurt, to intimidate and to smash.

128

> ## DISHONORABLE TO HUMANITY.
>
> ## THE POPE'S PROTEST.
>
> ROME, February 16.
> The Pope has telegraphed to the Vien-
> nese Nuncio, protesting against the bom-
> bardment of the churches and basilica
> at Ravenna, and urging the Kaiser to
> abandon the aerial bombardment of open
> towns and an unarmed population as
> dishonorable to humanity.

What they do at Ravenna is a mere variant upon what they are attempting here, and, while we chatter about reprisals for the blows inflicted on us at home, they are steadily renewing their vigour on the Western Front. The authorities know it and are now bringing back units which have only just got into rest camps after prolonged duties in the trenches. If only the Derby Scheme had been inaugurated six or eight months earlier, we might be able to give a real rest to some of these men whose labours have been incessant – but even today, it is defective numbers which haunt us at every turn.

In August 1914 the Earl of Derby had recruited four battalions of Liverpool men, at his own expense. The principle of 'pals battalions' – that men from the same area would want to enlist alongside friends and neighbours – was implemented all over the country. In October 1915, as director of recruiting, he set up the so-called Derby Scheme. Under it, all males aged between 18 and 41 were to attest to their readiness to enlist. Married men responded well, as they had been promised that they would only be recruited once single men were no longer available. Of the single men, only fifteen per cent attested. Nearly half did not respond, while others claimed exemption for medical reasons or their work's necessity to the war effort. The lack of volunteers had made it necessary, in January 1916, to introduce conscription.

## Thursday, 17 February 1916

A band played in the square this afternoon. I think Coldstream but we could not get away to listen. All day long waiting for evacuation train. When it came in from Remy siding it was overcrowded and only two of our cases could be taken on board. Patients were lying in the passages and many had to be left behind. Nevertheless our motor ambulance convoy has done very little today. The orders are to evacuate by train so as to save petrol. The result is that men are left behind who should be got to the base or at least to Hazebrouck. And the cars which could do the work are lying idle meantime. Men who come from the line today and yesterday all speak with horror of the German offensive which has been very closely concentrated, though on relatively small fronts. Haig admits the loss of 600yds of front line trench on Monday and Tuesday – but it is generally agreed that in certain cases at least two lines were captured. A curious rumour is current that Turkish troops are against us in the salient. I am inclined to doubt it. Bulgarians perhaps, but hardly Turks. Were Ottoman soldiers transported to Flanders one would scarcely know whether to assume it means a grave shortage of German reinforcements, or to admire the Boche for his genius in slave-driving.

## Friday, 18 February 1916

A *Taube* visited Hazebrouck last night – at midnight we were awakened by three or four violent explosions. Nunn, Lisgo and I thereupon went to bed again after looking out of the window, but Dawson made us come downstairs as our attic is unsafe – and all the patients from the upper wards were likewise removed shivering to the cellar. We got to bed again about one o'clock. One bomb fell about 80yds from us into the RFC billets and wounded several men of whom one has since died. Another bomb fell about 100yds from us in the main street, so we had a fortunate escape.

## Saturday, 19 February 1916

Quiet day and few admissions of interest except one or two exceptionally severe cases of shell shock. Cantley, the town major, is preening himself on the prospect of becoming a real major – for he is quite certain he saved the Prince of Wales's life. It appears that Cantley was certain the *Taubes* were coming the night before last – so certain that he insisted on the Prince's leaving Hazebrouck. The Prince went, the German airmen came, so Cantley saved his life, so Cantley must be promoted – and yet promotions miscarry. Has not the excellent Captain Grant, DADRT, and the most soldierly looking squire in the town, long been disappointed of preferment?

## Sunday, 20 February 1916

Had a talk with the colonel today. He tells me that, after five months, he has at length received permission from the munitions department to patent his famous stretcher, a provisional patent having already been sanctioned. What fee or reward should he get? What compensation for an equipment handed over to the government is he entitled to ask? I said that he might so easily ask too much or too little if he acted on his own initiative, that in my opinion he would do well to suggest that six or twelve months hence the matter should be referred to assessment by arbitrators, one of whom would be nominated by him.

He seems to share the view constantly attributed to high quarters that we can break through the German lines whenever we please – in other words whenever our allies are ready for a simultaneous effort. But he thinks that to make a substantial incursion into Belgium, say, from ten to twenty miles along our whole front, would involve casualties of up to 200,000. Were we to make this sacrifice with some such outcome, and assuming that France and Russia could affect proportionate gains, the blow inflicted upon Germany should be fatal; the internal discontent and domestic problems must by now be so acute as to end the war. Nonetheless, I hesitate to accept the premise that we can 'get through' even at such a cost.

Erzeroum is comforting – and if the Grand Duke could push on 300 or 400 miles (across the damnable mountain range) we should *ipso facto* be able to withdraw 100,000 men from Egypt.

Grand Duke Nicholas of Russia was leading the attack on Eastern Turkey. Erzeroum was captured, before the Turks could exploit their victory in the Dardanelles. Crawford hoped that the Grand Duke could relieve the British in Mesopotamia, but he could not follow through in time. Revolutionary feelings were permeating the Russian forces.

To return to this subject of souvenir hunting, I fancy that the lax discipline of our new armies, and the souvenir-hunting propensities of new officers, will entail much trouble if ever we can make an effective advance. When a German trench is captured it is always difficult and sometimes impossible to get the men to advance for an hour or two until they have ransacked the place and picked up all they can carry. It is innocent enough under such conditions, but dangerous and reprehensible. The French on the other hand, once they get on to German soil, will pour out the venom and animus of the most deep-seated bitterness, and woe betide the German homestead which falls into their hands. Our colonel seems to think that the Zeppelin raids at home have bred a spirit of personal vindictiveness in our men. I rather doubt it. The actual suffering entailed to relatives and friends of the soldiers out here is too sparse to colour the sentiment of a whole army.

## Monday, 21 February 1916

*Taubes* again bombarded us last night, and this afternoon four or five of them sailed round and round us for an hour or more. Some of our shells I am glad to say showed a better aim than usual, but the imperturbability of the German craft was the most noticeable thing of all. They are so much prettier than our aircraft, these *Taubes*, though why they should be called after doves I know not. They closely resemble kestrel hawks. We imagine that they were out hunting for our 12in howitzers which passed through the town today. Several bombs were dropped, but the expedition was for observation and little damage was done. All day long the heavy guns have been roaring continuously in the La Bassée region.

> Further south, on this day, the Germans began an immense bombardment of Verdun and the surrounding ring of forts. It was the battle in which General Philippe Pétain (later president of Vichy France) first became prominent. Having expected to retire without reaching the rank of general, he suddenly emerged from obscurity to become the hero of Verdun. At Verdun, he rallied the troops with the order *'Courage! On les aura'*, a phrase used on war posters.

## Wednesday, 23 February 1916

A number of bombs were dropped on Hazebrouck last night, one of them about 100yds away. It now seems a recognised practice of the Germans; they think they are terrorising the French as much as the English, but they are mistaken. People here look upon these inflictions with disgust, but with philosophy too. They know how insignificant are their sufferings compared with what is undergone by people fifteen and twenty miles off, within the German lines, and here as elsewhere the military result of these raids is negligible. It is however an infernal bore for us NCOs, for when the explosions begin we are ordered out of our attic until the visitation is past. It ruins one's continuity of repose. Snow again today – hard frosts, and the roads shocking. The local boys turned up in scores and had a snowballing encounter with a dozen of our fellows – they stormed, enfiladed and whizzbanged us until we were compelled to surrender, to the huge delight of the onlookers.

## Saturday, 26 February 1916

This morning we woke up to find Hazebrouck, which has been groaning under wintry conditions for the last three days, smothered in snow. How it alters the silhouette of the Grande Place, and gives great distinction to the steep pitched irregular roofs – but this evening we are in all the throes of a thaw, and a few degrees of frost tonight will make life on the roads impossible. As it is, the skidding has been very bad all day long.

I was giving out the tobacco ration today – scarcely one man would take a large tin of good tobacco in preference to a couple of small packets of indifferent cigarettes. Pipe smoking has quite gone out of fashion, fags being all the rage. One man told me that twenty-eight big tins of Black Cat tobacco were used in their trench to buttress up some sandbags – nobody wanted to smoke them, and, within five minutes of making their sandbags secure, a whizzbang scattered the lot. We all smoke too much.

There are scores of patients whose nerves are wrong and who are entered as neurasthenia or something of the sort, whereas their real complaint is nicotine poisoning. Of course the outdoor life neutralises a good deal of smoke, but even so there can be no doubt of the danger. Some units complain that their tobacco ration is short – but one way and another, partly by gifts from home and largely by spending the weekly pay, the amount of baccy consumed is stupendous. All sorts of brands of tobacco can be had cheaply from the canteens – neither British nor French duties are paid which reduces the price immensely. It would appear that new brands are contrived or else new firms have been created in order to cater for the BEF – at any rate new styles and mixtures constantly appear and are often very poor in quality. Charitably minded people at home subscribe largely for sending us tobacco – the merchants may make a fortune out of it, but their stuff is too often unsmokeable. Matches too have sadly deteriorated in quality.

The local matches were known by the troops as 'Asquiths' because one had to 'wait and see' before learning if they would light; the Prime Minister's much derided use of this phrase symbolised his dilatory method of leadership which was to lead to his replacement by the more impetuous Lloyd George. A Canadian unit in a British assault was given instructions in code, to foil any Germans eavesdropping on their communications: 'Asquith' meant 'wait and see', while 'Lloyd George' meant 'attack at once'.

### Sunday, 27 February 1916

I was picking up patients at the station when Jim Mason turned up – looking very white I thought, but upright and distinguished in civilian clothes. Soldiers mistook him for a general in mufti and saluted him. We had a good long talk. He has been touring about France with the parliamentary deputation and has seen interesting places and people – he is now at HQ Fromelles, and going to be shown something of our front. His impressions should be worth recording. I must urge him to put them on paper while fresh in his memory. He has seen lots of things I would give much to see, but, stationary as my lot has been, he hasn't had the faculty of observation and knowledge which alone pertains to the underworld.

James Mason was Crawford's brother-in-law, MP for Oxfordshire.

## Monday, 28 February 1916

Sloppy day. Saw a quadrille of seven planes start for the German lines. Verdun news rather better – but the sensational reports of a great French success are unbelievable. The colonel is to leave tonight for the Riviera. Lucky man! He has been laid up with an asthmatic cough, and Major Campbell, our Presbyterian chaplain, accompanies him. What would one not give for a glimpse of the blue Mediterranean and the Côte d'Azur sunshine! Somehow the war has made me long for leisured warmth more than for any other blessing of peace. I should like to know something about this convalescent home at Cimiez; I think Lord Michelham has something to do with it. Tonight Captain Church goes there after enjoying six weeks of boisterous health in our hospital. I can't help feeling that some swinging of the lead goes on there.

> The banker, Herbert Stern, ennobled as Lord Michelham, set up a convalescent home for officers at Cimiez, near Nice. The Michelhams were well known in society for lavish parties at their house, Strawberry Hill, once the home of Horace Walpole. Crawford was uncomfortable with *nouveaux riches*, but would have appreciated Lord Michelham's munificence to the National Gallery to which he himself gave a painting by Ugolino. He funded the quadriga on top of the Wellington Arch at Hyde Park Corner, in London, his son being the model for the charioteer.

O'Grady tackled my tooth this morning and has raised a mighty molar where last night there was a dejected stump. If he saves the old fellow, I shall owe him a real debt of gratitude. He complains of his poor and defective equipment. The surgeons get pretty nearly all they want, but dentistry is still the pariah of medical science out here – and yet in some ways more ill health and suffering is caused by bad teeth than by the ordinary maladies of the trench. The establishment at Arques where the dental mechanics work is quite inadequate for the tremendous demands upon it; men waste weeks waiting for their treatment. The colonel, who supervises the dentistry of the Second Army, isn't a dentist himself and knows nothing of the subject – complains, for instance, that O'Grady uses gas in extracting a few teeth out of one single jaw. The wretched man should have them pulled out without anaesthetic. O'Grady has firmly refused to receive dictation on these technical matters – but he is fed up with the whole business and wants a commission in a combatant unit.

Dentistry, though the pariah of the medical services, got a boost when the C-in-C, Sir Douglas Haig, got toothache and increased the recruitment of dentists into the RAMC. It led to the formation of the Royal Army Dental Corps in 1921.

### Tuesday, 29 February 1916

The colonel didn't go to the Riviera after all. Perhaps he thought that he could not well go with one of his own majors – perhaps also the expectations of a new leave before long may have dissuaded him. Anyhow he is still here and in rather a querulous mood.

Lord Caledon must rank as a fifth cousin of mine – at any rate he should be descended from Earl James. He has come in suffering from scabies. Connie sends me a most delightful photo of Barbara.

Lord Caledon was Crawford's fourth cousin. His younger brother, Major Harold Alexander, was a gallant and inspirational soldier who won a MC and DSO on the Western Front. In the Second World War he became Supreme Commander of the Allied Forces for the Mediterranean and, as Lord Alexander of Tunis, Governor General of Canada.

The quality of our loaf is again deteriorating. The bread itself is all right, but owing to some fault in the baking there is a renewed tendency (as was the case while we were at Le Havre) for the whole of the upper crust to detach itself from the rest of the loaf. This crust is leathery, and, without the substructure of bread, uneatable. The lower part, by being exposed to friction when its upper protection has gone, quickly runs to waste and a high percentage of loss ensues. It is a pity. I hear of bread sacks, each holding forty loaves, which reach their destinations in the line almost in a condition of crumb – all because there is something faulty in cohesiveness. The bread itself is good – not very palatable, but genuine and unadulterated. It lasts in the most extraordinary way and preserves its freshness for longer than the ordinary household loaf at home. Its degree of sustenance is high. It is said that the chief baker in France (probably a major of the ASC) has got the DSO for his baking. On the whole we are well served by him and have reason to be grateful to him. The French bread remains the food of our choice – always delicious, though short-lived.

On his return to politics, in addition to ministerial appointments, Crawford became chairman of the Wheat Commission, which was to ensure the supply of cereals and bread. He was responsible for the 'standard loaf', which was supposed to be nutritious, tasty and economical. His experience in the ranks no doubt was of great value in this task.

## Friday, 3 March 1916

The French press seem to show a renewed anxiety about Verdun – partly based on Repington's view that the enemy will renew the attack, either there or elsewhere, on the French lines. Meanwhile, except for the local action, we remain pretty quiescent. My feeling is that Joffre has ample reserves to meet any fresh attack.

Colonel Charles Repington was a former army officer who had served with General Plumer and General Smith-Dorrien, among others. After more than twenty years as a soldier, he had to resign his commission over a divorce scandal and he became *The Times* military correspondent and author of several books. His connections and background gave him an access to GHQ which was unique among journalists.

## Saturday, 4 March 1916

As the military qualities of the officers deteriorates – the experienced men gradually being killed or falling sick – the demands of the new officers become less tolerable. One hears complaints of the disparity between the treatment of officers and men based on the old theory that one officer is worth twenty men. In old days the varying treatment was justified (or at least balanced) by the soldierly virtues of the officer. Nowadays his qualities seem scarce and his needs insatiable. The AS will stand much from a gentleman, but he is quick to detect the bourgeois and asks himself why he travels in filthy cattle trucks, by the forty, while the officer is installed further down the train in first class carriages. How often have I heard these criticisms and felt their existence, even when unspoken.

## Sunday, 5 March 1916

General Plumer went over the hospital today. Staff majors and staff captains came to see Captain Spencer, an inmate from GHQ. Lots of aides-de-camp and orderlies accompanied all the red-capped officers and all the aides-de-camp wore red caps too. The reddest note of colour in all this galaxy of crimson tones was the maroon of General Plumer's countenance. The German attack on Verdun has reopened with fresh vigour. I don't quite like the comments of the French critics that, even if Verdun falls, their army will remain intact and the line unbroken, though further back. This almost suggests preparation for bad news.

## Monday, 6 March 1916

Another of our orderlies driven out by Alexander, Private Webster, one of the best bandagers I ever saw – but she made his life burdensome and has finally got him transferred to No. 1 where he won't find work congenial to his tastes and capacity. We are all sorry to lose him. It was most amusing to hear him tell off a refractory patient. 'There are no officers in my wards', he would say to a critical or domineering officer, or to one who gave too many orders. 'There are no officers in my wards, except my own medical officer: everybody else is a patient'.

Colonel Sprot came to see me. He says that one French general at Verdun will be court martialed. He was entertaining a fairy at the crucial moment – and a second general has already been called back to give explanations of his conduct. Why General Pétain who has come into such prominence was quite unknown to the public, is explained by the fact that he was third or fourth in the Verdun hierarchy. The crisis has found him prepared, and all France is talking of his modesty and prowess. Let us trust he can hold firm for another week – and then we can face the future with greater confidence. I assume what Colonel Sprot tells me is true; this version is accepted by our GHQ and probably is only too well founded in fact.

> The alleged scandal behind Pétain's promotion is not generally confirmed by historians.

## Tuesday, 7 March 1916

Weather vile. Very busy day, great difficulties with our evacuations which are now very unpunctual. One hundred and twenty cases due for evacuation from No. 1. I don't understand why supplemental ambulance trains are not run in Hazebrouck; also we have 500 patients who should be sent to the base. The railway traffic seems to have increased greatly compared with the volume of say six months ago – but we haven't built a yard of new siding, though the technical difficulties of doing so are small. What comfort and economy would have been gained if a light footbridge had been built to join the different platforms, a week or two and a few hundred pounds would have done it – but on such things we linger. At Abbeville, we have spent as many thousand on railroad improvement as we have spent pence at Hazebrouck. Yet seven lines converge at our station.

A rumour is abroad that GHQ is migrating to Hazebrouck. I feel that they ought to move from St Omer, which is at the far end of our longish line. Hazebrouck is much nearer the controlling centre of our strategy. But if they move at all, they should surely go farther south towards Béthune. I doubt, however, if Hazebrouck could provide accommodation for the myriad suite of GHQ. We have none of those spacious mansions which abound in St Omer and our substitutes would prove meagre for the red hats. As regards ourselves, we in Hazebrouck would prefer to retain our provincial obscurity. We are worried by our police here – but nothing compared to their inflictions at St Omer where the AS is expected to keep his buttons polished as though he were at Aldershot. In point of fact, the restrictions on the ordinary freedom of the AS at St Omer make the town one of the most unpopular stations in France. The police have been needlessly severe and far from tactful in carrying out their orders.

## Wednesday, 8 March 1916

Heavy snow all night, thaw all day. The French news is disquieting – a village apparently on a height taken on the west bank of the Meuse. How critical the next ten days will be and how far-reaching their effect upon the subsequent campaign. I notice in some Paris papers and notably in the articles by René Bazin and Maurice Barrès, vigorous replies to violent criticisms chiefly emanating from southern writers. The *Toulouse Presse* seems very bitter in its attacks upon priests, millionaires and the authorities in general. The allegation is that there are many shirkers, *embusqués* shielded and encouraged by influential people. It may or may not be true in the fraction of cases where such allegations may be well founded, but that such a thing is general cannot be believed. Anti-clericalism and a passion for levelling would seem the foundation for such charges, and the replies are spirited and well-reasoned. Why Barrès and Co give needless advertisement to such attacks I don't understand, because otherwise their vogue would be limited to the obscure Midi – but it is possible that these counter appeals for unity of the nation, admirably maintained hitherto, are based upon a fear that analogous criticism is simmering in the heart of France. A reverse on the Verdun salient would intensify latent discontent and perhaps produce a serious outbreak of criticism. Clemenceau, I gather, is again suppressed. His paper, the *Homme Enchaîné*, has long been a nuisance, egoistic beyond belief and crabbing, grousing, minimising everybody and everything except Clemenceau himself and his little clique. There is a capital onslaught upon him in Gustave Hervé's paper *La Victoire* – calling him 'the wrecker'. Clemenceau will presumably reappear in a few days in a fresh gabardine and behave better for a while – but the egregious vanity of his later years will reassert itself. He cannot forget his own greatness and has lost all the brilliant qualities which I remember in him ten years ago.

> Georges Clemenceau, a medical doctor and journalist by background, had been Prime Minister of France in 1906–9, but then had resumed his career as a hard-hitting journalist. In 1917, he again became Prime Minister and was a principal architect of imposing harsh penalties on Germany at the Versailles Treaty in 1919.

## Thursday, 9 March 1916

New equipment served out to us – belt pack and haversack – we have to surrender our old tackle, which is a pity as, after all these months, I have grown attached to my gabardine – when I call the new stuff 'new', I use an army euphemism for it is second and third hand – the equipment of dead soldiers or of men sent to the base hospitals. H.P. was a recent owner of my new pack. Where is he now, poor fellow?

Major Kay bade me farewell this morning. He is a calm, phlegmatic Scotsman, genial as an officer, decisive as a surgeon and has taught me much surgical science in his quiet, undidactic way. I said I wished he would take me to his FA. But I fear we are still stuck at Hazebrouck for some time to come. The French news this morning is bad, though the military critics persist in looking on Verdun as an important, but not all-important, item in the long French lines. My fear is that were the fortress to fall, the internal and political results would be even more serious than the military setback.

## Friday, 10 March 1916

Churchill's speech on the navy estimates fills me with disgust. He suggests inertia in the Admiralty because they have had no Antwerp or Gallipoli and he alleges that AJB has slowed down the progress of shipbuilding, not a word of which I believe. Finally, he makes a covert attack on the First Sea Lord by overpowering flattery of his predecessor. I suspect that Churchill begins to grow frightened of Fisher. The latter seldom forgets and never forgives. The rancour of Churchill's final attack went unanswered. Fisher's silence is ominous and one day, perhaps quite unexpectedly, Churchill will find himself the target for bitter, smashing and conclusive counter attack. This *ex-post facto* sycophancy was calculated by Churchill (whose diplomacy is Teutonic in clumsiness and ineptitude) to soften the wrath of a great man whom he has belittled. He acted without taking AJB into account – the last man in the world to be blackmailed by this form of repentance. Churchill always was a sneak – all his courage, energy and conviction is tempered by this dominating feature of his character. By now, I trust he is sufficiently discredited to prevent this last outburst from being seriously mischievous.

> Sir Henry Jackson was First Sea Lord and Lord Fisher his predecessor.

Why can't he leave matters alone! Hasn't he plenty to do looking after the battalion whose command he filched? But he appears to get leave every six weeks. He ought to be kept to his work out here. The soldier alas is always afraid of the politician and weakly surrenders. Were it not for political squeeze, neither Churchill, nor Seely, Colonel Ward, Hamar Greenwood and lots of others, would ever have received their high promotion on military merits alone – but as MPs they had influence, and stooped to make best use of it. Haig is less tractable on such matters than French. Thank heavens.

> Jack Seely (Conservative, later Liberal) and the trade unionist Jack Ward (Liberal-Labour) did notable military service. They, together with Hamar Greenwood (Liberal, later Conservative) all changed their party political allegiance, as did Churchill; this might explain Crawford's negative remarks, since he was a staunch Conservative loyalist.

## Wednesday, 15 March 1916

France's endurance during this protracted crisis of Verdun fills one with admiration. The French have suffered serious losses, and notwithstanding the conventional argument that Verdun is no more important or essential than any other fort, there is a deep and fundamental anxiety about the outcome. Yet the absence of fussiness and criticism, the confidence in the troops whose motto is '*n'passeront pas*', the reserve and self-control of the press – all these things somehow would be impossible under similar circumstances at home.

Today is the anniversary of the day when I realised the terrific failure of Neuve Chapelle and the inevitable prolongation of the war – up to then we had all based hopes on our spring offensive which took seven months of preparation. But our hopes were belied in spite of our great efforts and the truth made itself known, although the official reports made many people believe we had won a victory. I shall never forget the horror of that week – there was a similar time early in the South African war, when we had a casualty list about the scale of one hour at Neuve Chapelle. How the standard of slaughter has mounted since the winter of 1900, how engines of destruction have been developed, and a spring offensive, which last year caused us a casualty list of 35,000, may in 1916 entail the loss of 200,000 killed and wounded.

> The forthcoming Battle of the Somme was to result in more than 350,000 British casualties.

### Thursday, 16 March 1916

Last night O'Grady was complaining about the management of dental cases out here. A man was actually sent back to duty who only possessed one tooth. The ownership of teeth is apparently looked upon as a luxury in the British Army.

Our washing is now being sent to Dunkirk. Of course the quantity is immense, but, with the three big CCSs here, one would think that some central laundry could be established – the cost and waste of time involved in conducting it to and fro are heavy, though Dunkirk is cheaper than Hazebrouck. None of our soldiers are there and prices are consequently half those in vogue where British cash is available. Dunkirk has the reputation of speaking the purest Flemish in all old Flanders. If a cheap meal with good rum can be got, there will be competition among the boys to do the washing fatigues. At our officers' station the linen is sent to the Ecole Menagère round the corner, where a sweet nun of the order of St Vincent de Paul looks after the refugees who do the washing. My own washerwoman, poor thing, is mourning the loss of her son, killed a few weeks ago in Champagne.

### Friday, 17 March 1916

Some spring and summer bulbs have been given us for our garden. I am fond of bulb gardening and have been responsible for planting out many thousands – but this gift fills me with dismay. Late summer flowering tulips – planted late in March. Why, they may not bloom until July – are we going to sit at Hazebrouck till the autumn – is there no confidence of an advance, of a move eastwards? We want a move and we want it badly. We are getting stale like the air and atmosphere of our big station, where no less than five of our staff reported sick today! There is no change, no rotation of rest and hard work which the troops in the line secure, there are few half days off – as regards myself I am technically on duty, day and night, and I haven't been away from the hospital for an hour at a time since I came back from leave, except when I go to Madame Renault for a bath. And now this evidence that the colonel expects us to stay here almost indefinitely shatters one's hope; though many think that there will be little if any movement eastwards, it was at least expected by some that we should replace units who are in Belgium, units in which the wastage has been tremendous and where the quality of work suffers from the perpetual and grinding strain.

## Saturday, 18 March 1916

Every day I see a train load and crowded platform of elderly French territorials working their way up the line – their uniform and equipment are happy go lucky beyond belief – but the vigour and solidity of these good citizens impress me more than I can say. Every man seems to have character, to be a character. Lots of them may be scoundrels, but all have force, astuteness, patience, resource – something or other of military value. It would be impossible to pick out one of our regiments and see these unfailing rows of faces which count. How easily one misjudges these old French *poilus* ; their costume is so variegated and their kit such a potpourri of odds and ends and their ridiculous habit of carrying small canvas portmanteaux with parcels tied on here and there with bits of string – all these things combine to make him an object of indulgent smiles to our old soldiers, and an object of ridicule to our young ones. Both are wrong. Study these men's faces and one sees many and often great qualities which more than counter balance their lack of military bearing. The younger troops are different metal. Their faces and characters too are formed, more so than in our army for the Frenchman reaches his fixed physiognomy quicker than the Briton – but somehow these young troops don't seem to have the qualities of race so marked among the territorials. Is the young generation inferior to the old, or will an added fifteen or twenty years give them the temperament and stomach so noteworthy in their elders? I rather doubt it. It is perhaps not only in France that the married men are to save the state.

## Monday, 20 March 1916

Verdun still holds firm and I now believe the *poilu's* motto '*n'passeront pas*', will be realised. The German casualties, measured by our own experience as attacking party at Loos, and taking into account the density of their infantry formations, may well approach a quarter of a million. What is the influence of Verdun upon our GHQ? Does it not show the terrible sacrifice of the offensive? May it not perhaps delay our own forward movement until more and more troops are accumulated on our front? We hear of men coming back from Egypt, which is good news. I can't help admiring the Germans for submitting us to the biggest bit of strategic bluff ever conceived. These reinforcements will be welcome, but after a certain point we cannot use men advantageously on a limited front, at least not in proportion to their numbers though they are invaluable to make wastage good.

Austen Chamberlain writes to me about an officer on whose behalf I wrote. He adds: 'I had hoped that I might have got you for India, but *Dis aliter visum*,' an observation which intrigues me a good deal.

Austen Chamberlain was Secretary of State for India at the time; his quotation from Virgil's *Aeneid* means that the gods saw it differently. He was a son of Joseph Chamberlain, an outstanding politician of the late nineteenth century. Joseph's Liberal Unionists, a splinter group of the Liberals, joined the Conservatives to form the government in 1895. Largely due to policy differences over free trade, they lost heavily to the Liberals in 1906. Austen held some of the highest offices of state over more than thirty-four years, but the premiership eluded him, as it did his father. He was a gentleman in politics and it was said of him 'He always played the game and always lost it'. As Foreign Secretary he won the Nobel Prize in 1925 for his role in the Locarno Pact, which was intended to prevent war in Europe. After his death in 1937, his half brother, Neville, became Prime Minister before being replaced by Winston Churchill in 1940.

## Wednesday, 22 March 1916

Dawson left us today. He has been MO at our little hospital since we opened eight months ago. One reason why Dawson has left us is that he feels it imperative to safeguard his practice and we hear of other RAMC officers who joined the army for limited periods doing likewise. I don't quite understand how this comes about as one imagined that, apart from certain territorials, nobody could resign a commission during the war.

One feels for people in this predicament, especially for such professional men as doctors who see the shirker absorbing their practices, and yet the trouble must exist in every grade of occupation. It all comes from the fantastic timidity of our rulers who are afraid of phantom electors and create deep injustices by their patchwork schemes and promises. Jack Sandars writes that the married men problem may well produce a serious political crisis at home. I am not surprised. The government has been afraid of compulsion in its logical and consistent form – and accordingly devised a network of exemptions through which able-bodied men are escaping their civic liability in thousands. This produces a counter irritation among those who are prepared to enlist in their proper rotation and Blighty seems divided into two camps, married versus single. And all the time, while a wave of bitterness and recrimination is welling up at home, the army abroad fights on in partial oblivion of our domestic strife. It is recognised, in the dull way of those who have no time to read newspapers and whose correspondence is limited to family matters, that something is wrong, that the government doesn't govern. The general view that ministers seem at loggerheads internally and in collective action supine.

> Jack Sandars was A.J. Balfour's secretary. The 'married men problem' refers to the bitterness felt by married men, who had been told that they were unlikely to be recruited, but now were to be subject to conscription.

### Thursday, 23 March 1916

Colonel Skinner, twenty-five years' service, North Hants Regiment, is a plucky man. He has been suffering agonies for weeks past from a badly treated whitlow in his hand – came into us today driven in by pain, to be operated on. Our new MO, Captain Owen Taylor did it – the first time I have seen him operate. It was a nasty thing, but somehow I felt he should have been a little more decisive.

The fighting goes on at Verdun. Germany gains little ground and suffers heavy loss – but how long can France stand her casualty lists? Their army is big but its wastage has been immense and they have smaller reserves to fall back upon. The French newspapers too contain many acid comments about the *embusqués* – their equivalent of our shirker. Dishonest doctors have been amassing fortunes by manufacturing the *embusqués* – by means of fraudulent exemptions on the ground of ill health.

# VI

# 24 March to 6 June 1916

*The Anzacs and Canadians come to town – twelve months in the ranks – Australian indiscipline – second trip with General Porter – Zeppelin over Edinburgh – local currencies – Anzac lung troubles – German brutalities anger America – Dublin shame – Crawford's family want him home – complex accoutrement – preparing for Somme – promotion to corporal – Jutland's stupefying losses.*

Although there were already small groups of Australians and Canadians on the Western Front, 1916 saw a big increase in their numbers, together with New Zealanders. The latter had combined in Egypt with the Australians to form the Anzac contingent; hardened by their experience in the Dardanelles, the Anzacs were to be a formidable fighting force on the Western Front. Crawford sees the worst of them as they turn up in Hazebrouck, exemplified by drunkenness, rowdiness and indiscipline – the British troops were ashamed of their British Empire compatriots and the stolid citizens of Hazebrouck were disgusted. However, once in the heat of battle, they were, as in the Dardanelles campaign, exceptionally courageous and effective. Indeed, they were to show particular gallantry at Hazebrouck itself, the subject of major hostilities in 1918, as the Germans made their last desperate efforts to turn the tide.

A notable feature of the Anzac presence in France was their susceptibility to infectious diseases, such as mumps, measles and scarlet fever. There were many cases of VD. Many Anzacs were particularly vulnerable to pulmonary illness, due to their unfamiliarity with European weather. This created problems for No. 12 CCS, which was more geared to surgical than medical cases.

As always, wild rumours spread among the NCOs and men, for example about the forthcoming hostilities, leave suspensions and a possible transfer of the No. 12 CCS's seminary to the Anzac medical services. Most alarming was a rumour to the effect that the Germans were going to 'throw an electrical shock of tremendous voltage' across the British trenches. After all, in the previous July the Germans had used a terrifying flame thrower – *Flammenwerfer* – against the British. Crawford is very critical of the spin coming from government and newspapers, such as the claim that wounded men at home longed to 'have another shot at the Germans', when in fact they longed to stay at home or that Neuve Chapelle and Loos were anything other than 'great tactical defeats'.

Home Rule for Ireland had been the hottest issue in British politics before the war, but it went into abeyance as tens of thousands of Irish soldiers (notably in the RAMC) served loyally and bravely for the British Empire. However, it burst into life again with the Easter Rising of April 1916. This was seen at the time as an act of basest treachery and it was brutally suppressed. After the war, the Irish Free State was created, while Ulster remained part of the United Kingdom.

## Friday, 24 March 1916

A Canadian Brigade has arrived from Egypt. I never saw a more robust looking lot of men, nor more miserable – for, coming from the temperate climate of Egypt, they found themselves with very insufficient billeting plunged into the snow, sleet, and demoralising winds of Hazebrouck. They had two blankets each in Egypt – last night only one. But they are cheerful and confident people, who, if only their discipline holds good, will render excellent service.

## Saturday, 25 March 1916

The Australians think that nearly the whole of their overseas army is shortly to find its way to France, perhaps 100,000 men. They are loosely built men, long in the leg, deep in the chest, rather round shouldered, but broad. They slouch about anyhow with their hands in their pockets, rather like the French territorials – and as for saluting officers – well such a thing never occurs to them. The town major had words with a puttee-less private in the Rue Merville and the Australian was very eloquent. Corporal Lisgo's brother appeared today; he has been seven years in Australia and looks a fine resourceful fellow. His meeting with our benevolent chemist was quite melting.

Australian indiscipline was a nightmare for the British generals, who were very set in their ways; Sir Douglas Haig attributed it, in part, to the absence of death penalty. In reality, the main cause was that the Australian troops were citizen volunteers, imbued with a cheeky and informal individuality, who did not see their officers as their superiors. Their attitude to saluting officers is summed up in Cecil Hartt's cartoon: *British officer:* 'Don't you know what to do when you see an officer? You're a soldier, are you not?': *Australian reply:* 'No, I'm a farmer'. Despite their indiscipline in what they saw as routine matters, the Australians were gallant and effective soldiers, who suffered more than their fair share of casualties in battle.

### Sunday, 26 March 1916

Corporal Patterson ASC tells me that he was told to look round the Second Army workshop store, close to the ammunition works. He says that there are hundreds of pounds worth of new steel bolts lying on the ground rusting and depreciating in value and efficiency, that there are Sunbeam cylinders worth £15 and £20 apiece chucked aside, tyres, rims, spare parts of all kinds – a general exhibition of waste and muddle – and it is like this elsewhere. It is all deplorable and scandalous too, and we shall be paying for these follies all our natural lives – but are these things avoidable? I doubt it.

### Monday, 27 March 1916

Last night about ten o'clock we heard explosions of wrath in our courtyard. Captain Cantley, with the wind properly up and the whisky properly down, had detected a light in Captain Owen Taylor's window. In vain Stanley Harrison the night orderly explained that the light wasn't being used to signal to Zeppelins. 'I tell you there is signalling going on from that window', persisted the town major. 'Look the light gets high and low' – as gusts of winds make it flicker. Nothing would pacify the poor man who stormed and raved round the yard like a lunatic. It was all very funny, but a man who can lightly accuse an officer (whom he knows quite well) of treachery, should not fill an important judicial position through which he can control the liberty of any wretched man who incurs his displeasure.

Our old friend Uncle Sam is here; Captain Lang was taken ill at Remy siding with acute rheumatism, and we had to carry him up to our only vacant bed in the attic. I paid him a visit this afternoon and he was eloquent about his x-ray apparatus, but said that he wondered if he was really doing good work in view of the great obstruction he recently encountered when some repairs became essential. Personally I think this unit is invaluable. Apart from the actual location of the foreign body, the fact of the equipment being available gives confidence to surgeons and useful instruction as well. Lang is an enthusiast, but as he assures me, not an 'expert', and he can't get the expert subvention for his work which is onerous and dangerous. He will have to be transferred to the base tomorrow – but wonders how the skiagraphic work can continue as he is the only officer in the unit.

There are other units in the RAMC which have only a single officer such as the mobile field laboratory. This unit is interesting – a smallish ambulance wagon with equipment for analysis and pathological research. All local examinations of blood for typhoid and so forth are promptly dealt with there – and, considering the small scale of their apartment, it is wonderful how quick and accurate they are.

## Wednesday, 29 March 1916

We are to move from Hazebrouck. This morning a bevy of generals swarmed into the hospital about midday. Sir Arthur Sloggett, General Porter with various Australian officers and retinue. They made a lightening inspection of the place, and as bad luck would have it I got pinned in an angle of the hall staircase. Then there followed a conversation which was most embarrassing for me. Sir Arthur asked how I was. I replied suitably. Then, in presence of everybody else, including our colonel and medical officer, he asked me if I was happy and contented and finally said point blank, 'Would you like to be exchanged to another unit?' I told him I would prefer to stay with the unit where I was born and bred – but how tactless both towards my colonel and myself to put such a question under such circumstances. General Porter quickly saw that Sloggett was putting everybody in a false position and interposed with the remark that he was going to take me with him on one of his tours of inspection. This changed the venue of talk and extricated us all from an uncomfortable impasse. The cohort walked down the yard, and disappeared in a fleet of well-appointed motors.

> Sir Arthur Sloggett was Director General of the RAMC in France.

The colonel came back to the hall (back teeth gleaming) and said, 'So we are to be taken over by the Australians'. It transpired that, without a word of warning to our colonel, this important news was told him, and in presence of his Australian successors. Here again surely Sloggett was at fault, for the colonel in turn was placed in a most awkward and vexatious position. At least they might have told him privately what was contemplated for he has created both hospitals and some consideration is due to him. So much for form. As to the substance. Where are we going and when? Rumour has suggested Nieppe as our destination between Armentières and Steenwerck. Not a bad spot, though probably the clearing station would be wholly in marquees as the town is unlikely to have a palatial building like our Petit Séminaire here – and there are real inconveniences attached to tent work. The SM is delighted at the prospect of migration so are most of us, and luckily we are approaching the advent of decent weather.

### Thursday, 30 March 1916

Are we to go after all? Anyhow, we have been forbidden to pack and are directed to continue our work as usual. It is believed that Sloggett has achieved another gaffe, having publicly announced our migration without having obtained the sanction of Douglas Haig; his consent is of course essential and, until this little formality is completed, further action is suspended.

### Friday, 31 March 1916

It is said with apparent authority that we are not to move. The satisfaction at our prospect of going from Hazebrouck was so spontaneous that the reaction on being told we are to stay has suddenly revealed to the whole unit what has long been clear to some of us, that we are all thoroughly stale. Had no migration ever been suggested, we should have plodded on stolidly and stupidly; but having now been baulked of the prospective move, disappointment will formulate itself in many minds. For my part, taking all disadvantages into account, or rather all the advantages we enjoy in Hazebrouck, I should welcome a change of scene. Officers don't understand how killing the monotony of our life has become. There are scores of men here who during the last ten months have never once been more than a mile away from the hospital – and, apart from the ridiculous concerts we organise amongst ourselves, there is no such thing as an entertainment – no cinema, no reading or recreation room. Such conditions can't fail to atrophy interest in one's work and I am not surprised at the disappointment verging on sullenness with which the news today of our immobility has been received.

I have been more fortunate than most. I recall a visit to St Omer with the colonel, another journey there with dirty linen, an evening at Mont des Cats with drugs, two tours of inspection with General Porter, and above all I have been on leave. So my perspective has been lengthened from time to time, and, so precious has each occasion been, that I feel real pity for those who have been continuously stuck here.

### Saturday, 1 April 1916

It is twelve months today since I went to Aldershot and was attested – twelve months since I wore civilian clothes or looked at the world as a man of affairs. What reflections does this past year evoke? In the first place, notwithstanding discomfort and every kind of inconvenience and being surrounded by all kinds of horror, I have kept wonderfully well. Thank heaven for that. Then again occupation of a specific character and within the danger zone of France has calmed my conscience which was distraught by Neuve Chapelle and much which preceded it. I could not have remained at home old as I am. Then a few months after I enlisted came the offer of a post in the coalition government. This, in spite of severe pressure, I declined, being opposed to the formation of a coalition. I have never regretted that decision – yet I get odd letters and hints from home suggesting my return – on the ground that I could be more usefully employed there. How? As a minister or as a critic? I could fill the latter role with *éclat* and the former with decision, but I had better *endure fort* out here. To return to political life *in medias res* would entail many mistakes as it would be impossible to pick up the threads of public business and the general temperament of the country – while the civilians at home who govern us would never understand the point of view of one who is back from the expeditionary force.

'Endure fort' is the Lindsay family motto.

But all the time my heart aches for wife and children, homes, pictures, books, papers, flowers, trees. As time goes on, this nostalgia must increase. The fundamental fact borne home to me is the ennobling influence of discipline and uniform. How splendid the army is – notwithstanding its seamy side and its plague spots, the courage, character and good will of the average soldier fill me with boundless admiration – and my opportunities of seeing and assessing soldiers of the line are constant and innumerable.

## Sunday, 2 April 1916

The Australians do small credit to our army or their continent. They drink a great deal too much and are followed about by crowds of open mouthed French children – one sees men brandishing empty bottles, making speeches, reeling about, and in general behaving in a foul and disgraceful manner. About fifty military police had to do the town picket tonight, in place of three or four men who are adequate when we have 10,000 of our own men here – and today, although the town is out of bounds, the place is still swarming with them. So long as they don't try to push past the sentries on the main roads, nothing much is said, as indeed to apprehend all the offenders would involve putting the whole brigade under arrest. It appears that twenty-eight days first FP is the normal punishment for being drunk and disorderly. Pay also is stopped. With us the pay is forfeited, but the Australians say that in their case it is only deferred and will be credited to them at the end of the war; moreover with us the weekly allowance made to men undergoing first FP is one shilling (to buy necessities such as soap or candles), whereas the Australians get five francs a week, so there again there is less deterrent from misbehaviour. Our fellows complain that the rich and reckless Australians are raising the price of everything in town.

> The Australian allowance was more than three times the British one. The official rate of exchange promulgated by the Adjutant General was three shillings and seven pence to five francs or about eight and a half pence to the franc.

I would rather command a well-disciplined division of second class courage than an equivalent number of men of first class courage and second class discipline – and nowhere does faulty discipline entail its punishment more quickly than in the trenches. It is not merely that the Australians cannot control themselves, but from all accounts they are in constant conflict with their officers. The ordinary boast of the talkative Australian is how he said this that or the other to his officer, how the officer apologised or didn't, and so forth. Perhaps German discipline will teach them a lesson though it may be too late.

In fact, in the heat of battle, the Australian soldier's informality made it easier to improvise the replacement of killed or wounded officers.

## Monday, 3 April 1916

I went for a long tour of inspection with General Porter – a most glorious day. We began at the Mont des Cats whence we walked a couple of miles across country following the line of water pipes which collect the water from a dozen valleys and place thousands of gallons at the hourly disposal of our troops at Poperinghe. Down the long slope of the hill are scattered tiny remote farm cottages, not many of them. I asked what steps were taken to prevent pollution of the streams by farm sewage. He told me that this difficult and responsible work is entrusted to the Quakers' 'RAMC'. Their head-quarters are at Dunkirk. They are men of substance, maturity and wealth, and I doubt not fulfil this delicate task (which also involves medical inspection of the houses and their inhabitants) with tact and discretion. I don't think our own men could do the work; at least the life of complete isolation involved would soon prove demoralising.

Thence to Boeschepe, a melancholy spot where a field ambulance takes charge of men suffering from self-inflicted wounds. At present there are about fifty patients. Some of these wounds are frankly suicidal, others partly accidental, and a third category is where the man has been talking about a 'Blighty touch' – points a rifle at his foot and somehow or other the thing is loaded or goes off subconsciously. It is a very serious crime in the army to try to slay or mutilate a comrade, but even more serious to commit any such trick towards oneself.

Thence to Remy siding. This must be one of the biggest groups of hospitals in the world – when at high pressure they can treat some 5,000 cases a day! Through Poperinghe, to Vlamertinghe on the road to Ypres where we went over some advanced dressing posts – the stage preceding the field ambulance. Then westwards through Houtkerque, Herzeele and Wormhoudt to Esquelbecq, all towns of character.

I had been hoping that General Porter would tell us something about the prospects of No. 12 – only when getting out of the car at the end of a long and tiring day did he vouchsafe a remark on the subject; and his observation was so obscure and ungrammatical and mumbled in such an odd way that, for the life of me, I haven't the smallest idea what he meant to convey.

Porter told me some home truths about Hector Munro who is believed to have inspired R. McNeill in that ill-advised and uninformed attack on the RAMC. I remember Munro when a patient at our hospital and a real swinger of the lead; he was a snob too. I said to myself at the time of his departure that some day we would come into conflict – a disappointed and incompetent man, he wasn't treated with the deference he expected and has evidently gone home to make mischief.

> Hector Munro, also known as 'Saki', was a prolific short story writer. Like Crawford, he had joined the army as a private soldier, at the age of 43, having refused a commission. He was killed in France by a German sniper in November 1916. Ronald McNeill, later Lord Cushenden, was MP for St Augustine's, Kent. On 15 March, he made a 'very bitter personal attack' in parliament on certain RAMC officers and declared that the RAMC was 'utterly unsuited to the fighting of today'. Some MPs sprung to the defence of the RAMC, including Crawford's friend, Arthur Lee, MP for Fareham.

## Tuesday, 4 April 1916

Australians marched past our hospital for forty minutes this morning. They are no doubt an exceptionally lithe and active lot of men, but the longer they stayed here the worse their reputation became and their departure is hailed with satisfaction, even by those who have been coining money from the newcomers. The town is full of Australian stragglers who got left behind. Many were marched off under armed guard with the main brigade. A certain number, who were not sober enough to march, were chucked onto the wagons and later on a big squad of police rounded up a lot of men, perhaps forty or fifty, but even at five o'clock this evening there were men hanging about, diving in and out of the estaminets and asking where their friends had gone. Our men, even those whom we qualify as boozers, are frankly ashamed of our compatriots. The French are disgusted.

## Thursday, 6 April 1916

I see the report of a debate in the French chamber which would indicate that in some parts of France agriculture is by no means as prosperous as here. It represents a weak feature in French administration where so much depends on the personality of the local prefect or mayor. It is the same with the problem of the *embusqué* – in certain parts he is scarce, in others lamentably numerous, and it is in the south, well away from the pressing horrors of war, that the laxity is most prevalent.

Connie writes that she went into Edinburgh on Sunday and that the Zeppelins dropped a bomb into the very street where she slept! What a merciful escape. *Taube* bombs which have dropped all round our hospital are disagreeable enough, but those from Zeppelins are ten times worse.

The bomb from which Connie had such a narrow escape is commemorated in a plaque in the Grassmarket, Edinburgh.

Owen Taylor tells me that the surgical policy of the RAMC is practically determined by Anthony Bowlby, for example whether, as a rule, head cases or abdominal cases should be dealt with at the CCS or sent on forthwith to base for treatment. At present, the idea is that head wounds should go to base; this means a delay of drainage. As for abdominals, Owen Taylor says that the statistics are much too optimistic, and that, by including a number of superficial cases, the percentage of recoveries is unduly inflated. Can this be so? General Porter takes a very different view of the matter.

### Friday, 7 April 1916

I see constant references in our newspapers to the wonderful health and robustness of our soldiers. I can't help feeling that this view may be incorrect. They look hale and hearty, they are bronzed by the sun and tanned by the rain – often enough, they put on weight, and with their breezy manner are pronounced splendid. There is a reverse to the picture. Thousands of men belie their appearance. Their stoutness is often owing to the sedentary life in the trenches, where the food is bad, bowels immovable and exercise out of the question – followed by a spell behind the line where there is often too much beer. It is an illusory health in many cases, and the constant state of shock under which the men live makes them susceptible to wounds and all the ordinary human ailments. It is after the man has left the front line that he frequently breaks down – just as gassing shows itself a fortnight and even three weeks after the man has been attacked. The reaction is always serious and I look forward with apprehension to the inevitable sickness after the war, when men who have apparently passed unscathed through the terrible ordeal will succumb to influenza, bronchitis, myalgia – all aggravated by the festivities which will accompany our return.

In 1918 a flu pandemic spread over the whole world, its distribution perhaps strengthened by the war. Many soldiers, having survived the hostilities, succumbed to the flu.

## Saturday, 8 April 1916

Patient No. 19 woke this morning with a black eye. He can't say how he got it. What can one expect in the field from those who can't even behave in hospital? An ASC man just back from Steenwerck tells me that quite a number of Australians who have just entered the line have been sent back with head wounds, some of them dead. The first order a man gets on approaching the trenches is not to expose his head, but the Australians are both inquisitive and undisciplined; hence a score of needless casualties. The Canadian loss of trenches is deplored as we must regain them and at some considerable cost.

Recently enlisted Canadians were trying to defend an important ridge, Messines near Ypres, where they experienced an enormous cannonade.

## Tuesday, 11 April 1916

No evacuation today, the train being filled by Canadians who have suffered pretty severely. New liquor regulations posted in public places seem to be issued to bring the French more into line with the drastic regulations affecting our troops. Some French papers argue that there is a serious amount of drunkenness. This may be the case in Marseilles or Paris, but neither here nor at Le Havre did I ever detect anything comparable with what exists at home. In Hazebrouck, the sobriety of the population is notable – though they have no objection to selling and smuggling liquor to us. Absinthe is stopped; it certainly was a rotting and dangerous poison. There is a movement to schedule certain other strong drinks, *Byrrh* is the name of one of them; the public as a whole acquiesces in this partial prohibition and the agitation to have general prohibition, based on the Russian model, doesn't seem to make much headway. So many are concerned in the retail business that it would be difficult to bring about so far reaching a change.

Byrrh is a wine based aperitif, still manufactured by Pernod Ricard.

## Wednesday, 12 April 1916

Today at the railway station we learned that the cause of the Cassel train being an hour late was a dispute between the fireman and driver, both having taken a glass too much! They deserted the footplate and argued the toss on terra firma. The fireman dabbed the other chap on the nose. Traffic was considerably disorganised.

## Thursday, 13 April 1916

Our unit at No. 1 received a lengthy and solemn telling off from the sergeant major yesterday afternoon. Everybody was drawn up on parade in the big dressing room. I would have given much to hear his eloquence. To put it briefly, everything is going wrong with the unit – too much slackness, a noticeable penchant for liquor, undue familiarity between NCOs and men – in fact the whole detachment is demoralised and ill-behaved. Some of it is true, much of it exaggerated, but there is certainly disquiet. This I have long since observed and the cause is obvious – the grinding monotony of our work and surroundings and the absence of all change and recreation. All that surprises me is that the colonel seems ignorant of the source of our troubles, but officers are officers all the world over; not one in a thousand has the faintest idea of opinion in the underworld.

One special matter calls for criticism – the allegation that convalescent patients were worked too hard. In one case this certainly was so, but it seems to me essential that, during their last few days in hospital, men in pretty robust health ought to be given some occupation. They have to be kept in hospital nearly all day owing to the town's temptations; while there, it is right that they should clean the wards and do easy fatigue work. In fact without the help of the patients themselves, it would prove quite beyond the staff to look after 400 to 500 patients. There are always willing workers available, men who are glad to postpone their return to the horrors of the front – and they are so frank and honest about it that nobody can object to their swinging the lead a bit if they work hard during the process.


## Friday, 14 April 1916

What seems to annoy our men at No. 1 more than anything else in the sergeant major's scold was the absence of any acknowledgement of good work accomplished. From his language one would have assumed the whole work of the unit to be a disgrace, whereas, notwithstanding defects here and there, the men have toiled with devotion and loyalty. The nurses, in particular the matron, are held responsible for the slating. From them one receives a ceaseless barrage of vituperation and belittlement. Everything is wrong, always wrong. The matron nags and worries us all day long, and, to do her justice, she bullies the other nurses as much as she fusses the officers or slangs the orderlies. All are denounced with impartiality, and her subordinates naturally enough try to pass on some fragments of the infliction.

## Saturday, 15 April 1916

I got a Marseilles note for one franc in change today, rather a pretty little green document. For a long time, Hazebrouck (acting, I dare say, under the guidance of the mayor, a partisan of sound money) resisted the temptation to use local paper money – but now we are flooded with it. The notes of the Dunkirk Chamber of Commerce are officially recognised by the authorities, but Lille, Havre, Rouen, St Omer and a dozen other towns in the north send their paper here – and now Marseilles follows suit. It is odd to record that

*Marseilles bank note* (Internet)

synchronous with this inflation of local and municipal paper, there has been a marked increase in the amount of silver in circulation. I can't quite make this out.

> The reason may have been distrust of the new local paper money. At the start of the war, coins were hoarded because of their gold and silver content, so local chambers of commerce issued small denomination bank notes to lubricate trade, under the control of the central bank, Banque de France; these notes, made of inferior paper, easily became ragged through usage.

Among other things in this routine order sheet of April 13 is the news that three men have been tried by Field General Court Martial on the charge of 'when, on active service, deserting HM service'. In each case the sentence of the court was 'to suffer death by being shot'. The three sentences were carried out on March 20 and 26. It is harsh, but necessary and just to inflict the supreme penalty, and I doubt not that the offenders received careful and even sympathetic trial. Still one feels the disparity between these hideous sentences and the immunity enjoyed by positive traitors at home. They escape scot free. These others who voluntarily enlisted have to sacrifice their lives for desertion which can at least be understood by those who know what the front line may mean.

> In fact, almost 90% of those condemned to death were reprieved by the C-in-C.

### Sunday, 16 April 1916
Palm Sunday. Here the symbol consists of bunches and boughs of green box trees, and very pretty it is. Great congregations in church off and on throughout the day – and the bell has not been tolling. Is this liturgical or is the octogenarian bell ringer dead, or is it some new precaution against *Taubes*? Several bombs were dropped in our neighbourhood last night but I hear of no special damage being done. Lieutenant J.C. Campbell RFA returned to duty today. He wears a pair of leather breeches (resembling corduroy to the uninitiated eye) which he boasts cost him nine pounds. His effects weighed well nigh a quarter of a ton.

### Monday, 17 April 1916
I came across a bulletin which contained some German correspondence captured during one of our attacks; it shows an entertaining picture of the German connubially minded *hausfrau*.

159

Application for furlough for _Landwehrman_ and stretcher bearer Meier, 3rd Bavarian Div:

Sir, I have the honour to request that a suitable period of furlough be granted to my husband, stretcher bearer Meier, so far as the exigencies of the service will permit, in order that he may see his son born last January, and also that he may contribute further to the fruitfulness of the nation at this time when so many men's lives have been lost.

I have the honour to be, Sir, your obedient servant, Hildegard Meier.

To GOO 3rd Bavarian Div:

Forwarded and recommended. Pte Meier is an industrious and persevering worker.

_[Signed]_. Schafkopf Oberstabsarzt

To DDMS 27, 3rd Bavarian Div:

Pte Meier is granted 14 days furlough. A report should be rendered in due course to this office.

_[Signed]_. Kress von Kressenstein Generalleutnant.

As I copy this out, and notice that somebody signs himself Schafkopf, I confess I begin to wonder whether the whole thing isn't an imposture – but I feel its unconscious humour, such as 'rendering a report in due course', is too genuine to be the product of German fiction.

Schafkopf, literally sheep-head, was a trick taking card game popular in Bavaria.

## Wednesday, 19 April 1916

Australians and New Zealanders are beginning to come into hospital suffering from lung troubles. There are some pretty bad cases. Somehow the New Zealanders seem less robust than the Australian which surprises me a good deal. Their temperament is certainly less effervescing. A large percentage of both contingents are British born, though less than in the original units.

## Thursday, 20 April 1916

The New Zealanders are still hereabouts, some few thousands of them. They can say nothing too bad of the Australians – and their complaint is that New Zealand always follows Australia in date of movement, and on arriving at any place find that their Australian friends have set the place on fire, and New Zealanders suffer in consequence by suppression of passes. It happened in Egypt, at Marseilles and now the same farce is repeated at Hazebrouck.

The newspapers offer gloomy reading, Kut in deadly peril and a new ministerial crisis is reaching its apex – a crisis which should involve the resignation of one group or other of ministers. Churchill is back intriguing in Downing Street, while the adjutant general is alleged to have given special extension of leave to MP officers now at home. Haig seems as weak as French where politicians are concerned. What a dossier one could compile on this aspect of wartime favouritism and sycophancy. I should like to submit it to whatever royal commission enquires into the conduct of the war.

## Friday, 21 April 1916

For a long time past I have missed the sick horse train which used to come into the station just before our midday ambulance train. The enterprise is useful, interesting and humane – sick and wounded horses are collected and forwarded to the base remount depot where they are doctored by a host of clever vets belonging to the Army Veterinary Corps. It sounds a dull job, but for the horsey man this corps must be ideal as thousands upon thousands of steeds parade before them and are criticised in the familiar terms and above all with the customary gestures. But the cost of this 'Blue Cross' work must be great and I often wonder whether it would not be a better economy to kill outright many of the disabled beasts, for lots of them fail to recover from wounds and sickness.

## Sunday, 23 April 1916

I took General Wilson RE to No. 14 general hospital at Wimereux. The distance is sixty miles or so, and it is odd that on a broad highway we didn't pass a single place which appeared to have more than 5,000 inhabitants. The country seems sparsely populated and yet agriculture is well forward – perhaps rather more behind-hand and with less manure to the acre than here, but none the less an example and model to many districts at home. At Arques, a street has been named after Miss Cavell.

Edith Cavell, from Norfolk, became matron of a new nursing school in Brussels in 1907; she also provided training services to several other

After depositing my general, I went to see the *Sussex* lying in Boulogne dock, a recent and important episode in German submarine warfare which greatly annoyed President Wilson; he has written a firm note with not more than three phrases which will enable him to accept any washy explanations which Bernstorff may deign to offer. I was surprised at the effect of the torpedo on the ship – the fore part has been clean cut off and the whole centre of the ship is exposed and flooded. How she ever regained port seems a mystery.

Johann von Bernstorff was the German ambassador to USA and Mexico. In 1917 the Germans secretly offered Mexico territorial concessions in return for joining the war against USA; the offer, coupled with unrestricted submarine warfare even against neutral ships, and von Bernstoff's spying and sabotage activities in USA, led to the entry of USA into the war.

## Tuesday, April 25 1916

Today is the secret session in Parliament. I would give much to be able to tell them the truth as I know it from a thousand and one sources – from daily talks with men from the advanced lines. I doubt if any officer, with the exception of some who have risen from the ranks, could give Parliament the information at my command. Neither has Parliament been told that Neuve Chapelle and Loos rank as the greatest tactical defeats of the western campaign – still less can they know that shortage of men, in addition to faulty leadership, was responsible for the disproportion between our losses and the advantages gained. Yes, I would give much for the chance of telling them the truths so persistently withheld.

## Thursday, 27 April 1916

Oh the shame and disgrace of this morning's news – Dublin controlled by rebels – the first concrete breach in national unity, the product of Birrell's scandalous pusillanimity I suppose they will shoot Casement but there are others who deserve execution still more. Then the report of the secret session Churchill mentioned as one of the speakers – is he back again or is his leave indefinitely prolonged?

Sir Douglas Haig is expected today. It is rather sad how small an impression he has made on the mind and imagination of the AS since he took command on French's withdrawal. He made a mark during our first retreat, but somehow or other we have no commanding personality which makes its impact on soldier and civilian alike.

The French have so many men of great character, the Germans of great force. I think I could quote more names of highly placed German generals than of our own men of high standing. I feel I can see Hindenburg, with his vulture-like countenance, and Mackensen, Pétain, Castelnau, Cadorna and the Grand Duke. On the other hand, I have seen French and Plumer and a score of others, but saw nothing which led me to say 'That is a big man' – alas, how low and depressed I become.

Paul von Hindenburg, having retired in 1911 after a long military career, was recalled to service in 1914 and became a national hero by virtue of the German victory over Russia at Tannenberg. In 1916, he became chief of the general staff and in 1933 president of Germany, to be succeeded by Adolf Hitler.

## Saturday, 29 April 1916

Glorious weather. The government can scarcely survive the double blow of civil war in Ireland and the ignominious collapse of their military service bill. Had one of the last Zeppelin attacks been a biggish massacre, I really believe that the nation would have had to incur the 'disaster' of a change of ministry – but failing this *pièce de conviction*, I suppose the limpets will continue to limp along their ignoble path. One hears pretty direct criticism about the Irish rebellion. Our mildest and most pious non-conformists all clamour for blood of the traitors.

Conscription, introduced in January, exempted married men, but this exemption proved unsustainable.

Lloyd George, I gather, is being scurrilously treated by the radical press – in fact the disquiet and unrest of the last three months seem to have ripened into a general lack of confidence, before long to be translated into a vote of censure in the House of Commons. But I still fail to see even the nucleus of an alternative government. If the so-called opposition had had an organiser during the last six months a fresh ministry would be almost ready to one's hand – but the fear of breaking the truce has kept the unofficial party in a fluid state and has too often diverted its energies into wrong channels.

The French press is very discreet. It talks about the German emissaries in Ireland, attributed all to the cunning bribery of the Boche, and reassures the French public, already puzzled and perhaps distressed by our recent inaction, by minimising the Dublin affair. But even so, there is no disguising the fact that there is civil war, that the authorities must have foreseen some such outbreak, and that even now the rebels show fight and actually extend their activities. What should we say if Munich or Dresden were in the hands of a pro-English mob?

### Monday, 1 May 1916

Last night, a New Zealander came and offered to fight us all in turn; a dozen of us were standing there. A small group of his friends came along and I ordered them to carry the hero away. The Anzac is very vain and boastful – and he annoys the incomparable soldier of our county regiments by every kind of disparagement. My own impression is that the Anzac prowess has been overrated. His reputation is largely based on Ian Hamilton's florid panegyrics. The Australians, who could talk about nothing but their Gallipoli feats a month ago, now say that the German is much more formidable than the Turk – and the Turk must either have been badly led or corrupt to have allowed that bloodless retreat. The New Zealand divisions haven't had much experience of Flanders and are still boasting about their greatness.

General Sir Ian Hamilton commanded the force trying to capture Gallipoli in the Dardanelles campaign.

And Kut has surrendered. It makes me sick. Another ten days and the Grand Duke would have saved the situation – that I firmly believe in spite of fresh menace on his main front. And having cut the Turkish communications behind Kut, I furthermore believe that Constantinople would have rebelled – and that within a month the whole Eastern situation would have been reversed – and now we are too late. If anything can upset this wicked government of ours, surely this must. Antwerp, Gallipoli, Mesopotamia,

164

Egypt, Dublin and all the rest of it, thoroughly mismanaged. Yet the more I look at the problem, the more certain I am that Asquith must remain head of the government and that the cabinet cannot be substantially changed.

## Tuesday, 2 May 1916

MacCrae, the matron, is making herself intolerable, so much so that the nurses from whom we have so often suffered are now much more civil and considerate towards us, actually effecting rapprochements in order to fortify themselves against the Common Foe. But how humiliating it is, the vulgar way this tiresome woman tries to boss all alike, officers, NCOs and men. However, she has been told off with emphasis during the last day or two.

> A different perspective is found in the diary of 'Mother' McCarthy who had recently visited both hospitals of No. 12 CCS and found 'everything in excellent condition, the CO thoroughly satisfied with everything, Miss MacCrae most capable, her staff working well, and properly'.

## Friday, 5 May 1916

Jeanie writes to the effect that I should return home and 'lend my aid in any fashion however much in the background'. Lady Wantage writes in the same strain, or rather she endorses a letter from Robin Benson to the same effect. Evidently, my friends and family are talking among themselves. There is a fundamental fallacy in Robin's letter – where he says that I should be at home so that, if wanted, I could be offered a post. That might be feasible if I were an officer – but I suppose he thinks I am only playing at work out here and can skedaddle home whenever I want to. Far from it, I enjoy no privilege not accorded to others of my own rank, and take my share of work just as anybody else – let that be recorded for those who seem to fancy that I am a free agent. I am nothing of the kind. And the soldier of twelve months experience in France is far too precious to be readily released by the authorities.

> Jeanie, Lady Wantage and Robin Benson were relatives of Crawford.

Supposing I went home, what could I do? Awaken the public? I have no histrionic devices, the House of Lords has been eviscerated and I am dis-qualified from sitting in the Commons. I am able-bodied with twelve months behind me in France. I don't quite see where my sphere would lie. The Red Cross and RAMC don't want any more civilian help in hospital administra-tion at home. Could I become assistant Provost Marshal of Kensington or

Knightsbridge? But what good should I be doing? What more good than keeping our unit together out here which is my practical task? The fact is that I instinctively dislike leaving a job half finished. I came out here because example was needed and because I found that speech making and criticism at home had lost all vital value. No active and profitable sphere was available: to return now, though I may have to do it, would be distasteful to me and perhaps of little service to the cause.

## Saturday, 6 May 1916

I have noticed latterly that elderly Frenchmen are wearing the little black and green rosette which is the medal ribbon of those who fought in the Franco-Prussian war of 1870–1. I wonder if it is Verdun which has brought out this blossom of a long neglected decoration? Verdun indeed continues splendid and the French seem at last to have regained the initiative. Nobody believes that any German offensive can overcome the miles of new works which the French have now prepared behind their present lines. One rather anticipated a fresh outburst on some other section of the front, but hitherto nothing much has occurred.

## Sunday, 7 May 1916

Some more of the Irish traitors have been executed. I feel that all the signatories of the Republican proclamation will have to suffer the supreme penalty – and I doubt not that in times to come they will have their monuments in Ireland and be lauded as martyrs. This will be the test of inherent disloyalty which has thriven so much during the last few months, supplemented by German cash. The ugliest feature of the tragedy is the ease with which the movement degenerated into cowardice and rapine.

## Monday, 8 May 1916

Hot bath. My company was an ASC man from the x-ray unit, a Flying Corps man and a railway engineer driver, a 'lad in blue'. He told me that a huge siege gun on its own special truck with sixteen pairs of wheels has now reached Vlamertinghe, having been two days on its journey from the coast. During the forty-eight hours there have been half a dozen breakdowns as the enormous weight keeps breaking through the rails. The gun is followed by a special train with a breakdown gang which creeps along with a massive crane to raise the monster. What will this gun be used for? I take it to be a 17-inch howitzer. Until we get a little farther along the line, it can't be of much service; for instance, we can't throw such shells into Lille. There the Germans have an incalculable advantage over us for we are naturally reluctant to bombard allied cities. If only we were across the German frontier, the impact of our artillery would be tenfold.

### Wednesday, 10 May 1916

The colonel tells me that tomorrow he is going on a tour to distribute the new stretcher which has at last attained perfection. He wants to visit Amiens among other places, but today was shown a new order forbidding all access to the town to officers below the rank of major general, unless furnished with special permission. A brigadier general must have a pass! I wonder what can be in the wind. The general view seems to be that our front bristles with so much artillery that we can scarcely find emplacement for another battery and that there is an inconceivable reserve of ammunition. Yet we make no move, awaiting Russian preparations. But can Russia ever be prepared in the sense of equipping all her men? A hundred thousand men sent to France might form a more effective army than 200,000 left at home. By the way, for days past there has been a rumour spread by a leaflet dropped by a *Taube* that on the ninth of this month the Germans were going to electrocute us, throw an electrical shock of tremendous voltage across our trenches. I would give much to see this printed warning. Let us hope that the whole thing is only a soldier's tale.

### Friday, 12 May 1916

This is the anniversary of our landing in France. I look back on these twelve months as a wonderful experience during which I have done much hard good work. I have learned many things and seen curious and awful sights. I do not wish to celebrate a second anniversary out here. None do, even the freshest arrival quickly acquires a horror of it all, and it is only for newspaper consumption that we hear of wounded men at home longing to 'have another shot at the Germans'. So strong is the German, so well dug in and so plentiful is his ammunition, that the favourite topic of speculating on the date of peace has long since been abandoned. One sees no signs on which to make an estimate. Yet I can't help feeling that were a successful breakthrough to be achieved before the next harvest, internal and economic difficulties across the Rhine might drive the Germans into capitulation.

Germany was suffering from the blockade imposed by the allied navies, to which the German response was unrestricted submarine warfare – from which Britain equally suffered serious losses.

### Saturday, 13 May 1916

The colonel is concerned by the high proportion of infectious cases developed among the Anzac troops. Every day we send away half a dozen or more men suffering from mumps, measles, scarlet fever, etc. This represents a large and costly wastage. It is generally assumed that pulmonary complaints are commoner among the Anzacs than with those acclimatised to the horrors of European weather – their lungs are very susceptible. But why these other illnesses should be so prevalent is not clear. I think prophylactic work is a good deal neglected by the Anzac medical service.

Another and more serious source of anxiety is the prevalence of VD among officers and men. I have seen no statistics, but cases are apparently much more frequent than a few months ago. We are already getting cases from the 41st Division which has only just arrived. Indeed this division starts life with the unenviable reputation of the 17th which has always been noted for its high rate of sickness. I doubt if the public has any idea of the tremendous losses we incur from ordinary sickness – that is to say the group of maladies wholly unconnected with war. It is a grave problem. I wish that it was being grappled with in a firm and systematic manner.

> VD was the commonest sickness and an enormous cause of inefficiency, particularly among the Anzacs and Canadians, who lacked the safety valve of home leave. The incidence of VD among British troops was 24 out of 1,000, among Canadians 110 and Australians 130.

### Sunday, 14 May 1916

I can't help being rather amused at Asquith's voyage to Dublin, where he will partake of the best for a week, talk tall to representatives of every interest and end by persuading them and himself that a peaceful solution is in view. He hopes to be the *Deus ex machina* who will avert a crisis far more dangerous than that recently passed – and I fear he makes a mistake in so quickly superseding the military rule. I doubt if there is room for a Prime Minister who takes control while the country is still under martial law.

### Monday, 15 May 1916

The colonel has issued orders that, when on duty outside the hospital, we are all to wear belts, and the sergeant major has added verbal instructions that we are to burnish our buttons. This is hardship bordering on persecution. During hot weather, the addition of a belt adds fire to flames when one is engaged on stretcher bearing or any other heavy work.

## Tuesday, 16 May 1916

Oh the nuisance of our accoutrement. I counted its items yesterday. Pack, haversack, belt and water bottle. There are twenty different straps, twenty-eight buckles and no less than 193 strap holes – and this without the complicated chain of ammunition pouches and the trenching tools carried by the infantry. Nothing is more ugly than the French equipment, but it seems well balanced and is more easily subdivided than ours, and they appear to carry all essentials, including a spare pair of boots. Our packs are enormously heavy and whenever any serious work is on hand they get thrown aside. The pictures of our troops crossing the parapet in full rig are pure imagination.

## Friday, 19 May 1916

The heavy guns are beginning to gossip this morning and the aeroplanes have been busy chatting with the Boches overhead. While we are waiting, Germany is wearing down French divisions before Verdun and is maturing her defence against ourselves. The most solid of the AS with whom I discuss the question in private agree that, in trench warfare, the Germans are our equals if not our superiors. In the charge or in an open campaign our men are incomparable, but the Germans are the parents of this new war of fortifications and all our equipment is based on or copied from theirs. Even today, we have nothing to approach their whizzbang. Then again, the German reserve trenches far behind their firing line are admittedly more thorough than ours. It may be said that this measures our confidence of never being driven back, but the German strategy contemplates and prepares for all contingencies. To them, everything is worthwhile and no trouble or expenditure too great to assure the main issue.

## Sunday, 21 May 1916

I read the air debate in the House of Commons with attention but it leaves me unconvinced, though rejoicing that Mr. Billings' vulgar pusillanimity should have received so stinging a rebuff. All these assurances about our superiority over the Germans have been heard before. The RFC men I meet every night are much more humble in their estimate of Boche aviation.

Pemberton Billings was an aviator who became an MP and promoted the idea of a separate air force. His efforts contributed to the creation of the Royal Air Force in 1918; until then the RFC had been part of the army.

## Monday, 22 May 1916

The last three or four weeks have marked a great reaction in the attitude of the nurses towards us. After months of scolding and vituperation they have become amiable and at times friendly. The transformation has been caused by the matron MacCrae who has bullied and harassed the wretched women to such an extent that they feel the need of support, and have entered into a tacit alliance with us! The burden and weariness of our lives is greatly reduced. Let us hope there will be no counter reaction – anyhow, for a fortnight we have lived in peace. The matron is, of course, more insistent than ever finding the hands of all turned against her, especially since this unholy entente between the sexes! Today she gave orders that in future, when going up and down stairs, orderlies are not to put their hands on the banisters – which strikes me as really droll. Had she not treated us with contumely and the nurses with brutality, one would be charitable enough to assume the woman was going potty.

## Tuesday, 23 May 1916

I am today promoted full corporal after being lance-corporal for eight or ten months; I suppose a just and fitting recognition for faithful service. The colonel is almost as pleased about it as if he had got the KCB for himself; for my part, I double my stripe with feelings of regret. I see no reason for preferment and in many ways it limits my freedom – for instance were circumstances to make me desire change, possible spheres would be reduced in number – and moreover, I become one step nearer a sergeantcy in our own unit – a post I certainly don't want, for it would involve my commanding men which is the last thing I should want to do. A special reason which makes me fear another promotion is that it would debar me from acting as theatre orderly.

Crawford's view had changed since October (page 69) when he thought that he would like to end the war as a sergeant.

## Wednesday, 24 May 1916

Two German airmen were buried today. All the RFC contingent acted as guard of honour. This seemed a little ridiculous. It is true that the Fokker and Aviatik have not been associated with the Zeppelin massacres; nevertheless it is unpardonable for the whole local strength of the RFC to have wasted a precious morning on such a quest.

## Thursday, 25 May 1916

Written in a cheap novel which has been going the rounds of our hospital for months – 'with best wishes for good luck to the Tommy or Reggie who receives this book, from R and M Heath (misses) 22 Gartmoor Gardens, Southfields, London, SW'. God bless them both – such anonymous kindnesses touch the heart. Tonight comes the sickening rumour that the French have lost Douaumont, which they had recaptured at so serious a loss. The Germans are beating us at Vimy, beating the Italians in the Trentino, waging an astonishing offensive against the French. It all looks more and more as if their fresh forces and equipment are still in advance of our own; if once this proves true, our joint staff will probably abandon all idea of a summer campaign. Technically they would be right from a military point of view, but the number of potential surprises is so great that the course would be attended by grave risk. Who knows what Norway, Holland or

There was much concern about the intention of neutral states; some were bribed or bullied to join one side or another. Louis Raemaekers' cartoon 'The Friendly Visitor' depicts a German soldier saying 'I come as a friend' and a Dutch lady replying, under the gaze of Queen Wilhelmina, 'Oh, yes. I've heard that from my Belgian sister'. Holland remained neutral throughout the war.

Greece may be thinking six months hence or what troubles might arise in India, what friction between Japan and the United States? There are many contingencies which would urge us to attack the moment we can do so with safety.

## Saturday, 27 May 1916

Churchill's speech about the aspect of manpower in relation to the war on our front contained good points. I note his remark about grooms and officers' servants. There is undoubted scope for improvement here, but that this reform should be advocated by Churchill of all people amuses me. He has the reputation of having looked after his bodily comforts with care during his brief stay at the front, interspersed as it was with frequent leaves. But Churchill only takes the superficial point. He declaims against the number of soldier servants, whereas their existence in such quantities measures the high standard of comfort and luxury enjoyed by officers. The number of servants should be drastically reduced, for in the process officers would have to diminish the scandalous bulk of their kits! The routine order limiting their weight is a dead letter.

And if the officers were forbidden to carry these vast wardrobes filled with needless costumes and weighty souvenirs, they should also be strictly limited in their days and half days off duty. They should be made to work harder, or at least more regularly; they should be taught some of the professional temperament of the Navy. Alas we multiply men, but the quality of our officers does not improve.

## Sunday, 28 May 1916

The French news is rather more reassuring today and acute anxiety may perhaps be laid aside: but it has been a critical week. Can one begin to hope that the Crown Prince will desist from his holocausts? Or is it somebody behind the Crown Prince who is responsible for these mad onslaughts? I often think that some obstinate old general is more likely to direct the strategy than the young featherbrained prince – who, I should imagine, would scarcely have nerve and character to have so long continued the slaughter of his own troops.

Crown Prince Wilhelm, son of the Kaiser, was in command of the German forces at Verdun, aged 32, with limited military experience. He was known as the 'Butcher of Verdun'; later, he claimed that he tried to stop the slaughter, but was overruled.

Mother writes to say that Walter is home with nephritis – a dangerous illness – but we have had so many cases where rapid and apparently fundamental cures have taken place within a few weeks of the patient's removal to the base that I am very hopeful of equally good fortune for Walter. Our doctors are much puzzled by the prevalence of this disease and are conducting careful experiments to detect its origin. Some ascribe it to bad water, others to exposure, others to a definite *nephritis coccus* – for the moment, the investigations are still empiric, but there seems some confidence that precise information will be forthcoming later on.

## Monday, 29 May 1916

A circular is being issued to medical officers warning them against too frequent use of the tourniquet, on the grounds that the dreaded gas bacillus (*perfringens*) is most likely to thrive in closed tissues. I wonder who has detected this important factor in the life history of the germ. But the tourniquet is not easily replaced in advanced field dressings.

Today, a French ambulance convoy passed southwards, also two or three searchlights mounted on swift cars and manned by sailors. There were also some of those long motor buses one sees in Paris – not to compare with ours for compactness, or speed – one can easily put forty-five men onto ours, and very much used they are. The French ones hold many less. The French transport as a whole is less *bien monté* than ours, but somehow they seem to get along with their indifferent equipment just as well as we do with our first class stuff. The most marked contrast of all is in the ambulance trains. Ours are sumptuous to a degree, theirs generally improvised and adapted. Here we no doubt don't see the best of the French equipment, though a pretty important line of front is controlled by the French authorities. The fact is that, except in the actual fighting material, the French government takes cost into account, whereas economy never seems to have entered into our consideration.

## Tuesday, 30 May 1916

An officer introduced himself as Chapman, whose work is to attend Anzac courts martial. He is presumably a barrister put in by GHQ. He tells me that there is an improvement in the Australian discipline. They have learned from bitter facts that discipline is needed for life and limb – and moreover a field punishment camp has been established pretty close to the firing line, where the prisoners are made to work hard, and where all luxuries in the form of sugar, butter, milk and tobacco are forbidden. This drastic treatment is bearing good fruit, but the lack of discipline is very obvious – not merely in disobedience of orders, but in those who give the orders. There is no idea of the promptness, exactitude and clearness which should mark any order issued to any man. Orders are given in a vague slushy way; often enough taking the form of casual requests, with the result that a prisoner can often show that he did not understand the order. Chapman rather thinks that this sloppiness is incurable. He says that the only way to teach the Anzacs discipline, that is to say discipline in its noble and inspiring form, is to send battalions in rotation to work with some division where true discipline exists, to the Guards Division, for example, or the 9th – where they would see how the qualities bred of discipline would make the retreat from Mons possible – in fact which converted a retreat into a grand military movement.

> The British retreat from Mons in August 1914 permitted vital British participation in the Battle of the Marne in the following month. This destroyed the German war plan of capturing Paris before turning to the Eastern front.

This afternoon had an interesting talk with Edward Wood, major in the Yorkshire Yeomanry, which I suppose now ranks as divisional cavalry. We talked a good deal about home politics and he told me about the chaotic condition of things in the House of Commons. Among other statements of fact were:

(1) That, after the initial success of Germany at Verdun, the Kaiser was prepared to effect a satisfactory peace with and for France, the war to continue against us. This is quite credible.

(2) That we have difficulty in enforcing the blockade against Scandinavia because Russia is frightened of an invasion via Finland. This must have elements of truth.

(3) That new leave passes have a statement printed on the back, that in the event of peace being declared, the holder of the pass is to report to his depot. Surely this is impossible.

> Wood was MP for Ripon and went on to have a prominent career in politics as Lord Halifax. He was nicknamed the Holy Fox by Churchill for his interest in hunting and in religion.

### Wednesday, 31 May 1916

I went for a walk to La Molte, a pretty village five kilometres away nestling in the heart of Merville forest. It is the headquarters of the Forest Control

Department, one of the odd by-products of our army system. A week or two ago there was a tree felling competition there between lumbermen of the various allies out here. The French woodcutters were beaten, but in the opinion of some, their work was more thorough than that of the Canadians and Anzacs. Vast quantities of timber are used in trench warfare, but it is difficult to believe that we need to import foresters to France. Our men are all soldiers of course and they seemed to be having a cushy time.

Coming home, I was overhauled by the car of Colonel Barclay, whose companion was Griffith-Boscawen, now a colonel. He commands a garrison battalion of elderly or infirm men, most of whom have been disabled at the front, though still capable of sentry and guard work. This battalion is scattered in thirty-one different places between Calais and Poperinghe! Boscawen's duty is to inspect this unit which is powdered over half our area! A job which apparently takes the best part of a fortnight.

Arthur Griffith-Boscawen, MP, had a particular interest in social housing and church matters. He held ministerial positions after the war.

### Thursday, 1 June 1916

The unit was paraded today for an inspection by the town major who brought a woman with him. She was detected selling army stores – and was brought to identify the culprit whom she supposed to be in our unit. No success – and she was quite frank in her statement that none of our men had sold her the stuff. The town major must now parade other units, beginning with No. 50. No great quantity of government material was found in her shop (the raid having taken place yesterday), but there is no doubt that in the aggregate French houses, above all the farmhouses, contain masses of our stores. Some of it, especially in the areas over which we retreated, was collected legitimately enough after being abandoned by our troops. Much also has been left behind in billets and farmhouses behind the line when some detachment has moved and found its transport insufficient to carry all the stores away. The stuff stays and the *indigène* collects it, conceals it and awaits an opportunity of peddling it out locally. In this recent case, the woman says she had bought everything before Xmas – apparently thinking that a few months' delay would reduce the danger of detection. She will be prosecuted by the French authorities for being in unlawful possession of British government property.

175

## Friday, 2 June 1916

Deans our SM is mentioned in General Barnardiston's despatch relative to the capture of Tsingtao. We only had a handful of men there, and I don't think the SM formed a very high estimate of the Japanese troops. He served throughout the campaign and, like so many who have lived in the Far East, distrusts our gallant ally.

In 1902 Britain had formed an alliance with Japan, both holders of intrusive concessions in China. So it was natural for Britain to help a fellow imperialist. Japan captured the German concession in Tsingtao which had become a town of notably German character. It was a major step in Japan's encroachment into China, which had catastrophic consequences over the next thirty years. Although China declared war against Germany and provided 140,000 labourers to the allies mainly for road and rail maintenance (of whom 10,000 are estimated to have died), her claim to recover her territory was subordinated to Japan's imperial aims at the Versailles Treaty. Amidst the ensuing protests in China, known as the Fourth of May Movement, the young Zhou Enlai emerged as a radical activist. He was later to be Mao Zedong's long serving premier and foreign minister.

## Saturday, 3 June 1916

When hard at work clearing up in the theatre, a staff man came in telling us of the disastrous news from the fleet. I nearly fainted. Another officer was talking about the serious attack on our front here, mentioning that the PPCLI had suffered very severely. In comes a subaltern called Hopcroft, was told the naval news, and the only comment he offered was, 'oh, how very annoying'. I could have knocked the man down. At night, there are rumours that we did better than the official despatch indicates. But our actual losses are almost stupefying.

The British and German fleets fought the Battle of Jutland. British losses were considerably larger than German ones, but the result was that German battleships never emerged from port again. Instead, the Germans developed their devastating submarine strategy.

## Monday, 5 June 1916

What we have lost is known to us and the world, what the Germans have suffered is still speculative – and the impression on our minds though grievous is hopeful – the rumour that we have bottled up some German ships in neutral waters gives another ray of hope. This naval action caused deep dismay at first – men threw down their newspapers and swore it was all a pack of lies – could not eat our breakfasts, then got up and had another angry look at the news. One or two optimists assured us that our ships must have sold their lives dearly and that more loss had been inflicted than we know.

We are still curiously deficient in news from our own front. The Canadians and Australians are bad observers on the battlefield – unaccustomed to our simple assessment of results and too anxious to explain away their own rebuffs. Ambulance trains very busy all day. So we are puzzled, though uncomfortably certain that the Germans, whether momentarily or for the forthcoming summer campaign, are as strong and well equipped as ever. The attacks on Verdun seem to grow in magnitude every day. Can the French continue to incur these appalling losses notwithstanding the greater casualties inflicted on the Germans? The fall of Verdun now would be graver catastrophe than if it had occurred in February, for I believe the blame would be placed upon our shoulders.

### Tuesday, 6 June 1916

Much better spirit among our men as further news of the naval action seems to confirm the severity of the German losses.

# VII

# 7 June to 9 July 1916

*Lord Kitchener's death and assessment – his succession –
Colonel's stretcher plagiarized – Colonel's well earned
promotion – French press urging British action – Russia's
success at Czernovitz peters out – allies bogged down in
Salonica – Crawford offered commission in Intelligence
Corps – Battle of Somme – Crawford accepts cabinet post,
encouraged by his senior officers.*

Lord Kitchener of Khartoum was drowned on 6 June when his ship hit a
mine on his way to Russia. It was seen as a huge loss, so great was his
prestige and status among all classes; but his cabinet colleagues had
been trying to ease him out of his office as War Secretary for some time.
In November 1915, they had sent him to report on the Dardanelles,
hoping that he could be given a major posting based in Egypt or further
afield. He had been seen as hampering the war effort by his addiction
to traditional methods, his aversion to new technologies, such as the
machine gun, and his reluctance to widen the range of armament
suppliers. Lord Northcliffe unkindly opined that his death was a great
stroke of luck for the British Empire.

Family members and others had been lobbying to get Crawford
transferred to work more appropriate to his talents; on 26 June, he was
offered a commission in the Intelligence Corps, with the object of
improving relations with the French press – he spoke excellent French
and was well equipped for the task. Just as he was about to take up his
new job, he was invited back to London to join the cabinet as Minister
of Agriculture; Kitchener's death had necessitated a cabinet reconstruction. In the last days before he left France, he witnessed the opening
salvos of the Battle of the Somme, which was to last a further four months
and inflict huge casualties on the British and allied forces.

WEATHER

**New York ⚓ Tribune**

*First to Last—the Truth: News·Editorials·Advertisements*

CIRCULATION
Over 100,000 Daily
Net Paid, Non-Returnable

Vol. LXXVI No. 25,406.

WEDNESDAY, JUNE 7, 1916.

• • •

ONE CENT

# Kitchener, Staff and 400 Others Die When Cruiser Is Sunk Off Scotland

"K. OF K." LOST AT SEA.

## WAR SECRETARY KILLED ON MISSION TO RUSSIA

England Staggered by Death of Hero of Khartoum in the Destruction of the Hampshire.

### VESSEL WAS MINE VICTIM, NAVAL OFFICERS BELIEVE

King Calls Council to Consider Question of Successor—Sir William Robertson, Chief of Imperial Staff, Most Likely Choice.

## Wednesday, 7 June 1916

Kitchener drowned in a cruiser struck by submarine or mine! The news caused us stupefaction. What does it all mean and involve? The AS thinks Kitchener irreplaceable. In a sense this is very true, but I can't help feeling that Sir William Robertson is a tower of strength. Kitchener's role during the early stages of the war was to inspire confidence in the public mind and to maintain a feeling of stability. That province he filled with distinction. In administrative matters his hands became overcrowded. Gradually his control was loosened while the influence of the war staff was enlarged. Therefore he insensibly became of less importance than at the outset especially when the special department was created to look after the munitions of war.

Kitchener went to the Near East, and on this fatal voyage was bound for Russia. In neither case, particularly in this last expedition, could his absence from England be justified. Cabinet ministers should stay at home during such times of crisis. Asquith's jollification in Paris and Rome was utterly wrong, and this journey of K to Russia could have been advantageously entrusted to the more skilful hands of some trained diplomat. I dare say he welcomed the opportunity of a fortnight's change of perspective.

179

He must have had a bad time in the Cabinet. He had neither the coolness nor the subtlety to grapple with the politician, and I doubt not that any element in the Cabinet which disapproved of Kitchener's view would have upset him in argument, bamboozled him and probably roused his temper into the bargain. I expect moreover that the course of argument must often have led him to abandon propositions and to contradict himself. None of this, which I instinctively feel to be true, is apprehended by the AS. Neither is it quite realised how small a part Kitchener has played in forming public opinion. How often the civilians in the Cabinet have had to defend, without a public word of help from Kitchener, some scheme which issued from the WO itself. Asquith and Co have a right to complain that Kitchener's unmeasured authority and prestige was so seldom offered in aid.

But about the future. I take it that there would be a serious outcry were a civilian to become Secretary of State. Yet for the life of me, I can think of no soldier who could undertake the task. French is out of the question. My chief fear is that Squiff may prevail upon Robertson to succeed Kitchener. No choice could be better in one sense; no selection could be more disastrous in another. The vital need is to uphold Robertson's good work at the WO and to keep him out of the intrigues of the House of Commons. Put him into that vortex and his services to the country will be reduced tenfold. And we shall now perforce undergo a fresh Cabinet reconstruction – how terrible that will be, just when one had reason to hope that the government was beginning to feel its legs after the long sequence of stumbling from crisis to crisis. This week we have lost two admirals, three generals and a field marshal – 500 other officers and I suppose 5,000 to 6,000 men.

Sir William Robertson was Chief of the Imperial General Staff. Squiff was a nickname for Asquith the Prime Minister, also known as Pol Roger, because of his fondness for good wines.

## Thursday, 8 June 1916

A rumour that after all Kitchener has been saved – but considering that the disaster occurred on Monday, surely such a hope can only be dispelled. Tonight, a telegram which almost admits the loss of Vaux Fort. And a rumour that a German division has mutinied, shot its officers and surrendered to the amount of 13,000 men. How can we believe these things, and yet the tale passes from mouth to mouth with ever growing precision? To illustrate our credulity, I note also that in a naval action in the Baltic the Germans have lost twenty-eight more ships. Ribot's death is also rumoured. Who invents fairy tales for us?

Which of two distinguished Frenchmen did he mean? Théodule Ribot, a French psychologist, who died later in 1916 or Alexandre Ribot, a French Prime Minister, who died in 1923?

## Friday, 9 June 1916

The circumstances of Kitchener's death have silenced all critics. And few men, not even Lord Roberts who died under analogous conditions, have received so handsome and ungrudging obituary notices. Robertson seems designated as Kitchener's successor, which I should still regard as unfortunate. Would not Lloyd George, with his great knowledge of one cardinal war factor and his abilities to master the other essentials, make the best of S of S? This would leave Harold Tennant out in the cold, so Asquith would instinctively dislike the idea. With Robertson as S of S, even were he not made a peer, Tennant could still retain his position and status in the House of Commons – for presumably Robertson would be freed from all the normal duties of an MP.

Harold Tennant's sister, Margot, was Asquith's second wife.

## Saturday, 10 June 1916

The colonel in a tantrum. His famous stretcher was sent to the ordnance works at Calais for reproduction. The work was badly done and had to be done over again. Now to his surprise and disgust he learns that an acting colonel has coolly cribbed the main design, made one or two trifling alterations (adding six pounds to the weight in the process) and is now issuing his for trial and inspection by the troops. Our colonel patented his own design eight or ten months ago – and is pretty wild at this larceny.

There is a very odd communiqué from our Press Bureau which states rather defiantly that Douglas Haig has settled his strategic policy, indicating that nothing will deflect him from pursuing the course allotted us by the allied war council. What can this mean, why this reassurance? The only deduction one can legitimately draw from these assurances, that Haig will choose his own time and place, is that some violent and possibly successful assault upon the salient is expected and that public consternation may then be discounted in advance. Let us hope that one is reading too much into the paragraphs.

## Monday, 12 June 1916

I came across an old routine order issued on 4 November by the Adjutant General relating to the restoration of old buildings. 'It is intended to reconstruct damaged or demolished historical buildings, such as the Cloth Hall Ypres, cathedrals and churches, and to use as far as possible the original ornamental stone and masonry ... so no such materials to be removed for any purpose whatever.' Fancy reconstructing the Cloth Hall at Ypres and using the original ornamental stone now crumbled to powder. The task of rebuilding Ypres will not only be a delicate problem from the aspect of town planning and of art, but it will be terribly dangerous as well. The number of live shells embedded in the streets and among the ruins must be huge; in the agricultural lands as well, there will be deadly aftermaths of the war.

During the last week we have had hundreds of Canadian officers and men sick and wounded from the salient where they got so terribly hammered. They are so boastful and aggressive that they forfeit our sympathy. They assure us that never have the Germans attacked with such persistency and vigour, that their own prodigies of bravery are unparalleled, etc. Our English and Scottish troops usually accept these tirades with good humour and tolerance – but occasionally some specially bombastic hero from Canada carries his scorn of what he calls 'Imperial troops' too far, then there is an explosion.

> The Battle of Mount Sorrel, in the Ypres salient, began with a huge German bombardment on 2 June, in which one Canadian battalion suffered ninety per cent casualties, but the Canadians were to score a good victory two days later and recover 1,500 yards of German positions at nearby Zillebeke.

## Tuesday, 13 June 1916

Sergeant Nunn and I attended the memorial service held in the town hall to ask repose for the soul of Lord Kitchener. The place was crowded and all the units in the town sent their contingents. Abbé Lemire attended. It was a short and simple service, not disfigured by a sermon. These ceremonies have been held today up and down the length of our line. I observe great laxity in fulfilling the order about mourning. Some officers have never 'put it up' at all. Others masquerade with a bit of crepe 9 inches deep – some with a narrow ribbon. Crepe is the commonest of textile commodities in France.

## Wednesday, 14 June 1916

The colonel is leaving us! He becomes ADMS of the 4th Division, which I think is in the Third Army. It is promotion and he has earned it, having worked incessantly for the care of the wounded and the credit of our corps. We are ordered today to send in to GHQ a list of our men who have worked in underground mines – coal, ironstone, etc. I think we have ten in the unit. Whether these men are to be withdrawn for tunnelling work out here or for colliery work at home we don't know. Some of our colliers are excellent fellows well suited to the heavy work of the RAMC.

The first Canadian Division has done well in this last Zillebeke affair, removing a slur which rested upon the Canadians as a whole. Many troops moving, but moving in all directions so it is difficult to see whether the salient is really being strengthened or not.

This was the build-up to the Battle of the Somme.

### Thursday, 15 June 1916

The DMS issues a circular stopping all leave from tomorrow, but there is a special exception for men who have been out here for twelve months. So all our boys who haven't been home yet will be able to get away. That is good. Meanwhile, RAMC officers are being detailed to move up to the CCSs at Remy, which looks as though many casualties are expected in the immediate future. I am afraid that the gradual though slow encroachment upon Verdun is producing fresh nervousness in France. After a certain point it may be dangerous or superfluous to defend the actual city, and at the same time catastrophic from the political aspect to abandon it. The Germans are now within four miles of the citadel, and were it not for these political and sentimental reasons, strategy might well demand an evacuation.

Some of our men rejoice in the colonel's promotion, and are already making their dispositions to use the interregnum between his departure and replacement, to redistribute working parties in the hospital and men are being provisionally grabbed for this office or that. The wards, the QM stores, the passages – all in authority want more help and each NCO is trying to strengthen his own staff. Meanwhile, the atmosphere of our big station does not improve – too much beer and too heavy gambling.

### Friday, 16 June 1916

Gustave Hervé in *La Victoire* has an article called '*En attendant les Anglais*'. It is ostensibly a reply to letters he receives from soldiers and others asking what our army is doing. He answers the question very well, and the press has noted Bonar Law's and Asquith's assurances that we only await the summons of

General Joffre. There is another article, I think in the *Journal*, urging action – all these things are symptomatic of the fear that the next week may witness a fresh and final attack on Verdun during which the French resistance will be paralysed by new artillery which the Germans have been preparing ever since we advertised our munitions policy eight or ten months ago. Gustave Hervé answers the case well – but his title and the statement of the case he sets out to demolish show the widespread apprehension. I fancy le Père Joffre is not going to delay overlong his instructions to the British and allies. That too is the general opinion in France, but Verdun is a place which might almost be taken by a *coup de main*, and one has a vague fear that before our offensive could mature in the north, a disaster might occur south of our line.

## Monday, 19 June 1916

The railway station is *pavoisé* for the fall of Czernovitz. One hopes that a big haul of prisoners has been effected and that it will bring some influence to bear upon the sneaks of Romania and Greece. The old Belgian refugee who lives with my washerwoman asked a station official the cause of the flag flying. '*Silence madame*', he said, '*les oreilles ennemies vous écoutent*', and, not having heard the news, she came away completely mystified. If only this Russian offensive can proceed for another month at this crushing standard! Here it seems generally assumed that a move will be attempted pretty soon, the idea being that the salient will be held securely and the pressure take place between Arras and Béthune. Were a move brought about down there, I suppose Lille would fall, and a tremendous wave of pride would sweep through France. Meanwhile, it is assumed that Père Joffre is confident about Verdun, for the next three days must witness a terrific attack.

The capture of Czernovitz, capital of the Austrian province of Bukovina, with a huge haul of war materiel and prisoners, was the high point of the Brusilov Offensive, itself Russia's most successful enterprise of the war; but the Russian effort petered out, with enormous losses. After the war, Czernovitz became part of Romania and is now in Ukraine. It was important to enlist Romania and Greece as allies, still uncommitted, particularly as Bulgaria had joined the Central Powers in September 1915. Romania did join the allies in August and was to be comprehensively defeated by the year's end. Greece was divided against itself (see 22 June below).

## Wednesday, 21 June 1916

I had a talk with Arthur Boscawen who told me about Asquith's portentously dull speech at the secret session of the House of Commons of two hours and twenty minutes, containing nothing which well-informed people didn't know by heart, except his important statement that after August the French will be hard put to it to find reserves. Apart from this, there appeared nothing which was essentially secret. I dare say Squiff didn't quite trust his audience; can one be surprised?

France too is now having its secret session which seems likely to last as long as the assault on Verdun. All the French deputies must be airing their grievances, but the public takes no interest in their lucubrations. I fancy however that the position must be rather more dangerous than appears on the surface. Had Briand's explanations been satisfactory, the debates would have concluded by now. The unknown factor is the amount of hostility aroused in the minds of Clemenceau, Caillaux and other born intriguers. It would be a disaster were the Prime Minister to be displaced in such a fashion as to give power to such a man as Caillaux. His antecedents are both nebulous and sinister.

Aristide Briand was serving his fifth term as French Prime Minister. Joseph Caillaux, as Prime Minister in 1911, had made concessions to Germany to avert war over Agadir, provoking bitter charges of unpatriotic conduct. Spice was added to his reputation, when his wife killed the editor of *Le Figaro* who threatened to publish compromising letters about him. During the war, Caillaux led a peace party wanting to make peace with Germany and, as a result, was put on trial for treason in 1918, but later rehabilitated.

Boscawen says we aren't ready for our push – that in three weeks' time we shall have greatly increased our numbers and striking power. This may be true – must in fact be true, but we shall always be stronger three weeks hence. The question is whether we or France can afford to wait much longer – taking into account the detrition of French troops before Verdun, the beginning of an effective reaction in the Trentino and above all the Russian push in Volhynia. Are we to be the too late brigade again? Moreover the coming weeks are those during which military pressure of the allies will most quickly arouse economic pressure within Germany. We can't afford to wait much longer.

The Battle of the Somme was in fact to start in less than two weeks' time.

## Thursday, 22 June 1916

Army Council instruction 280 of 1916 issued in February says, 'Throughout the country A and D books are being very carelessly kept ... thirty per cent of diagnosis in A and D books are so indefinite as to be valueless for statistical purposes'. I think, in fact it is pretty clear that this notice only applies to hospitals at home – great care is taken here to ensure complete and correct records for the A and D book. But I dare say that we out here are often indefinite in diagnosis. There is much PUO and NYD, though Captain Taylor never inserts such a description except when transmitted by a field ambulance. 'Debility' is also frequently employed. Our conditions make a scientific diagnosis impossible. I never quite know where the colonel (who hasn't moved yet) gets the information on which he talks so freely – nor do I think he is very sound in assessing evidence at his disposal. But tonight I was rather struck by his forecast that unless the war ends in the next few months the whole French frontier will have to be taken over by British troops. This is a reflection of what Boscawen told me about the difficulty of finding French drafts after next August.

PUO stood for 'pyrexia of unknown origin' or trench fever and NYD for 'not yet diagnosed' or shell shock. These were two of the war's new ailments, which were not yet properly understood.

Salonica remains a huge reservoir from which diplomacy might extract hundreds of thousands of allies, but Tino appears to grow more recalcitrant towards us and more treacherous to his country every day. The Athens situation becomes very disagreeable – and, as our blockade increases in stringency, public annoyance will injure Venizelos upon whom all our hopes are fixed. Altogether, we have muddled the Greek business badly – too washy and benevolent when firmness was required; in this one traces British influence, British sloppiness. France or Russia alone would never have allowed the crisis to be so long protracted.

The British troops in Salonica had arrived too late to help the Serbs and could not depart lest Romania and Greece defect to the Central Powers. King Constantine 1 (Tino) of Greece, brother-in-law of the Kaiser, wished to stay neutral. The Prime Minister, Eleftherios Venizelos, wanted Greece to join the allies. In August 1916, a coup effectively divided Greece into two entities. Reunification came next year, with Tino's son taking his father's place on the throne and Venizelos assuming leadership of Greece, which joined the allies.

## Saturday, 24 June 1916

Considerable movement of troops and the air is full of expectations and speculations about a great attack. Rumour has it that the two big churches in the town will be cleared for hospital purposes. I hope not. Hundreds of marquees are available and the germ-laden churches should only be used in the last extremity. X-raying all morning.

## Monday, 26 June 1916

Received notice to proceed to GHQ to interview the Intelligence Corps. I don't like the name of this department which leads the scoffer to scoff. The colonel strongly urges me to take any post which the authorities may offer. He says that, apart from gaining experience in the sphere of surgical operations, I can learn no more than I already know of the RAMC and he adds his assurance that I can be of material service elsewhere. I am sorry to go. After fourteen or fifteen months with the unit such a *déracinage* cannot fail to make itself felt. Everybody in our station whom I met today spoke despondently of themselves and of the station which I have largely helped to keep together during the last six months of weariness and squalor. The next few weeks may, if all goes well, restore mobility, and with it give fresh life and interest to all.

## Tuesday, 27 June 1916

I bade farewell to General Porter who has shown me great kindness during my stay at Hazebrouck. He was as emphatic as our colonel in recommending me to exchange. Major Martin drove me as far as Hesdin, via Aisne. I had lunch with a jolly old sport with a bosom gleaming with ribbons – the first time I have sat down to a tablecloth for ever so long. Two or three other officers present, I haven't an idea who they were, one of them exceptionally stupid. Hesdin is the overflow of Montreuil GHQ. It is a pleasant hamlet, but lying in the bottom of a saucer is pronounced unbearably hot and stuffy during warm weather.

From Hesdin, I came on to Montreuil in one of the first ambulance cars sent out to France. Notwithstanding protests made by the RAMC before the war, the authorities had always refused motor transport for the wounded, probably on the ground of expense. The scheme of evacuating wounded was that they should be sent to the rear by the 3-ton motor lorries, which would otherwise return empty. The idea was of course farcical and soon broke down. The stores and ammunition taken up to the line by the lorries were dumped at points where it was difficult and often impossible to collect the wounded; and naturally nothing could be more unpunctual than this method of evacuation. Moreover, the build and vibration of these huge wagons made them utterly unsuited and often most dangerous for the transport of wounded men. The WO had to recognise this and a number of chassis, fifty I think, were commandeered and ambulance bodies built on to them. Thus the first motor ambulance corps came into existence, and the system has been splendidly developed. It was a pleasure to me to ride in one of the pioneer cars today and especially to be driven by one of the ASC men attached since the outset to this convoy.

Reported at IC headquarters where the clerks give a great lesson and example in civility to any other army clerks I have ever met. At 2.45, I was told to report in the square to Driver Clarkson, there to await Colonel Hutton Wilson and to accompany him to see General Charteris. I assumed this meant a drive to the other end of the town, but to my surprise found that to Beauquesne and back meant a journey of 150 kilometres or more. Anyhow it was a lovely day and I had a charming journey through Frévent and Doullens to the back of the line.

Colonel Wilson en route, and between intervals of slumber on the shoulder of Driver Clarkson, told me that General Charteris wants me to act as a kind of political liaison officer between the FO, GHQ and the Maison de la Presse in Paris. Tom Legh and John Buchan are already engaged in this work and want a commissioned officer to act as their local correspondent and intermediary in France. The programme sounds rather vague and, on interviewing General Charteris at Beauquesne, I was not much the wiser though he is very keen on this branch of his propaganda organisation. I suppose he sees some shortcoming in his present machinery and is evidently confident that I can help to put the matter right. I sat by John Buchan throughout this long journey and we slept together in the Hotel de France. He is a good fellow besides being a strong Tory and successful writer. As colleagues, we shall get on together. I dined at the journalists' chateau a few miles out of Montreuil, rather an amusing milieu. Late to bed.

Tom Legh, a former Conservative MP, had been Paymaster General. John Buchan's thriller, *Greenmantle*, was published in 1916, A prolific writer, he also had a distinguished career in public service; as Lord Tweedsmuir, he became Governor General of Canada. General John Charteris was the C-in-C's favoured intelligence advisor. In a lecture in 1916, he said that the desire to please was the most important pitfall that every Intelligence Officer must avoid, but he was himself accused of

### Wednesday 28 June 1916

Slept well in a very comfortable bed. I must admit that a floor with two or three blankets to mark it and to keep the body warm may have Spartan merits, but has its drawbacks as well. At nine o'clock, Buchan and I went to the Military Intelligence room. It appears he is going to get a commission and must therefore be vetted. He thinks he passed the test all right – and departed for Amiens. We are to meet at the Foreign Office a few days hence. I also had to be examined, quite a familiar process to me. The MO was greatly pleased with my eyesight – this gratified me for I have recently thought that the strain of reading and writing in very bad light had weakened my vision. 'Have you been in hospital?', said the surgeon. 'Yes, sir', I replied. 'How long?' 'All the time, thirteen months', was my answer, thinking he wanted to know whether I was CCS or field ambulance. 'As a patient, I mean'. 'Oh never, sir' … and there are very few in my unit, not more than two or three, of whom such a thing can be said. Captain Fenn of the Intelligence Corps, whose time seems largely occupied in arranging the rota of motor cars of all sorts of people, gave me my pass to London, from tomorrow until July 5. I am to order a uniform, but shall still be an RAMC corporal on my return as the commission won't be granted by then. This is tiresome as it involves a lot of trouble in bringing back, and then sending home, my duplicated outfit. It grieves me to have so little time as I shall have much to do, and my visit to Connie and the children must be all too short.

### Wednesday, 5 July 1916

GHQ France, Montreuil. I got here at five o'clock this evening. Connie saw me off at Charing Cross, and I travelled in great ease and comfort with Sonny Somerset a King's Messenger. He was overloaded with parcels and packages for various people, including a huge portrait of the P of W. At least that is what we supposed it to be, a compliment no doubt to some amiable French Mayor.

I carry away vague impressions of London and the political situation. It is so long since I was there that all my many acquaintances insisted on talking to me – and soon as I had begun a conversation with one of them two or three others would break in. Accordingly, I scarcely gathered any fixed impressions. It is however clear that the Irish imbroglio has introduced a dangerous element of intrigue and discontent. And it is still needful that the government should be kept up to the mark by constant and vigorous control from outside. The politicians are thinking too much of themselves and their futures. In the Carlton Club the great offensive now in progress for which we have toiled and moiled ever since last September is less a topic of discussion than the domestic problem of Ireland. Anything which distracts attention from the central issue is to be deprecated.

London itself seemed very busy and quite satisfied with itself – apparently placid beneath a military bureaucracy which has grown up with the war – for every other man one meets from Piccadilly down to Westminster seems by his deportment and uniform to be governing somebody or other. The material prosperity of the place seems phenomenal. Vast posters lecture one upon the etiquette and propriety of one's costume, motor cars, etc., and every pillar box has a small bill inviting the sum of fifteen shillings which is to be returned later on (with interest) and which in the meantime is to supply the army with 125 cartridges.

### Thursday, 6 July 1916

A beautiful drive from Montreuil to Amiens through magnificently cultivated land. General Charteris wants me to go to Paris forthwith, whereas Colonel Hutton Wilson would like to keep me here to help him and to get an insight into the press censorship. Later, I went to the cathedral. The porch and many internal monuments sandbagged, and they are now, notwithstanding our advance, engaged in sandbagging the choir. It occurs to me that the Hotel de France at Montreuil must be the inn at which the sentimental traveller engaged his French servant; was he called La Flache? I forget. Anyhow, this association endears Montreuil to my heart.

The reference is to *A Sentimental Journey* by Lawrence Sterne; the servant was La Fleur.

### Friday, 7 July 1916

Our troops tried to take Mametz Wood today and failed. Likewise, after a momentary success at the important hamlet of Contalmaison they were unable to hold the position.

These were the early stages of the Battle of the Somme which was to last four more months.

190

Captain Fauncroft, ex India Civil Service, took me out to see the action with the official cinematographer and the government snap-shooter, both of whom have been doing admirable work for our propaganda. The latter tells me that the government charges ten shillings, six pence per plate for the English press and that thousands of pounds have been thus paid into the exchequer. He is a personal friend of the late Lord Kitchener's valet, taught the Royal family how to Kodak, and used to spend a few weeks every summer photographing eminent shooting parties in Austria and Germany. These were my companions during an eventful day. We started from Amiens pretty early and drove through the town of Albert – smashed to bits – this is where the great church was most cruelly shelled – and the huge Madonna who crowned the lofty steeple hangs downwards at a threatening angle. The superstition runs that as soon as she falls peace will be declared.

We made our way as far as Bécourt, whence we passed along a mile or so of communication trench till we got to the neighbourhood of Mametz Wood. We were there soon after 8.30 our attack having begun half an hour, earlier, and Boche prisoners and our wounded men began to pass us on their way back almost immediately. Shelling on our side was heavy, on theirs practically negligible except now and then for machine gunning which once drove us into a dugout. We moved about the trenches for a couple of hours until we noticed signs of greater German activity. Their shrapnel was bursting about a quarter of a mile east of us and, as the explosions come towards us at an increasing interval of 50 or 80yds (say 100yds), the enemy made us move, and we were followed by shrapnel for a quarter of a mile during our retreat. By now it was midday and we had some food. I spent most of the afternoon watching our 18-pounders and 4.5-inch howitzers keeping up a somewhat intermittent fire – at times really heavy and then slackening off.

We got back to Amiens by 5.30 and after a good bath I retired into pyjamas while my clothes were dried. I have nothing but what I stand up in as my kit hasn't got here from Montreuil yet. There were drenching rainstorms at intervals during the day and one waded through flooded trenches. Poor fellows; how my heart goes out to those heroes whose good humour and pluck are invincible.

We got into the first line or two of trenches in the wood and were almost entirely driven out. The Prussian guard counterattacked with great vigour at Contalmaison and we lost during the afternoon all our gains of the morning. The prisoners were a very mixed lot as regards age, but all well fed, well shod and adequately clothed. Our men treated them with great consideration.

Made them useful by gently persuading them to do some stretcher work. Too many of our men are sent back as escorts to these prisoners – one man, going back towards our lines, where he is in constant touch with our fellows, can perfectly well supervise five or six unarmed Germans – whereas sometimes there were as many guards as prisoners. I laughed at one fellow (East Lancs) in rear of a party of about a dozen. Distrusting his rifle and bayonet, he carried a Mills bomb in his right hand to prevent any attempts at escape.

What a scene of desolation is this area of battle. One stumbles across a corpse distended by gangrene, half hidden by luxuriant flowers, and then a few yards further on a patch of land from which every vestige of vegetation has been completely burned. What is marked on the map as a wood is in reality a seared row of skeleton trees. This is the most violent and wasteful of all the invasions of nature which a bombardment involves.

## Saturday, 8 July 1916

Last night Colonel Hutton Wilson told me I was to see General Charteris at nine this morning. I drove there (to Beauquesne) expecting to have my instructions to tackle the French editors. The instructions with letters from the FO were all there on the table, nicely typed, but to my surprise another message was there as well. A cypher telegram he had received from General McDonough – the head of Intelligence at the WO. Here is the full text.

'Please communicate the following message from Bonar Law secretly to Lord Crawford' Message begins: 'The party is very much divided and I am certain that in view of the Irish difficulties you should render a greater service to the nation by joining the government than is possible to you in your present position. AAA. If you agree shall propose you as Minister of Agriculture and I earnestly hope you will accept'. AAA message ends 'wire me answer.'

The prose comes from Bonar Law's heart. But imagine my bewilderment at the message. The moment I had come out to France, AJB made a similar gesture. Now that I have transferred from the RAMC and am about to enter upon a sphere of work which promises to be exceptionally valuable and long overdue, comes a fresh invitation to join the government – not at the unblemished outset of its career, but late in the day, after grave discredit and serious failures. Moreover, I am asked to join a bankrupt concern during a crisis which threatens the very existence of our own party, having been bamboozled into a hopeless commitment on the Irish question.

How can one be of real service in such conditions? The idea of returning to the familiar fields of party life does not smile on me at this juncture. Had I been in the government at the birth of the coalition, this Irish trouble at least would not have taken my friends unaware – but now, to join at this stage when all the signs of vigour and vitality seem at their lowest ebb, the task is repelling.

General Charteris strongly advised me to accept. I think he regrets the possibility of our severance as he thinks I could help him considerably, and we get on well together. Accordingly, a telegram was sent in the afternoon to say I am returning to London. It occurred to me after the wire had gone that Bonar Law might consider this as assent. Let us hope he won't, for one or two things must be made clear before I could join the government; I should at least have to know that further resignations need not be expected, and that a proper scheme is prepared to safeguard England from new Irish dangers during the next six months. On other matters too, e.g. my position in Wigan Coal & Iron Company, I must be cautious. Charteris said that it would be useful for the government to have a man who knows something of the French aspect of our army. I dare say he is right. There is nobody in the government with any concrete knowledge or experience, bar F.E. Smith and one or two other weekenders at the front. This view impressed itself on my mind as worthy of exploration. I shall go to London tomorrow and think further on these matters en route. It is tiresome being made to ponder when one has so long only had to act! And this evening I found little help, consolation or encouragement in St Thomas à Kempis.

Crawford was Chairman of the Wigan Coal & Iron Company and there had been 'a good deal of acrid comment' about ministers with director-ships. He resigned his directorship and served as Minister of Agriculture without pay.

### Sunday, 9 July 1916

Left Amiens by car at midday and drove to Boulogne via Montreuil, where I lunched at the Intelligence Corps mess. There are too many officers knocking about at GHQ. I was to add one more to the roll. Perhaps indeed I may still do so. Eighty miles drive, lovely day, good crossing.

I am afraid it is pretty clear that the Contalmaison business was bungled. The village lay north of the point where I spent several hours on Friday. We saw it well shelled. We occupied it, and in the process inflicted heavy loss on the so-called Prussian guard. Then our troops retreated as a fresh counter attack was threatened. Why they abandoned their ground is not clear. They seem to have vacated it in a steady and well-disciplined manner and suffered no serious loss in the process. Who they were, I don't know. I wonder if they were territorials.

> Contalmaison was recaptured, with loss of 4,000, by the Welsh Division three days later.

Interesting talk with Repington, and interesting to him too. For as we discussed the morale, aspirations and shortcomings of the rank and file, I noticed he was watching me as though I were a strange animal – something quite new to him. My perspective, that of the AS, differs *in toto* from his own, which is based on observation of brigades and divisions, and coloured by talks with men of his own rank and generalissimos too. So he was interested in the novelty of hearing about the underworld from the underworld's point of view. No colonel in ordinary circumstances could ever get a NCO to talk with unreserved freedom.

> Colonel Repington, in his memoirs, recalling this occasion, thought Crawford 'very intelligent and interesting'.

I gave myself the pleasure of inspecting the South Midland Division CCS. They have been at Amiens since we took over their buildings at Hazebrouck last year. Their colonel, who told me that we were contemporaries at Magdalen, showed me the whole of his big and admirably managed place. It is luxurious compared with our tumbledown place at Hazebrouck. In a huge cellar used as the hospital store room, I noticed a lot of blue suits, pyjamas and expensive stores which are seldom to be found in casualty clearing stations. He told me that this equipment had a curious history. In the early days, No. 7 general hospital was at Amiens. It appears that the French authorities were jealous of our having an important base in the town, fearing perhaps that we should use our hospital as the thin end of the wedge for securing other administrative centres, in an area essentially French. Anyhow, No. 7 was cleared out. Churchill (then First Lord of the Admiralty) came to Amiens at the time and wrote an order presenting all the equipment of No. 7 to the French authorities. The actual document, which the colonel has seen, had a signature on it of some British officer whose name could not be found in our army list. No. 7 evacuated, leaving its tackle behind. The South Midland arrived just as General Foch took over the control of that zone, and he did his best to overthrow the permission given to the CCS by his predecessor. The South Midland people however managed to stay and have been there ever since and subsequently recovered much of the hospital stores which had been so coolly presented to our allies by that wicked busybody. Colonel Hutton Wilson says that WO Intelligence warned the government as to the exact date on which the outbreak of civil war was due to occur in Ireland.

# Postscript

Two days after leaving France, Crawford was appointed Minister of Agriculture (President of the Board of Agriculture and Fisheries). Food was low on the cabinet agenda and, towards the end of 1916, he found the situation 'terrifying', due to shipping losses, financial constraints, a thirty per cent reduction in the American wheat crop and an Argentine drought, accentuated by the locust travelling 'farther south than for many years past'. Most of Britain's food was imported, yet military and industrial recruitment had reduced the number of farm workers by a third and thousands of acres went to fallow and grass. Fishing risked 'total collapse'.

Starvation loomed. One day in cabinet Prime Minister Asquith was getting bogged down by a complex debate about aeroplanes in which two powerful Conservative ministers, Curzon and Balfour, presented opposing arguments. He did not heed Crawford's 'despairing cry for a few minutes consideration before lunch of his anxieties about the food of the nation', as Lloyd George recalled in his memoirs, 'the PM had a habit of turning round to the mantelpiece to see whether any temporary relief from his perplexities was indicated by the position of the hands on the clock.' It was lunch time and the food of the nation would be dealt with at a separate meeting. That meeting never took place under Asquith's chairmanship. Soon, he was replaced as Prime Minister by Lloyd George. Crawford held several ministerial positions throughout Lloyd George's premiership, retiring from politics in October 1922. He declined Stanley Baldwin's attempt to recall him to ministerial office in 1924.

Crawford chaired the Royal Commission on Wheat Supplies from its start in October 1916 till its end nine years later; it was 'a gigantic and delicate task'. Its function was to buy, sell and deliver Britain's wheat needs, which were seriously dislocated by war and governmental neglect. Soon, its remit extended to all cereals and its clients included allies, neutral states and, after the war, former enemies. By the end of the war, the commission controlled almost all the world's exportable grain and began an orderly process of decontrol. America, through its Food Administrator (later President) Herbert Hoover, then came to dominate the wheat trade and provided vast amounts of food to stave off famine in Europe and the Middle East. The Wheat Commission was finally wound up in 1925; for Crawford it had been a 'long and serious responsibility' and, characteristically, he rejoiced that the work was so done 'that it always eluded public attention'.

After returning from war service and between his public duties, he was able to see much more of his family, which he sorely missed while serving with the RAMC in France. He also resumed or assumed his leading role in various artistic and cultural institutions, which at one time of another encompassed the National Portrait Gallery, National Gallery, British Museum, British School at Rome, Council for the Preservation of Rural England, Royal Fine Art Commission, National Fine Arts Collection Fund, the Victoria & Albert Museum, and several smaller institutions. He was indeed the 'Uncrowned King of British Art', as described by John Vincent in the *Crawford Papers*. He was a Fellow of the Royal Society and Chancellor of Manchester University. He chaired the Broadcasting Inquiry, which led to the creation of the BBC, whose chairmanship he declined.

The family business, Wigan Coal & Iron Company, suffered financially in the late twenties and was split in two in 1930 under the Bank of England's rationalisation policy. Its coal interests were absorbed into the Wigan Coal Corporation and its iron and steel interests into Lancashire Steel Corporation. Crawford took a dim view of the Bank's actions: 'they are too much detached from the realities of production; they are usurers and nothing else'. Industrial activities in Wigan were much reduced and Crawford's special relationship with the business could never be the same, to his sorrow. After the war, Wigan Coal and Lancashire Steel, together with other leading British iron, coal and steel companies, were nationalised.

Crawford died in March 1940, aged 68, having become reconciled to Winston Churchill, of whom his reservations are apparent in the war diary, where he is described as a 'traitor', 'cad' and 'wicked busybody'. A quarter of a century later, he was fully convinced that Churchill was the right man to lead Britain in the Second World War. He was succeeded by his elder son, David, the 28th Earl, who had a notably distinguished career as a leader in the same fields of art, education and culture as those where his father had been so prominent.

# Aftermath of the Great War

35 million casualties – 50 million killed by flu, aggravated by the war.

Three monarchies converted into four republics, with reduced territories.

Eight new states in Europe, some aspiring for democracy, but becoming unstable.

Unsettling minorities in new states such as Czechoslvakia, Romania and Yugoslavia.

First overtly durable Communist state, the Soviet Union.

Ottoman Empire reduced to Turkey in Asia and small piece of Europe.

Five new nations, under quasi-colonial mandate, formed in the Middle East.

Seeds laid in Arabia for seven more states, previously under Ottoman or British sway.

The 'big five' lost much of their gold reserves and became large debtors.

The neutrals were enriched, such as Netherlands, Argentina, Spain.

The limited participators, such as Japan, and late entrants, such as USA, were enriched.

USA became the leading global power, but embraced isolationism and spurned the League of Nations, despite the efforts of President Wilson.

Financial dislocation of the war, coupled with harsh terms of the peace treaty, caused devastating inflation. In Germany, they spawned the rise of Nazism and led to the Second World War.

## Trends accentuated by the war

- Improvements in health care.
- Technology advances, land and air vehicles, phones, radio etc.
- Declining influence of the aristocracy.
- Aspirations towards decolonization and loosening of imperial ties.
- More power and rights to women.
- Rise of the working classes, industrially and politically.
- Global travel.

# Illustration Credits and Source Notes

## Plates section, between Pages 94 and 95, by image number

Family and personal sources – 1, 2, 8, 12, 13, 14, 24, 51, 54

National Library of Scotland, Edinburgh – 5, 11, 29, 33, 43, 56

Opera di Religione della Diocesi di Ravenna-Cervia, Ravenna – 45, 46

Wellcome Library, London – 6, 18, 19, 25, 26, 39, 40, 41, 42, 48, 50, 53

Army Medical Services Museum – 17

Victoria & Albert Museum, London – 15

Royal Observatory, Edinburgh – 7

Courtesy Council of the National Army Museum, London – 52

Ugolino di Nerio, Saints Bartholomew and Andrew © The National Gallery, London. Presented by the Earl of Crawford and Balcarres through The Art Fund, 1919 – 9

© Imperial War Museum, London – 55

Georges Degroote, Hazebrouck – 16, 28

Taylor Archive, Barnsley – 10, 20, 22, 23, 30, 32, 49, 57

John Duncan, Edinburgh – 47

Jean-Michel Saus, Hazebrouck – 27, 31

Wilson Library, University of North Carolina – 36

Fragments from France, by Bruce Bairnsfather, courtesy of Valmai and Tonie Holt – 21

Other images – internet

## Illustrations and maps in text, by page

Pages xiv & 198 – National Library of Scotland

Page xxxii – US Military Academy, West Point, Department of History

Page xxxiv – Wellcome Library, London

Page 26 – Jean-Michel Saus, Hazebrouck

Page 32 – Mairie, Hazebrouck

Page 39 – *Punch* magazine

Page 45 – National Archives, London, WO32/5460

Page 85 – *Fragments from France*, by Bruce Bairnsfather, courtesy of Valmai and Tonie Holt

Page 134 – *Bystander* magazine

Page 148 – *Humorosities* by Cecil Hartt

Page 151 – Family & personal sources

Other images – internet

## Source notes, by page

Numerous books, as well as the internet, have been used as sources for references to the Great War. Only references to sources of limited availability or specialised character are listed below.

Page xii & 197 'Uncrowned King' *The Crawford Papers* John Vincent, University of Manchester Press

Page xvi 'Montgomery' *Voices fron the Great War* Peter Vansittart

Page xvii 'Manchester' *Workman's Cottage to Windsor Castle* John Hodge

Page xxii 'CCS complement' *Official History of Medical Services in the Great War* WG Macpherson

Page xxii 'Kelsey Fry' *Royal Army Medical Corps* Redmond McLaughlin

Page xxv & xxx 'Cawkwell' *Corky's War* Ronald Fairfax

Page xxx 'American novelist' *The Forbidden Zone* Mary Borden

Page 1 'a great deal of unpleasantness' National Archives, London, WO95/498

Page 13, 'Charles Hoyt', http://www.wyomingtalesandtrails.com/powell7.html

Page 9 'Balfour surprised' *The Crawford Papers* John Vincent, University of Manchester Press

Page 39 'Graham Greene' *Voices fron the Great War* Peter Vansittart

Page 111 'Angela Forbes' *Memories and Base Details* Lady Angela Forbes

Page 133 'Canadian unit' *A surgeon in Arms* R.J. Manion

Page 197 'locust travelling further south' *Food Prospects in 1917* Report by Crawford, as Minister of Agriculture, to the Committee of Imperial Defence, National Archives, London, CAB/24/2

# Index

[Note 'C' refers to the diarist]

AS, Average Soldier: efforts to learn French, 5; respects sailors, 52; good judge of officers, 57; on political and military leaders, 81; rapid humour, 113; travel in cattle trucks, 137; C's unbounded admiration for, 152; *see also* Cattle truck

Aldershot: waste of food at, 20; stress on unessentials, 58, 115–6

Alexander, Nurse ('Bully Beef'): learns curtseying for King's visit, 74; remorse at scandal, 77; not a born mathematician, 88; careless medicine dispenser, 121; gives orderlies bacon fat, 127

Alexander, Major Harold (later Field Marshal): C's cousin, 136

ANZAC: 146, prone to VD and other infections, 168; *see also* Australians and New Zealanders

Asquith, Herbert H., Liberal Prime Minister: 34, 118; C against his coalition, 6, 151; 'wait and see' attitude, 133–4; must remain PM, 165; and Irish crisis, 168; jollification in Paris and Rome, 179; C joins coalition, 192–3

Australians: 146; rioting in Cairo, 27; unessentials, 147; drink too much, 152; stragglers chucked on wagons, 154; New Zealand critics, 162; talk only of Gallipoli, 164

Austria-Hungary: xv, 199

Aviation: an expensive fad, xvii

BBC: C's role in creation of, 197

Balfour, Arthur J., ('AJB'): former Conservative Prime Minister, 2, 8, 196; and C's refusal of ministerial office, 9; criticized by Churchill for inertia, 140–1

Baden-Powell, Lt General Robert, founder of Scouts: 38

Baldwin, Stanley (future Prime Minister): 196

Bath: after seven days dirt, 15; RFC monopolises C's bath place, 101

Belgium and Belgians: xvii, 171; refugees, 1, 22, 184; talkative dogs, 50; women mend underclothes, 85; RAMC inoculation methods impress, 87; sympathy for Belgium, dislike of Belgians, 106

Bonar Law, Andrew, Conservative leader in coalition: 183; asked C to join government, 192–3

Bowlby, Sir Anthony, Consultant Surgeon to BEF: 29–30

Braga, Vicomte De Souza, interpreter: 18; popular, but inaccurate, 53

Brandon, Mary, US novelist and nurse: feelings about war service, xxx

Bread: 20; C and standard loaf, 136–7

Briand, Aristide, French politician: 185

Buchholz, Lt., German prisoner: 74, 75

Buchan, John, author and politician: 188–9

Bulgaria: initially neutral, xv, 2; joined Central Powers, 184

CCS, Casualty Clearing Station: *passim*: 'power house of army medical services', xxi

Cadorna, Luigi, Italian commander: 163; army wondrously slow, 119; *see also* Italy

Caetanis, C's Italian cousins: 98

Caledon, Lord, C's cousin: 136

Cameron of Lochiel, Col Donald, wounded at Battle of Loos: 77

Canadians: 61, 146–7; loss of trenches deplored, 156; slur removed, 183

Cattle truck: 10; C and 30 comrades in, 12; AS asks why he travels in, 137; *see also* AS

Cavell, Edith, British nurse executed: Arques street named after, 161

Cawkwell, Private Percy: on service with RAMC, xxx

Censorship, xxv; C berated for using nickname, 4; of press, 190

Chamberlain, Austen, S of S for India: proposed C as Viceroy of India, 144

Chany, Pte: arrested by C, 40; court martial, 41–44

Charteris, General John: 188; proposes liaison task for C, 190; advises C to join government, 193

China: 176; *see also* Japan

Christmas: 83, 97–101; absurd fraternising, 99

Churchill, Winston, Liberal (former Conservative) politician: demoted because of Dardanelles 2; C's criticism, 80–1, 140–1; seeks command in France 64; wicked busybody, 195; C's belief in his Second World War leadership, 197

Clemenceau, Georges, French journalist and politician: 139–40; born intriguer, 185

Clothing: 82; new, 140; nuisance of 193 strap holes, 169

Coin and notes, 48, 158

Corporal, C as, 170, 188

Craig, new nurse: great hopes of her, 92

Crawford & Balcarres, Countess of ('Connie'), C's wife: sends Fortnum & Mason hampers, 4; wants C at home, 9; gives birth to a daughter, 102; and Zeppelin raid, 155

Crawford & Balcarres: 23rd, 24th, 25th Earls of, xix

Crawford & Balcarres, 26th Earl of C's father: xix; Derby's comment on 'latent unsoundness', xx; death duties, 124–5

Curzon, Marquess of, politician: 196; supported C as Viceroy of India, 124

Czernovitz, Austrian defeat by Russia: 184

Dardanelles and Gallipoli: 2, 117, 140; Australians talk only of Gallipoli, 164

Dawson, RAMC surgeon: 15–6; pinches choice instruments, 31; leaves to safeguard practice, 144

Death penalty: 159

Dentistry: 22; cement order needs Privy Council approval, 73; pariah of medical science, 135; ownership of teeth a luxury, 142; *see also* O'Grady

Derby Scheme, for voluntary recruitment, 82, 129

*Embusqués* French shirkers: 139, fraudulent medical exemptions, 145

Equipment of British Army sold, 50; abandoned, 70; rusting away, 148; in French farmhouses, 175

Erzeroum, Russian success: 131; not followed up to save Kut, 164

Espionage: 55; risk from interpreters, 85; careless talk, 105

Evans, L/C: keeps C awake in church, 30; decorates colonel's office with C, 56

Evesham: private from, C discusses asparagus with, 36–7

FP, Field Punishment: 44–45

Faivre, Abel, wonderful cartoon by, 93

Feeling: at ease with AS, xx; tender towards RAMC service, xxxi; touched by Livio's death, 98; suicidal at Neuve Chapelle, 9; stale, 11, 12, 33, 121, 150; regret at departing comrades, 15, 23; lousy, 23; shocked by enemy brutality, 128; stressed, 19, 22, 40, 67–8, 78; pride in work, 23, 41, 67, 167, 170, 187; concerned at immobility, 23, 54, 140, 150; nostalgia for home, 45–6, 57, 120, 152; pity for evicted people, 55; at home in Hazebrouck, 71; admiration for AS, 152; depressed at British generals, 163; faint at Jutland news, 176; stupefied by Kitchener's death, 179; bewildered by ministerial offer, 193

Fisher, Admiral Lord: 80, 140

Fokker, Anthony: aircraft designer rebuffed, xvii

Food: wasted, 20; officers complain, 75; foodstuffs analysed, 95; Britain seriously short of, 196

Foot problems: 8, 22, 97, army boots cause difficulties, 54; infernal cobble stones, 84; treatment methods, 88

Footitt, Tom, British clown, ex Foreign Legion: 69

Forbes, Lady Angela, establisher of canteens in France: 111

France and French, xv, 199; march astonishing distances, 5; amazed at our labour troubles, 33–4; complimentary about our efforts, 37, 46; view of British officers, 85, 89; dismissal of errant ministers, 91; endurance at Verdun, 114, 141, 143; disgust at Australian indiscipline, 154

Frémiet, Emanuel, sculptor of Joan of Arc: 117

French, Sir John, first British C-in-C in France: 31, 38; blamed for failures, 63; resigned, 95–6

GHQ, General Headquarters: 58; Lord
St Davids criticises, 82, 84; impossible rules,
90, 126–7; folly and tactlessness, 117–8;
rumour on Pétain's sudden prominence,
138; *see also* Staff officers
Gallipoli, *see* Dardanelles
Gangrene and gas gangrene, xxiii, 21, 192;
nurse experimentally injects herself with,
62
Garden, C works in, 31, 32, 34, 126, 142
George V, King: xxiii, xxix; jettisons German
titles, 38; flies by in superb car, 74
Germany and German, xv, 199; names, 38;
serious, 64; professional, 75; strength, 123;
bluff, 143–4; unconscious humour, 160;
suffering, 167; rumour of mutinuy, 180
Geyser: C purchases, 18
Gleichen, Count Albert: men's disrespect for,
38
Glubb, John (later known as 'Glubb Pasha'):
tips C for carrying luggage, 102
Grand Duke, *see* Nicholas Nikolaevich
Graves, Robert, poet: opinion of staff officers,
84
Great War: Aftermath, 198–9; Prelude,
xiv–v
Grech, Colonel: 10; C names new stretcher
'Gretcher', 46–7; C and comrades decorate
office, 56; resists impossible GHQ
regulations, 90; well deserved promotion,
182
Greece: initially neutral, 2, 63, 172, 186
Grey, Sir Edward, Foreign Secretary: xvii
Griffith-Boscawen, Arthur, Colonel: 185;
commands elderly battalion, 175

Haig, Sir Douglas, second British C-in-C in
France: 43, 111, 118, 126; succeeds Sir John
French, 63, 95–6; toothache, 136; on
Australian indiscipline, 148; weak on
politicians, 161; small impression on AS,
163; moves GHQ to Montreuil, 189
Hair: cut *en brosse* 7; C going grey, 36;
amicable robbery by barbers, 48
Hazebrouck, Nord, where C stationed:
*passim*; convergence of railway lines, 1;
C's affection for, 19; distinction of Grande
Place, 133
Head and head wounds, 7, 75, 97, 155;
wearisome helmets, 122
Head, Pte: carbuncle removed with scissors,
xxii

Hindenburg, Paul von, German commander
(later President of Germany): vulture-like
countenance, 162
Hodge, John, Minister of Labour, xviii
Holland: neutral, 171, 199
Horses banished: 43; C tipped for holding
officer's horse, 78; wounds from horse
kicks, 123; ideal job for horsey men, 161
Hoskyns, General: complains of champagne,
72

India, 90; C proposed as Viceroy, 124, 143
Inoculation: 87, 94
Intelligence Corps: 187–91; C offered
commission to liaise with French press, 188
Ireland, Home Rule: 89; 147; national unity
breached, 162; execution of traitors, 166
Italy: initially neutral, xv, 199; joins allies, 114;
doubts after Cattaro lost, 119

Japan: possible friction with USA, 171; SM
distrusts, 176; *see also* China
Joffre, Joseph, French commander: xvii, 74;
adored by AS, 81; allies awaiting his
instructions, 184
Jutland, Battle of: 176–7

Kay, RAMC surgeon: 66; operates on pigeon
fancier, 69; and statistical returns, 88;
C wants to join him at FA, 140
Kempis, Thomas à: *The Imitation of Christ*
C's regular reading matter, xxi, 107; on
patience, 8; little consolation from, 193
Kennedy, Cpt Leo, C's first cousin: battalion
came to grief, 67
Kipling, Rudyard: son killed at Battle of Loos,
118
Kitchener of Khartoum, Lord, S of S for
War: xvii, 31, 80, 81, 178–82; decisive, 65;
feared by men, 81; death stupefying, 178;
C's assesment, 179–80; memorial service,
182
Kut: British besieged, 89–90; in deadly peril,
161; surrender, 164; *see also* Nicholas

Lady Omega: C's nickname for new
daughter, Barbara, 102, 110
Lance Corporal: C reluctant to become, 15;
confirmed as, 68; aspires to become
sergeant, 69
Latrines and sewers: odious, 15; *poilus* cleanse
cheerfully, 61

Laundry: taken to St Omer by C, 58; taken to Dunkirk, 142

Leave: 103–113; unfair allocation of, 103–4

Lee, Arthur, MP: 33, 154; donor of Chequers to the nation, 34

Lemire, Abbé, Deputy, Priest and Mayor: a man of position in France, 18, 182; promotes fresh vegetables for allies, 32; saluted as king or pope, 41

Lille, German occupied industrial city: 1; refugees from, 3; recapture rumoured, 65

Lindsay family and clan: xix; family motto, 151

Lindsay, Barbara: C's eighth child, 102, 110

Lindsay, Eddy, C's brother: over age, enlisted as private, xviii

Lindsay, Lionel, C's brother: over age, enlisted as private, xviii

Lindsay, Ronald, C's brother: British diplomat in Egypt, later Ambassador to USA, 27

Lindsay, Walter, C's brother: over age, enlisted as private, xviii; has nephritis, 173

Liquor and alcohol, 22, 76; deadlier foe than Germany and Austria, 6; futile analysis of consumption, 88; Australians and, 152; see also Lloyd George

Lisgo, Cpl: dispenser, 29, 72; decorating colonel's office with C, 56; schoolboy behaviour at 40th birthday of, 78; melting reunion with Australian brother, 147

Lloyd George, David, Liberal politician (later Prime Minister): 2, 3 6, 81, 163, 180; on consumption of alcohol, 6; impetuous, 133–4; possible successor to Kitchener as S of S, 181; C serves in coalitions of, 196

Loos, Battle of: xxxii, 25, 61; a great failure, 61, 71; lack of troops, 83; see also Kipling

Louse: xxiii, xxvii; C's encounters with, 23, 108; characteristics of 79–80; see also Trench fever

McCarthy, 'Mother', chief matron BEF: 33; visit rattles nurses, 62; ignorance of scandal, 77

MacCrae, new matron: 72; inquisitive about C's peerage, 73; becoming intolerable, 165

McNeill, Ronald, MP: bitter attack on RAMC in parliament, 154

Machine gun: UK army chiefs sceptical, xvii; Kitchener's aversion to, 178

Malingering: 44, 92, 102; cowardly malingering reprobated, 67; see also Shell shock

Marne, Battle of: xvii, 37, 174

Married men problem: 143–5, 163; see also Derby Scheme

Mason, Jim, MP, C's brother-in-law: 134

Michelham, Lord, munificent banker: 135

Miners, needed for tunnelling: 10, 183

Moltke, Helmuth von, German commander: xvii

Montenegro: xv, 117; follows Serbia into Teuton's fist, 119

Montreuil, GHQ: 189; reminds C of favourite book, 190; see also GHQ, Sterne

Munro, Hector ('Saki'), author: 154

Museums: C's peacetime role in, xx, 197

Music making and bands: 37; unofficial music, 52; marching improved by, 11, 53

NCOs and men: will win war, 117; twelve bossed by thirty-one, 40; see also Officers

NYD (Not Yet Diagnosed) and NYDN (Not Yet Diagnosed – Nervous): xxiii, 186; see also Shell shock

Neuve Chapelle, Battle of: xviii, 1, 3, 46; effect on C, 9, 151; a great failure, 71, 83, 141, 162

New Zealanders: 160; complain about Australians, 161; offer to fight C and comrades, 164

Nicholas Nikolaevich, Grand Duke, Russian commander: 131, 163; might have saved Kut, 164

Nicholson, Sir William, CIGS: on uselessness of aviation, xvii see also Aviation

Non-effectives: C struck by number of, 12

Nunn, Sergeant: 122; guarding stores with C, 28; decorating colonel's office with C, 56; too tolerant of irregularities, 76

Nurses, passim: overview, xxvi–xxvii; bully orderlies, 16; not needed at CCS, 18; officers' zealous attention towards, 24; interfere in kitchen, 49; worried about McCarthy visit, 62; drunken sprawl, 64; prepare for royal visit, 73; scandalous conduct, 75–77; unbelievable waste caused by, 121; at last become amiable, 170; see also Alexander, Nurse, MacCrae, McCarthy

Officers, passim: overview, xxiv–xxvi; RAMC officers thoroughly good lot, xxiv; C won't salute officers with VD, 10; batman, officer servant, 12, 35–6, 172; officers' hospital, 15,

204

29; unwise attention towards nurses, 24; suicides, 28; looting by, 36; thirty-one bossing twelve NCOs and men, 40; excess kits, 47, 60, 77, 172; looting a church bell, 51; linguistic ignorance, 53, 85; men's unerring intuition about, 57; poor quality, 64, 85, 124; scandal with nurses and liquor, 75–77; forbidden to tip orderlies, 79; French opinion of, 89; should first serve in the ranks, 126; one officer worth twenty men theory, 137; don't understand men's boredom, 150

O'Grady, dentist: 73; tackles C's molar, 135; see also Dentistry

Operating theatres: C's main responsibility, 6, 16, 23; in lace factory, 14–5; sterilizing, 15, 72; making splints, 19; scrubbing, 24; in orphanage, 23, 27; in Petit Séminaire 26; see also Petit Séminaire, Warein

Ottoman Empire (Turkey): xv, 199

Perceval, General, patient: 49; courtesy compared to young swankers, 54

Pétain, Philippe, French general at Verdun, (later President of Vichy France): 132; scandal behind rise to prominence, 138

Petit Séminaire St Jacques, main location of No. 12 CCS: 26; boys pouring back after holidays, 70

Plumer, General: 37–8; popular and respected, 38; face like a parroquet, 83; does not seem a big man, 163

Poilu: French AS admired by C, 5; vigilance as railway guard, 60–1; shabby appearance, but deserves well of La Patrie, 101; Verdun motto n'passeront pas, 143

Pollen, Arthur, naval technologist: spurned, xvii

Porter, General, Surgeon General, Second Army: 24; C quizzed by over scandal, 76; takes C on inspection vists, 85–6, 153–4; kindness to C, 186

Quakers: controlling pollution, 153

Quartermaster: 20, 29, 35, 82; advises eating rabbit before decay, 91; C declines to become, 120

Raemaekers, Louis, Dutch cartoonist: 93, 94, 171

Railway & trains, passim: Hazebrouck as junction, 1; microcosm of base hospital, 86;

leave trains, 109–10; dangerous carrying stretchers across lines, 117; sick horses, 161; station pavoisé over Czernovitz, 184

Ravenna, St Apollinare: bombed, 128; Pope's protest, 129

Redmond, John, Irish politician: seeks Home Rule by peaceful means, 89; see also Ireland

Refugees: 1, 55, 142; sad shocking spectacle, 16; surplus food distributed to, 20

Religion: C against slushy churchmanship, xx; nods off in church, 30; Kitchener service not disfigured by sermon, 182

Repington, Colonel Charles: The Times military correspondent, 137; interesting meeting with C, 194

Return to UK: C's desired by wife, 9; urged by family, 165

Riga: Russian success at, 45

Robertson, Sir William: CIGS, 179; unsuitable to succeed Kitchener, 181

Romania, initially neutral: xv, 2, 63, 184

Royal Army Medical Corps (RAMC), passim: overview, xxi–xxiv; evacuation system, xxxiv

Royal Flying Corps: RFC men monopolise C's bath place, 101; jealousy of high pay and beautiful costume, 118; ridiculous guard of honour for German pilot, 170

Russia: xv, 199; see also Czernovitz

Salonica: too late to help Serbia, 83; huge reservoir of troops, 186

Sanitary: duties admirably done, 92–4

Scabies: simple to cure, 80; RFA man with our old friend scabies, 112; one of the army's greatest curses, 122

Serbia: xv, 2, 98; final cataclysm of, 117

Shell shock: seen as malingering, xxiii; also neurasthenia, 47; severe cases of, 130; confused with nicotine poisoning, 133; difficulty of diagnosis, 186; see also Malingering, NYD

Sloggett, Sir Arthur, Director General, RAMC in France: puts C in false position, 148; another gaffe, 149

Smith, FE, politician: weekender at the front, 193

Smith-Dorrien, General Sir Horace: relieved of command, 38

Somme, Battle of: xxxiii; build-up 183, 185, 190; seared row of skeleton trees, 192

Souvenir collecting: 51, 131; German prisoner spared for buttons, 28

Spin and propaganda, xviii, 66, 71, 117–8, 155, 162

Sports: C helps organise, 8

Sprot of Stravithie, Col Alexander, Fife neighbour: 75, 138

Staff officer: regular tyrant, 48; loafing about, 57; scandalous conduct, 75; and grand cars, 81; thoughtless routine orders; 89; galaxy of crimson, 137 *see also* GHQ

Stamp collection of 26th Earl, xix, 125

St Omer: marvellous cathedral, 18; beautiful town, 58 *see also* GHQ

Submarines 7, 112; attack on SS *Sussex* 162

Talbot, Lord Edmund: C's successor as Conservative Chief Whip, 8–9

Tank: inventor 'mad', xvii

*Taube* German plane: often over Hazebrouck, 15, 30; main line bombed, 45; their wonderful aim, 115; why called doves, 132; disagreeable, but Zeppelins ten times worse, 155; leaflet threatening electrocution, 167

Taylor, Owen, RAMC surgeon: 155; indecisive in hand operation, 145; on vague diagnoses, 186

Territorial Act: serious flaws in, 122

*The Times*: 62, 67, 82; C's letter against business as usual, xvii, 34

Tourniquet: circular warning against use of, 173

Trench fever: xxii, 88, 186; C curious about new disease, 47 *see also* Louse

Unessentials: 29, 58, 115–6, 168; Australian impatience with, 147; *see also* Aldershot

United Kingdom: xv, 199

United States of America: initially neutral, 199: wheat crop, 196 *see also* Wilson, President

VD or Venereal disease: breach of contract with King, 5; prevalence among ANZAC troops, 168

Verdun, Battle of: xxxiii, 115, 135, 137; Pétain at, 138; French endurance, 114, 141, 143; German assault yields small gains, 145; 'Butcher of', 172; catastrophic potential loss of, 114, 177 *see also* Pétain, Wilhelm, Crown Prince

Vincent, Prof John: editor of *Crawford Papers* xxvii

Volunteers: xvi *see also* Derby Scheme

Warein, Maison: orphanage, officers' station, 23, 27, 73

Wheat Commission, C chairman of: 136, 196

Wigan Coal & Iron Company: xix, xxvii, 71, 124–5, 197; C resigns directorship on joining government, 193

Wilhelm, Crown Prince: holocausts at Verdun, 172

Wilhelm ll, Kaiser: xvi, xvii, 114, 172, 174, 186

Wilson, President of USA: annoyed by German submarine actions, 162; vainly promotes League of Nations, 199

Wilson, Henry, General (later CIGS): 34

Wood, Edward, politician, (later Lord Halifax): 174

X-ray van: commanded by Captain Lang, 42; C got fearfully hot inside, 59; obstruction of invaluable unit, 149

Ypres and salient: xxix, 3, 10; as looting centre, 50, 58–9; peaceable and innocent old town destroyed, 50; instructions about reconstruction, 182

Zeppelin: panic at home, 128; sparse damage caused by, 131–2; Connie's narrow escape, 155; fear of massacre by, 163

206